The
Meaning
of
NATIONALISM

Political Nationalism has become, for the European of our age, the most important thing in the world, more important than civilization, humanity, decency, kindness, pity: more important than life itself.

—SIR NORMAN ANGELL

The
Meaning
of
NATIONALISM

by LOUIS L. SNYDER

Foreword by HANS KOHN

GREENWOOD PRESS, PUBLISHERS
NEW YORK   1968

TO

Joseph E. and Edith Wisan

HEREWITH MY DEVOTION

Foreword

Although nationalism has been the prime moving force of European history for the last one hundred years and has become of similar importance in Asia since the end of the First World War, the serious study of its meaning and implications has only recently begun. Yet such a study seems of urgent concern not only for the scholar but also for statesmen and citizens dealing with international relations. For nations—with their drives, emotions, and real or supposed interests—are the chief actors on the stage of present history. Errors of judgment about the persistence and variations of national traditions and character and about the nature of nationalism were responsible, among other factors, for the coming of the wars and the weaknesses of the peace treaties of the twentieth century.

In the middle of the nineteenth century, many Europeans believed that peace and unity would be achieved among nations as soon as each nation became independent and united. Common descent and language were proclaimed as the ideal basis of the modern state. The concept of national self-determination—transferring the ideal of liberty from the individual to an organic collectivity—was raised as the banner of liberalism. This faith in the nation exercised a determining influence on the political thought of a whole century. It was partly responsible for the principles which guided Woodrow Wilson sixty years later in his program for peace. The nineteenth century, in effect, abandoned the Rousseauan confidence in the natural goodness of individual man and accepted instead the even stranger belief that the collective individualities of peoples or nations would act as good

vii

and peaceful forces as soon as they had broken the fetters imposed upon them by multinational states or traditional dynasties. National independence was regarded as a panacea, which would by its magic establish individual liberty and social justice at home, and peace and benevolent cooperation abroad.

The events of the intervening century have raised many doubts about this optimistic faith. Nationalism arose in the West in the seventeenth and eighteenth centuries from the desire to limit the authority of collective power as represented by national governments and to assure an ever widening scope to the rights and liberties of the individual. Within the context of the intellectual traditions and the social structure of the modern West, as they originated in seventeenth century England, nationalism represented a movement for a more open society and the pursuit of individual happiness, for the security of civil liberties and the unfettering of thought. In the nineteenth and twentieth centuries nationalism spread to Central and Eastern Europe, to lands of entirely different traditions and social structure from those in the modern West and frequently hostile to, and contemptuous of, modern Western ways. In these lands nationalism became a trend towards collective self-assertion, towards a closed society, in which the individual counted for less than the strengthened authority of the national whole. The modern nation, as it developed in Central and Eastern Europe and later in Asia, no longer implied primarily a constitutional guarantee of individual liberty but was a semimystical body of separation from an alien world.

In the last half-century many new nation-states have been created and many peoples "liberated." Often these peoples had rightful complaints about the inequality of their status and about the curtailment of their individual freedom. But before the First World War, following the example set by Britain, the trend all over the earth went in the direction of greater equality of status and of growing recognition of individual rights. The creation of the new nation-states after the world wars has in no way strengthened this process. In many cases it has reversed it. Nationalities which had demanded release from oppression became oppressors themselves as soon as they were liberated. Innumerable disputes about historical and natural frontiers sprang up. Long established ties of economic and cultural interchange were disrupted. The ensuing feeling of insecurity led in many instances to a curtailment of individual liberty, to an increase in armaments, and to a heightening of international tensions. Though national independence brought a great emotional elation to many peoples at the time of achievement, the historian will ask himself whether this momentary elation was not too dearly bought. National independence and sovereignty, multiplied and sanctified in the last decades, have not turned out to be reliable formulas for greater individual freedom and more secure international peace.

Thus a study of nationalism becomes urgent and important. Nationalism is a phenomenon of great complexity. Its forms and consequences differ with historical circumstances. But the historian will need the cooperation of many other disciplines and their specific approaches to clarify the issues involved. Sociology, political science, and psychology, as well as the study of institutions and literatures will all have to make their contribution to the understanding of nationalism. Professor Snyder has written the first introduction to such an interdisciplinary inquiry. His objective and clearly conceived survey of the results and problems of the different approaches will be most welcome to scholarly workers and students in the various fields and may become the starting point for many further investigations leading to a better grasp of the nature of nationalism and its rôle in modern times.

HANS KOHN

Preface

It would be presumptuous to suppose that this book could give a definite explanation of the meaning of nationalism. At the same time, it would be mischievous and misleading to say that nationalism is inexplicable. We are dealing here with one of the most critical forces in contemporary civilization. Nationalism has long since passed beyond the academic interest of the cloistered scholar. It concerns all of us. Since it is within the sphere of human control, it must be examined ceaselessly and with extraordinary care.

The physical and biological sciences have given us the discovery of atomic energy and the development of biological warfare. The uses which can be made of these innovations have alarmed the entire civilized world. It has become vitally necessary for human beings to revise their thinking to cope with this new situation. It is the task of the social sciences to keep pace with the physical sciences by undertaking the responsibility for understanding the forces that work upon society. This is not simply an intellectual exercise. It is a matter of self-preservation.

It is the purpose of this book to present an appraisal from a multidisciplinary point of view of the meaning of nationalism. It concerns itself primarily with meaning. It is hoped that the material given here will provide a kind of extensive definition such as might have been presented by the editors of Webster's unabridged dictionary if they had had several hundred pages at their disposal instead of a few inches of space. Attention is directed to the definitions and clarifications offered by many disciplines, including psychiatry and psychoanalysis, in which much serious and fruitful work is being done on this subject. An effort has been made to include the findings of the best recent research. No extensive attempt is made to recount the historical evolution of nationalism and its practical applications from the time of the French Revolution, for this has been done capably many times. This work is limited to possible answers to one question: What is nationalism?

This publication has resulted from studies undertaken by the author during his tenure of a fellowship granted by The Fund for the Advancement of Education, established by the Ford Foundation, to enable him to broaden his qualifications for teaching. It represents the independent work of the author, however, and he is solely responsible for it. Grateful acknowledgment is made to Dr. Herman Ausubel, of Columbia University, who generously interrupted his own work to read the entire manuscript and to make many excellent suggestions for its improvement. The sections on psychiatry and psychoanalysis were read by a distinguished psychiatrist, Dr. Edmund Ziman. Professor Harry M. Shulman, of The City College of New York, made pertinent and valuable suggestions for the sections on sociology. Reference is made in the footnotes to Professors Eugene Dorfman and Isaac Mendelsohn, of Columbia University, and to Professor John M. Firestone, of The City College of New York, who assisted the author in their special fields. My colleague, Wallace Sokolsky, gave his time unselfishly in helping to read the proofs. I should like to express my appreciation also to members of the faculty of The William Alanson White Institute of Psychiatry, Psychoanalysis and Psychology, New York City, with whom I have spent many pleasant and fruitful hours during the last four years. I am further deeply indebted to my wife, Ida Mae Brown Snyder, for her counsel, encouragement, and inexhaustible patience.

LOUIS L. SNYDER

New York City
April 1954

Contents

The
Meaning
of
NATIONALISM

I

The Tyranny of Words

How many words have suffered corruption since Chaucer's days!
—Thomas Middleton

The Age of Nationalism

"Before God, and the world, my blood claims for the independence of Puerto Rico. My life I give for the freedom of my country. This is a cry for victory in our struggle for independence. . . ."

This penciled suicide note was found in the handbag of Lolito Lebrón, one of four members of the terrorist Nationalist party of Puerto Rico who, on March 1, 1954, sprayed bullets all over the chamber of the House of Representatives and left five United States Congressmen bleeding from bullet wounds. This completely irrational act (if a majority of Puerto Ricans had wanted independence, they could have had it) is typical of a special form that nationalism has taken in our time. Contemporary nationalism is a destructive force that often contains a high content of xenophobia—hatred of the foreigner. In recent years nationalism has spread in violent form from the great powers of the West to Egypt, the Sudan, Morocco, Iran, Tunisia, Indo-China, and Latin America.

The incident in Washington is symbolic of an aberrant phase of one of the most significant forces of our times. We live in an Age of Nationalism. Like all historical movements, nationalism is deeply rooted in the past. The product of political, economic, social, intellectual, and psychological factors, it emerged over the

3

course of centuries, gradually taking on common characteristics. Its first great manifestation was the French Revolution, which stimulated and spread the force already in motion. Its composite pattern has utilized some of the oldest and most primitive feelings of man, including love of birthplace and distrust of the alien. Its character has varied from benign love of country to destructive hatred for the foreigner.

The deceptively simple term "nationalism" is used to describe what is, in reality, a complex historical phenomenon. Several generations of scholars have devoted their efforts to the task of clarifying the meaning of nationalism. Despite their labors, they have not been able to achieve a unanimity of definition. The fault lies partly in the inadequacy of words as the transmission belts of social communication and partly in the varied implications of nationalism itself. A complicating factor is that the meaning of nationalism changes with the course of history. Another is that it means different things to different peoples—British liberals hailed it as a force for liberation and freedom; German Nazis welcomed it as a means for aggression and as a weapon against democracy; Russian Communists denounce it as a tool of capitalism and, at the same time, while claiming to be internationalists, seek to make use of it in satellite countries behind the Iron Curtain, in the Near East, and among Asiatic peoples. On occasion, different parties within one country utilize the word nationalism to express totally divergent views.

Much of the confusion may be attributed to nationalists who have a vested interest in maintaining a vagueness of language as a cloak for their aims. Since it would not be easy to win public opinion by a frank and open advocacy of national aggression and domination, nationalism is deliberately confused with patriotism to connote a deep love for country, protection against foreign encroachment, the desirability of national unity, the protection of national culture, civilization, and traditions, and the subordination of individual interests to those of the entire people. Hitler, among others, contributed to this abuse of terms: utilizing the banner of National Socialism in his drive for power beyond the borders of the Third Reich, he maintained that the continuity of German *Kultur,* the problem of *Lebensraum,* and the real destiny of the superior German "race" demanded an all-conquering application of the German national spirit.

In his *Expansion of England,* written in 1883, Sir John Robert Seeley, the British essayist and historian, complained that "we take no pains to conceive or define precisely what we call a nationality." [1] One of the greatest experts in this field, Frederick Hertz, the British sociologist, stated that the diversity of usage is often rooted in the antagonisms of ideologies or interests, and frequently it is due to a lack of critical sense. "Even careful writers," said Dr. Hertz, "are often compelled to use inaccurate terms because the public has become so used to employ the same word for different things that it would resent the introduction of new terms merely for the sake of scientific accuracy. Anyhow, the lack of a clear and stable terminology greatly contributes to the confusion of ideas." [2]

Some scholars consider the meaning of nationalism to be so complex a metaphysical fiction that they assume or explicitly state that definition is impossible. Israel Zangwill looked upon the principle of nationalities as "one of those tropical jungles of thought in which politics and journalism flourish." [3] Sir John A. Marriott has concluded that "the principle of nationality has defied definition and even analysis." [4] Viscount James Bryce modestly disclaimed the ability to define nationality.[5] According to George P. Gooch, nationalism is an organism, a spiritual entity, and "all attempts to penetrate its secrets by the light of mechanical interpretation break down before the test of experience." [6] H. L. Featherstone stated flatly that "nationalism is not capable of scientific definition." [7] The sociologist, Florian Znaniecki, pointed out that, in view of the terminological confusion, the editors of several encyclopedias have omitted the word nation altogether.[8]

[1] Sir John R. Seeley, *Expansion of England: Two Courses of Lectures* (London, 1883), p. 220.
[2] Frederick Hertz, *Nationality in History and Politics* (3rd ed., London, Routledge and Kegan Paul, 1951), p. 4.
[3] Israel Zangwill, *The Principle of Nationalities* (New York, 1917), p. 28.
[4] Sir John ·A. Marriott, Jr., *The Eastern Question: An Historical Study in European Diplomacy* (Oxford, 1917), p. 174.
[5] Viscount James Bryce, *Essays and Addresses in War-Time* (New York, 1918), p. 129.
[6] George P. Gooch, *Nationalism* (London and New York, 1920), p. 6.
[7] H. L. Featherstone, *A Century of Nationalism* (New York, 1939), p. 10.
[8] For example, *International Encyclopedia; Encyclopedia of the Social Sciences; Encyclopedia Britannica;* and *Handwörterbuch der Staatswissenschaft.* Cf. Florian Znaniecki, *Modern Nationalities* (Chicago, 1952), p. xiii.

Others are more optimistic. In a letter to the London *Morning Post* in 1918, Viscount Reginald Esher urged that "with a new world opening before us, it is just the moment to take stock of words and phrases in common use, and to give them precision and directness." [9] The political scientist, Max Sylvius Handman, disturbed by the indiscriminate use of the word nationalism by the social sciences, recommended it as a good idea "to have a sort of Nicene Council on the terminology used in connection with the social sciences." [10]

The Problem Semantically Expressed

Among the several causes for the unpopularity of Socrates among his contemporaries was his loud objection to the careless use of such words as beauty, goodness, and humanity. The great Athenian gadfly insisted that every word that has a single unequivocal meaning directly names a single similar object of a kind inaccessible to the senses and understandable only by thought. Such an idea he called ἰδέα or εἶδος, "form" (not "idea" in our sense). The sensible things we predicate from such words, he said, have only a secondary and derivative reality. It follows that the justification for a basic definition has to be found in weighing the acceptability of the consequences that would follow from its adoption. Therefore, before proceeding in argument, Socrates demanded precise, careful definitions, especially of words in the sphere of private or public conduct. The famous Socratic method of inductive reasoning (dialectic) was characterized by a constant insistence upon careful definition of terms as the very foundation of knowledge. This, in Cicero's words, "brought down philosophy from heaven to earth."

The problem of meaning in language has persisted since the time of Socrates. Alexander Pope spoke of the "power of words," and Disraeli noted that "with words we govern men." Francis Bacon, much earlier, put it succinctly in his *Novum Organum*

[9] Viscount Reginald Baliol Brett Esher, letter on "The Meaning of Patriotism," *Morning Post* (London), October 9, 1918.
[10] Max Sylvius Handman, "The Sentiment of Nationalism," *Political Science Quarterly*, XXXVI (1921), p. 104.

(1620): "There arises from a bad and unapt formation of words a wonderful obstruction to the mind."

Many of our most common terms have suffered corruption through popular misunderstanding and improper usage. Our current society has been subjected painfully to this tyranny of words. The terms democracy, liberalism, radicalism, constitutionalism, dictatorship, capitalism, socialism, communism, fascism, and pacifism have been used so variously that their meaning is often obscured. A case in point is the appropriation of the word democracy by the Soviet Union in a sense directly counter to the Western meaning of the term.[11] The Russians denounce Western capitalism as fascism, while the West labels the Soviet system state capitalism, social fascism, and red fascism. Neither at the diplomatic nor at the popular level is there any agreement on precise meanings. In a survey not long ago by an enterprising newspaper reporter in the Midwest, most persons interviewed had only the vaguest idea of the meaning of the word communist, their replies ranging from "a Russian radical," to a "foreigner" and a "spy." The keynote in a recent conclave of a patriotic society was sounded by a lady who described the United Nations as a sinister "socialistic society."

Among the terms which have been victims of obscurantism are nationalism, its corollaries, nation and nationality, and such composite terms as national character, national consciousness, national soul, national will, and national self-determination. Upon first thought, it would seem that the best way to understand the basic terms nation, nationality, and nationalism would be to consult the definitions given in Webster's unabridged dictionary. The editors of this compendium, popularly known as "the last word," have made, indeed, a valiant attempt to cope with these terms in the limited space at their disposal.[12] But it is a reflection upon the

---

[11] The word democracy has caused confusion elsewhere. After his recent world tour, Adlai Stevenson reported that in Japan he learned that 80 different Japanese words have been used to attempt to convey the idea of democracy. (*Look*, XVII [1953], p. 44.)

[12] NA'TION (nā'shŭn), *n.* [ME. *nacioun*, fr. OF. *nacion* (F. *nation*), fr. L. *natio* nation, race, orig., a being born, fr. *natus*, past part. of *nasci* to be born, for *gnatus*, *gnasci*, from the same root as E. KIN. Cf. COGNATE, INNATE, NATAL, NATIVE, NATURE, PREGNANT, PUNY, RENASCENT.] 1. *Obs.* a Kindred; race; lineage. b Nationality.

mystery of the word nationalism that nowhere in this definition is it stated where the line of demarcation lies between beneficial and harmful types. In the fourth definition of nationalism, the term is equated with patriotism, which means love for the homeland and should be distinguished from nationalism. Once again,

---

c A community or an aggregation of men or animals; esp., a caste or class formed by the common profession or interests of its members. d A country.

2. A people connected by supposed ties of blood generally manifested by community of language, religion, and customs, and by a sense of common interest and interrelation; thus, the Jews and the Gypsies are often called *nations*. See PEOPLE, I.

3. Popularly, any group of people having like institutions and customs and a sense of social homogeneity and mutual interest. Most nations are formed of agglomerations of tribes or peoples either of a common ethnic stock or of different stocks fused by long intercourse. A single language or closely related dialects, a common religion, a common tradition and history, and a common sense of right and wrong, and a more or less compact territory, are typically characteristic; but one or more of these elements may be lacking and yet leave a group that from its community of interest and desire to lead a common life is called a *nation*.

4. Loosely, the body of inhabitants of a country united under a single independent government; a state.

5. A division of students, determined by district or country of their birth, esp. in medieval universities. *Archaic.*

6. A multitude; a host.

7. One tribe of a group of Indian tribes; as, the Six *Nations*. Syn.—See PEOPLE.

NA'TION·AL'I·TY (năsh'ŭn·ăl'ĭ·tĭ), *n.; pl.* —TIES (-tĭz). I. State or quality of being a nation; racial, political, or institutional solidarity constituting a nation; national character; often, specif., existence as a sovereign nation; political independence as a nation; statehood; as, the *nationality* won by Greece.

2. State, quality, or fact of belonging to, or being connected with, a (or a particular) nation or state as by nativity or allegiance; as, *nationality* acquired by birth may be lost through naturalization in another country; state or quality of being generally characteristic of a nation; as, *nationality* of art usually springs from nationality of character.

3. National feeling or attachment; the feeling or sense of being of a people bound together by common customs, language, religion, or the like (see NATION, 3); nationalism.

4. A nation; a people united by common institutions, language, etc. (see NATION, 3).

NA'TION·AL·ISM (năsh'ŭn·ăl·ĭz'm; —'l·ĭz'm;59), *n.* I. National character, or tendency to it; nationality.

2. An idiom, trait, or character peculiar to any nation.

3. Devotion to, or advocacy of, national interests or national unity and independence; as, the *nationalism* of Ireland or China. Cf. INTERNATIONALISM, 2; NEW NATIONALISM.

4. Zealous adherence to one's own nation or to its principles; patriotism.

5. A phase of socialism advocating the nationalizing of industries;—essentially the same as *collectivism*. Chiefly U.S.

6. *Theol.* The doctrine that the people of a certain nation or nations are God's chosen people.

(By permission. From *Webster's New International Dictionary*, Second Edition, copyright, 1934, 1939, 1945, 1950, 1953, by G. & C. Merriam Co.)

we are faced with the Socratic admonition that the understanding of any word depends, in the final analysis, upon concepts inaccessible to the senses and understandable only by thought. In the case of nationalism, the variations in understanding, and the passions, prejudices, and interests of its advocates are so wide that we must go far beyond the limits imposed upon the best dictionaries by lack of space.

The Naturalization of Meaning

What is the explanation for the fact that words in common usage take on so many different meanings? One answer is provided by the science of linguistics. Scholars in this discipline say that words may be compared to citizens who cross the borders of nations; like citizens, words become naturalized.[13] The Latin *Caesar* became *Kaiser* in German and *Tsar* in Russian. In each case, the variant owed its basic meaning to the stimulus of the original word, but it took on specific regional connotations subject to its own peculiar milieu. In this continuous, fluid process of word formation, there is no guarantee that the original meaning will be retained exactly. Linguistically, it is neither natural nor desirable that this be done.

This naturalization of words is accompanied by a parallel process of nationalization, in which the meanings assume a national quality determined by the new habitat. The result is that many common words used throughout the world have different meanings to different peoples. An example is the word democracy, derived from the Greek *dēmos* (people) and *kratein* (to rule). For many centuries democracy designated a political movement. A revolutionary change in the meaning of the word was made in the nineteenth century, when democracy was given an economic connotation.

The words nation, nationality, and nationalism are similarly affected by this process of naturalization and nationalization. Derived from the Latin *natio,* the basic term nation would seem to indicate a people related by birth, and the quality of innateness would seem to be vital in its meaning. However, in the formation

[13] I am indebted to Dr. Eugene Dorfman, Department of Linguistics, Columbia University, for the general ideas expressed in this section.

of modern nations, the exigencies of historical development caused peoples to be thrown together by factors other than ethnic relationship. But the older Latin symbol for the nation—the *natio*—was retained as a descriptive term, even though there were variations in meaning from the original. Linguistically, this use of an earlier terminology is a common and understandable development, necessary to avoid a multiplicity of symbols that would result in even more confusion.

In its process of naturalization, the word nationalism was used in strikingly similar form in most major languages, despite the fact that it developed along different lines in various countries. Several examples may be noted: French: *nationalisme;* German: *Nationalismus;* Italian: *nazionalismo;* Spanish: *nacionalismo;* Polish: *nacjonalisme;* Slovak: *nacionalizmus;* Norwegian: *(en) nasjonalisme;* Danish: *(en) nationalisme;* and Swedish: *nationel egendomlighet.* In Dutch *nationaliteit* and in Portuguese *nacionalidade* are used to express both nationalism and nationality. In Roumanian *nationalitate* is similar to the English nationality.

In National Socialist Germany, the word *Volkstum* was preferred to *Nationalismus,* since the former term was believed to show more accurately the supposedly cohesive element of Nordic-Aryan blood relationship of the German people. While *Volkstum* was a realistic idea to the Germans under Hitler, its exact cognate in English, folkdom, has no meaning whatever to Anglo-Saxons and North Americans.

The use of the word nationalism in Hebrew and Yiddish presents an interesting commentary on how words and the historical process affect one another.[14] With their national independence crushed and their people scattered over all countries, the Jews were for more than 2,000 years a people without a state. The Old Testament employs many words for people and nation: *cam, le'om, goy,* etc. The Israelites themselves are referred to many times as *goy* (cf. Exodus 19:6, in which the Israelites are called *goy qadosh,* a holy people). It was only after the biblical period that the term *goy* (literally gentile, derived from gens) assumed the meaning of any other people than Jews. In Eastern Europe, where Yiddish has

---

[14] For the facts expressed in this paragraph I am indebted to Professor Isaac Mendelsohn, Department of Semitic Languages, Columbia University.

been spoken in the last few centuries, the term *Yiddishkeit,* the quality of being Yiddish, was used to express the sum total of the Jewish way of life, in both a religious and a secular sense. With the advent of the Jewish national movement in the late nineteenth century, the Hebrew word *le'ummiyyut* (derived from the biblical *le'om,* people, nation) came into use for nationalism. On occasion, the kindred German term *Nationalismus* was used in Yiddish. With the emergence of Israel as a national state, it became itself a *goy*—a nation. The Proclamation of the State of Israel used the term *cam* for people and *medinah* for the state.

In every case, nationalism, by this process of naturalization, took on a meaning consistent with national strivings. Thus, pre–1914 Austro-Hungarian nationalism must be differentiated from the Hungarian nationalism which strove successfully to break away from the Hapsburg Empire; in the former, nationalism was cohesive in nature, in the latter disruptive. Polish nationalism from the time of the Partitions in 1772, 1793, and 1795 until the creation of the Polish state in 1919 existed without a geographical setting. British nationalism became tinged with an existing imperial sentiment, German nationalism with a potential Pan-Germanism. In all these, and in many other forms of nationalism, one all-embracing linguistic term is used to describe what were actually varied naturalized concepts of a common word. Nationalism may mean whatever a given people, on the basis of their own historical experience, decide it to mean.

The Multidisciplinary Approach

Historians are prone to regard nationalism as their special province. Since they, generally, believe that nationalism is one of the strongest forces in modern life, they have emphasized it as a basic phenomenon in their studies of historical development. Every textbook in modern European history, as well as every course on the subject, pays more than passing attention to the meaning, characteristics, and implications of nationalism. This particularistic approach, while understandable, is not altogether satisfactory in judging the meaning and character of a sentiment that is linked closely with all aspects of human motivation. The complexities of human behavior are such that the historian is not equipped by training to understand all the factors that make up the conduct of men. Louis Gottschalk points out that man is at once a thing (having a physics and a chemistry), an animal (having an ancestry, an anatomy, a physiology, and a psychology), and a human being (having institutions, situations, traditions, and aspirations). "As a human being his behavior may be either rational or irrational, . . . determined by physical, biochemical, genealogical, social, and psychological factors." [15]

It follows, then, that the historian should call upon neighboring disciplines for assistance in understanding the meaning of nationalism. The nature of a polyhedron cannot be understood by observation, no matter how ingenious, of one of its plane surfaces. Yet, few historians are acquainted with the theoretical literature on human motivation, with the work of students of personality (whether psychologists, psychiatrists, or psychoanalysts), sociologists, anthropologists, economists, and political scientists. As long as we confine ourselves to a particularistic analysis of the meaning of nationalism and as long as we treat it as a single undifferentiated phenomenon, there is little prospect for clarification of its meaning.[16]

It is becoming increasingly apparent that interpenetration of the once segregated scholarly disciplines will be characteristic of research in the future. Multidisciplined thinking, however, makes greater demands than a particularistic analysis. It means, in the words of Eamonn F. O'Doherty, "that the corners be knocked off my too rigid schemata of conceptions by their clashes with yours, so that I emerge, not with, I think, a new concept—this seems to me to be psychologically repugnant—but with a drastically modified one." [17]

In their research on nationalism, scholars constantly discover debts to one another. Psychological analysis is not only possible but necessary in dealing with the meaning of nationalism, the na-

---

[15] Louis Gottschalk, *Understanding History* (New York, 1950), pp. 228–29.
[16] Cf. Max Wirth, "Types of Nationalism," *American Journal of Sociology*, XLI (1936), pp. 723–37.
[17] Eamonn F. O'Doherty, "Multidisciplinary Methods in Retrospect," *Psychiatry, Journal for the Operational Statement of Interpersonal Relations*, II (1948), pp. 355–56.

ture of national character, the content and function of tradition, and kindred problems involving psychological processes.[18] Sociologists also find it necessary to turn to other disciplines for assistance in the study of nationalism.[19] In discussing the growth and development of economic nationalism, economists find it helpful to call upon the field of history for substantiating data.

The late American psychiatrist, Harry Stack Sullivan, became the major architect of the culture-and-personality approach and was a pioneer in adding social scientists to the staffs of schools and hospitals. Sullivan was not simply an intermediary who brought disciplines together; he made many introductions across the boundaries of craft and clique—among anthropologists, physiologists, government officials, academicians, hospital administrators, students, patients, publishers, and writers.[20] Following the lead of Sullivan, psychiatrists and psychoanalysts have tended more and more to equate their work on individual cases with the social experience of groups, a tendency that, it is to be hoped, will be pursued further by social scientists in their search for the meaning of nationalism.

[18] Cf. Henry Lowenfeld, "Freud's *Moses* and Bismarck," in *Psychoanalysis and the Social Sciences,* ed. by Géza Róheim (New York, 1950), II, p. 277.
[19] "Despite the occasional allusions to sociology in the titles of books on nationalism, and despite the direct bearing of nationalistic phenomena upon important theoretical problems in sociology, no general sociological study of nationalism exists." (Wirth, *op. cit.,* p. 724.)
[20] Leonard S. Cottrell and Nelson N. Foote, "Sullivan's Contribution to Social Psychology," in *The Contributions of Harry Stack Sullivan,* ed. by Patrick Mullahy (New York, 1952), pp. 181–82.

II

The Concept of the Nation

What constitutes a nation is not speaking the same tongue or belonging to the same ethnic group, but having accomplished great things in common in the past and the wish to accomplish them in the future.
—ERNEST RENAN *

The Confusion of Nation and Race

The study of the meaning of nationalism cannot be separated from that of its basic component part—the nation. Let us eliminate immediately the kindred concept of race that invariably causes confusion. In popular thinking nation and race are often identified as one and the same thing. "The reason is," according to Frederick Hertz, "that most people find it difficult to conceive a close social unity without a physical bond, and that they cannot think of common mentality without common blood. An intimate solidarity of fraternity between members of a nation seems to them to imply a real relationship between members of a family." [1] Even in accepted usage, no sharp differentiation is made between the two terms. Webster's unabridged dictionary mentions common descent as one of the factors constituting the nation, making a concession to scientific conclusions on the subject by referring to "supposed ties of blood." The fact is that some parallels do exist between the two words, and it is often hard to keep them apart.

The average man may be forgiven for confusing the terms nation and race when so intelligent a statesman as Sir Winston Churchill, seeking to give emphasis to the idea of the nation, often

* Qu'est-ce qu'une nation? (1882).
[1] Frederick Hertz, Nationality in History and Politics (3rd ed., London, Routledge and Kegan Paul, 1951), p. 52.

14

speaks of "the British race," although it is certain that he does not mean it in a strictly biological sense. Many who consciously reject the racialist position unconsciously lapse into the use of its catchwords. Several distinguished scholars, moreover, have added to the confusion by insisting upon using the word race in unscientific fashion. Thus, Lord Bryce, in his *Race Sentiment as a Factor in History,* expressed the definite view that in the thought and imagination of every civilized people there is "an unquestionable racial strain" and that "race sentiment is one of the elements that go to make up national sentiment and national pride and help to make a people cohesive." [2] Similarly, the psychologist, W. B. Pillsbury, calls line of descent, i.e., race, a criterion of nationality and implies that a common physical descent is essential if a nation is to be made a unit in the best and fullest sense.[3] Defining a nation, the French philologist, Maximilien Paul Émile Littré, called it "a union of men inhabiting the same territory, whether or not subject to the same government, and possessing such common interests of long standing that they may be regarded as belonging to the same race." [4]

To understand the theoretical distinction between nation and race, it is helpful to remember that nation is a term used in social science, while race is one used in natural science: the nation designates historical and social characteristics which can be altered by society; race refers to hereditary, biological traits not easily changeable by education and assimilation.[5] Yet, there is so much disorder, nebulosity, and lack of precision surrounding the word race that it has been used as a synonym for a nation, a nationality, a language, or even artificial group customs. There never was, nor is there today, a German or American race, but there are German and American nations. There is no Aryan race, but there are Aryan

[2] Quoted in Bernard Joseph, *Nationality: Its Nature and Problems* (New Haven, 1929), p. 35.
[3] W. B. Pillsbury, *The Psychology of Nationality and Internationalism* (New York, 1919), p. 3.
[4] Quoted in George P. Gooch, *Nationalism* (London and New York, 1920), pp. 7–8.
[5] For definitions of the term race, see Eugène Pittard, *Race and History* (New York, 1926), pp. ix–x of the introduction by Henri Berr; Julian S. Huxley and A. C. Haddon, *We Europeans* (New York, 1936), pp. 7–9; Roland B. Dixon, *The Racial History of Man* (New York, 1923), pp. 3–4; A. C. Haddon, *The Races of Man* (New York, 1925), p. 1; W. Z. Ripley, *The Races of Europe* (New York, 1910), pp. 1–14; and J. de Morgan, *Prehistoric Man* (London, 1912), pp. 6–7.

languages. There was no Roman race, but there was a Roman civilization. Although race is used loosely to indicate groups of men differing in appearance, culture, or language, in the scientific sense it should be applied only to the biological groupings of human types.[6] Marcellin Boule's definition most closely approximates that generally accepted by scientists today:

> By race we should understand the continuity of a physical type, expressing affinities of blood, representing an essentially natural grouping, which can have nothing, and, in general, has nothing in common with the people, the nationality, the languages, or the customs corresponding to groupings that are purely artificial, in no way anthropological, and arising entirely from history, whose natural products they are.[7]

Used in this sense, the word race still retains a vagueness which is hard to overcome. It is possible that a nation may acquire a number of similar traits by isolation and inbreeding, and, when mixing with another group of different acquired traits, a population may result that possesses some characteristics of one parent group, of a second parent group, and of an intermediate, intermingled group.[8] It is difficult if not impossible to measure these variable factors. The definition by the racialist, Hans F. K. Günther, holding that "a race shows itself in a human group which is marked off from every other human group through its own proper combination of bodily and mental characteristics, and in turn produces only its like," [9] is not acceptable because such differentiations have never been successfully proven and may be dismissed as propaganda.[10]

[6] With reference to the word "human," Giorgio Pasquali, an Italian journalist, made the following pertinent observation: "I prefer the word *nation* when I speak of human beings, and the word *races* when I speak of Pekinese, racing horses, chickens, and Yorkshire swine." Man, although an animal, is a unique animal. From the biological point of view, his outstanding characteristic is his ability to transmit experience by tradition and without physical inheritance. Cf. Huxley and Haddon, *op. cit.,* pp. 116–17.

[7] Marcellin Boule, *Les hommes fossiles* (Paris, 1921), p. 322.

[8] Haddon, *op. cit.,* pp. 1–2.

[9] Hans F. K. Günther, *The Racial Elements of European History* (New York, n.d.), p. 3.

[10] "The important fact about race, so far established, seems to be that despite a degree of general overlapping in practically all physical traits, and despite the statistical stresses of common traits sufficient to recognize different populations, no single trait or known combination of traits appears to have any biological significance." (W. D. Weatherford and C. S. Johnson, *Race Relations* [New York, 1934], p. 7.)

We must distinguish in this complex problem between use of the term nation, indicating historical and political unity, and the word race, based roughly upon defined but generalized characteristics.[11] "A nation," according to the British historian, Ernest Barker, "is not the physical fact of one blood, but the mental fact of one tradition. A gulf is fixed between the race and the nation. The one is a common physical type; the other is a common mental content. The one is a natural fact which is already given at the dawn of history; the other is an artificial structure acquired by the thinking, feeling, and willing of human minds in the course of history."[12]

It follows, then, that in our treatment of the meaning of the nation we should exclude the highly fallacious and pseudo-scientific generalizations of the racialists and accept only those conclusions of natural science that impinge upon the subject.[13]

Nation and State

The widespread propensity for using the terms nation and state interchangeably is unfortunate. Webster's unabridged dictionary recognizes this tendency to use the words as synonyms in its fourth of seven definitions of nation and in its fourteenth of twenty-three definitions of state. It defines the nation as "loosely, the body of inhabitants of a country united under a single government; a state"; and the state as "a political body, or body politic; any body of people occupying a definite territory and politically organized under one government, especially one that is a sovereign, or not subject to external control."[14]

It will be noted in these definitions that the political aspect of the

[11] The British anthropologist, Sir Arthur Keith, objects to this distinction. According to Keith, when a land is peopled with a mixture of old races, a new effort at race-building is initiated sooner or later, just as a wren's nesting instincts are re-awakened as soon as the first nest is destroyed. "A nation always represents an attempt to become a race; nation and race are but different degrees of the same evolutionary movement." (Sir Arthur Keith, *Ethnos, or The Problem of Race* [London, 1931], pp. 26–28.)

[12] Ernest Barker, *National Character and the Factors in Its Formation* (London and New York, 1927), p. 12.

[13] The subject of race is treated in considerably more detail in Louis L. Snyder, *Race: A History of Modern Ethnic Theories* (New York, 1939).

[14] *Webster's New International Dictionary of the English Language* (2nd ed., unabridged, Springfield, Mass., 1949), pp. 1629, 2461.

state is emphasized and that the state is regarded as a coercive authority legally supreme over any individual or group. Yet, this political quality is so closely associated with social organization that it sometimes seems unreasonable to separate the two. The British political scientist, Harold J. Laski, declared that though "we must avoid the elementary error of identifying the state with the whole hierarchy of social institutions," many have done so.[15] Among those who have is the British philosopher, Bernard Bosanquet, who contributed to the confusion by this definition: "By the state we mean society as a unit, recognized as rightly exercising control over its members through absolute political power." [16] He further described the state as "the operative criticism of all social institutions." [17]

Some scholars claim that it is reasonable to use nation and state interchangeably when discussing international relations. The historian, Edward Krehbiel, reasons as follows. The term state, when applied to a unit like Great Britain, France, or Germany, clearly means the political unit. By nation some mean a state in which there is but one nationality, a national-state. These would be inclined to say that Austria-Hungary before 1919 was a state but not a nation; however, in international relations, Austria-Hungary was considered a nation, like every other. Hence, the terms nation and state should be used interchangeably when referring to a sovereign power in international affairs.[18]

The variation in attitudes toward the state as developed in different countries since the French Revolution presents an additional complication. In France, England, and the United States, under the influence of the rationalists Rousseau, Bentham, and Jefferson, the state came to be regarded as the over-all unit of sovereignty whose ultimate power lay in the people. On the other hand, some scholars diverged from this main stream and began to exalt the state as a mystical entity to be worshipped. Thus, the German philosopher, Hegel, who is regarded as one of the leading prophets of German nationalism, praised, with all the honorific phrases at his

[15] Harold J. Laski, *Grammar of Politics* (New Haven, 1925), p. 29.
[16] Bernard Bosanquet, *The Philosophical Theory of the State* (London, 1920), pp. 184–85.
[17] *Ibid.*, p. 140.
[18] Edward Krehbiel, *Nationalism, War and Society* (New York, 1916), pp. 1–2.

disposal, the omnipotent state, besides which the fate and happiness of the individual count for nothing. The state, to Hegel, is mind objectified. It is the Divine Idea as it exists on earth, the idea of spirit in the external manifestations of human will and freedom. The individual mind is only partly free, because it is guided by its own passions, its prejudices, and its impulses; therefore, of necessity, it must subject itself to the state. To Hegel the mere survival of the state was a test of national righteousness.[19]

Similarly, the German historian, Heinrich von Treitschke, regarded the state as the basis of all national life. The state appears, he said, in the image of a person; history itself is simply a great drama in which the various states are actors. Just as the individual possesses the abstract thing we call character, so do the states have permanent characteristics. It is wrong to think of the state as an organism; it is rather a person with distinct characteristics. The most important possession of a state is power.[20] But Treitschke was careful to distinguish between state and nation. Although the state is a moral community which is called upon to educate the human race by positive achievement, its ultimate object is that a nation should develop in it, a nation distinguished by "real national character."[21]

The Italian philosopher and historian, Benedetto Croce, defined the state simply, as "nothing other than the government."[22] Likewise, Harold Laski noted: "The state is, for the purpose of practical administration, the government."[23] Similarly, the political scientist, A. D. Lindsay, defined the state as "the organization of organizations, . . . comprehensive, therefore, in its scope as other organizations are selective."[24] An Asiatic political scientist, Mousheng Hsitien Lin, working in the United States, contributed a compromise definition: "The state is the power which maintains

---

[19] This was, according to the American philosopher, Morris Raphael Cohen, "a doctrine that misses the tragedy of history and is equivalent to Napoleon's dictum that God is on the side of the heaviest artillery." (In "Hegel," *Encyclopedia of the Social Sciences* [New York, 1937], VII, p. 313.)

[20] Heinrich von Treitschke, *Die Politik* (2 vols., Leipzig, 1899–1900), I, 29, 62–63.

[21] Treitschke, *op. cit.,* I, p. 74.

[22] Benedetto Croce, *Elementi di Politica* (Bari, Gius, Laterza, and Figi, 1925), p. 14.

[23] Quoted by George H. Sabine, in "State," *Encyclopedia of the Social Sciences* (New York, 1937), XIV, p. 329.

[24] A. D. Lindsay, "The State in Recent Political Theory," *Political Science Quarterly,* L (1914), pp. 128 ff.

a general hierarchy of values, upon which social life is organized, and of which social institutions are concrete embodiments." [25]

What, then, are the nation and the state? We may conclude that each term stands for something *sui generis*. Where the words are distinguished, nation takes on political, social, economic, and cultural connotations; the state refers primarily to legal authority.

Nation and Language

Language, like history itself, is never static; it is dynamic—ever in a state of change. It seldom dies but rather changes in form and construction, depending upon time and circumstances. It is a real living instrument of expression, which generally conforms closely in its structure to the mode of thought and expression of actual life. This may be seen in the development of language vis-à-vis the nation.

Before the age of nationalism, almost every village and region, every trade and profession, every social class had peculiarities of speech that were regarded as the special badge of that community.[26] In early medieval France, in the south the Burgundians and Visigoths used a dialect called *langue d'oc* (*oc* for yes, Latin *ac,* German *auch*), while the Franks and Normans in the north along the Seine had an idiom called *langue d'oïl* (*oïl* for yes, and pronounced like today's *oui*). The two dialects tended to merge from the beginning of the Crusades (1096) to the death of Louis IX (1270). The early Germans spoke two different dialects—Old High German (*Althochdeutsch*), used by the Germans in the midlands, and Old Low German (*Altplattdeutsch*), spoken by Scandinavians (Norsemen, Swedes, and Danes), Frisians, and Saxons (Anglo-Saxons and Dutch). The language of the Germanic tribes that conquered Britain in the fifth and sixth centuries is called Anglo-Saxon by some scholars. It mixed with Celtic, Latin, and Danish elements but remained essentially Low Ger-

[25] Mousheng Hsitien Lin, "Antistatism, Essay in Its Psychiatric and Cultural Analysis," *Psychiatry: Journal of the Biology and Pathology of Interpersonal Relations,* I (1938), pp. 391–92.

[26] The discussion in this section is necessarily brief. All major works on nationalism stress in detail the significance of language. Among the best treatments are those in Hertz, *op. cit.,* pp. 78–97, and Hans Kohn, *World Order in Historical Perspective* (Cambridge, Mass., 1942), pp. 70 ff.

man in character, similar to Old Saxon, Frisian, and Dutch. It is significant that the speech of the present residents of Hamburg, Bremen, and Lübeck is even today sometimes mistaken by English sailors as a corrupted form of English. All these dialects were accepted as natural, and were in no way looked upon as motivated by political or cultural factors. Language before the Age of Nationalism was rarely regarded as a fact upon which the prestige of the group depended.

As the modern nation emerged, its local, regional, and social rivals gradually lost their prestige and influence. Symptomatic of the new development were the translations of the Bible into English by Wycliffe and into German by Luther. National languages attained added importance under the impulse of new social conditions of the Renaissance and the Reformation and especially because of the appearance of the printing press and popular education. The rise of the middle and lower classes strongly stimulated the growth of national languages. Languages became uniform, eliminating the various vernacular dialects and, in general, reflecting the formation of the new nations.

Language reached a stage of idolization in modern nations. All nations tend to defend their language as the central symbol of their national life. Not only philologists and linguists, but the people themselves, regard language as a major expression of their independence and prestige, their personality, their characteristics, and their culture. Nationalists demand the domination of one language in their nation, the suppression of other languages, the purification of their own language from foreign elements, and the political incorporation of the nationals of other countries who speak the same language. National vocabulary, syntax, word formations, and word rhythms accurately reflect the intellectual and emotional qualities of a people. Moreover, it is through language that the accumulated historical traditions and memories of a people are transmitted from generation to generation to help maintain the unity of culture that partly distinguishes one nation from another.

Not only language but scripts, too, were influenced by the development of nationalism. Peculiar scripts are often regarded as signs of national personality. The rivalry between the Roman and the Gothic scripts in Germany and between the Roman and the

Cyrillic scripts in several of the Slavic countries has assumed a nationalist character. The process varies, but it is generally determined by nationalist aims. Turkey after World War I abolished the Arabic script in favor of the Latin, as a concession to the new nationalist spirit. On the other hand, the Irish revived their ancient Gaelic script as a recognition of their emancipation from England. Czechs and Latvians have changed their scripts from Gothic to Latin as a protest against German influence.

Language, then, plays a rôle in the structure of modern nations, especially as a determinant of national demarcation. We should not, however, exaggerate its importance. In popular usage, a nation is often identified as a people with a separate language, or it may even be assumed that a people speaking the same language form a separate nation. Hertz comments as follows:

> This identification of a nation with a language group is . . . untenable. It conflicts with both the legal and the sociological concept of a nation. The groups constituted by sentiment, citizenship and language very often do not coincide but overlap. In many cases, peoples of different tongues are citizens of the same State, and sometimes also regard one another as members of the same nation. On the other hand, many different nations in both senses speak the same language. Furthermore, demarcation according to language is occasionally made difficult by the fact that large parts of a population speak two languages, or a language intermediate between two others, so that it is not easy to determine to which other nation they have the closest affinity.[27]

Nation and Religion

Religion, a dominating force before the Age of Nationalism, was the object even of political loyalty. Europeans of the era preceding the Crusades did not divide themselves into nationalities; they described themselves, not as Germans, Frenchmen, or Greeks, but as Catholic Christians or Greek Orthodox Christians. The Reformation changed the character of religion as a factor in the life of nations when it introduced the idea of national churches. The struggle was a bitter one between a universal, all-embracing religious authority and individual nations which preferred their own Protestant versions of Christianity as more consistent with

[27] Hertz, *op. cit.*, pp. 95–96.

their own economic and emotional needs. The interminable religious wars that followed the Reformation threatened to destroy civilization itself.

The Age of Reason, the wave of Enlightenment that started in the late seventeenth century and dominated the eighteenth, was in one sense a reaction against the political as well as intellectual power of traditional Christianity. Newton, Locke, and their successors set up two great objects of faith, Nature and Reason, which were to the Enlightenment as such ideas as grace, salvation, and predestination had been to Christianity. The rationalists were responsible for the depoliticization of religion. "In this process," says Hans Kohn, "religion did not lose its true dignity; it remained one of the great spiritual forces, comforting and exalting to the human soul. It lost the element of coercion which had been so 'natural' to it for many centuries; its connection with the state, with political authority, was severed; religion retreated into the intimacy and spontaneity of the individual conscience." [28]

In the Age of Nationalism, the growth of nations was sometimes helped, sometimes hindered by the influence of religion. Even in its lessened rôle, religion helped to give to peoples that close sense of unity and cohesiveness implied in the idea of a nation. Catholicism in Ireland helped keep alive the Irish desire for independence, and in Poland it aided the demand for the re-creation of the nation after the Partitions. While it may be true that the formalized dogma of such religions as Christianity, Judaism, and Islam are supranational in character, the fulfillment of the religious spirit in the church community has proceeded in modern times along national lines.

Historically, then, nationalism may be regarded as a force that succeeded religion as a dominating power in the affairs of men; the two need not be confused, as are, for example, nation and language. But there remained an unconscious and indirect relationship between nationalism and religion. National consciousness is to some extent grounded on religion, in that it is thoroughly infused with a religious strain. In nationalism may be found many of the mystical and emotional manifestations that are ordinarily associated with religion, including pious idealization of the nation, worship of na-

[28] Kohn, *op. cit.,* p. 109.

tional heroes and martyrs, taking of military oaths, singing of patriotic hymns, construction of national monuments, creation of national myths, willingness to sacrifice life blood for the nation, and the urge to defend national customs and traditions against cosmopolitan tendencies. Defense of the fatherland is often depicted as the will of God (*Gesta Dei per Francos; Gott mit Uns*); the idea of a national mission is often clothed in religious terms ("the mission of a God-intoxicated people"). If nationalism becomes fanatical, dictators are hailed as saviors of the masses, as semireligious figures sent by Providence to lead a nation to its rightful place in the sun.

The Geographer's Concept of the Nation

Although the term nation had radically different meanings in the ancient and modern worlds, there is one point at which the two meanings converge: both regard the creation of the geographical unit as basic. The ancient world looked upon geographical unity as all-important in the origin of the nation, and the modern point of view retains it as one of the more important aspects of the existence of the nation.

Present-day geographers, like historians, sociologists, and anthropologists, take exception to use of the word nation as synonymous with race or stock. They admit the rôles of common ancestry, common language, and common institutions in any given nation, but they assert that exceptions to one or the other of these factors can easily be found. On the other hand, the criterion of an independent government is not so much open to objection. In arriving at the concept of a nation, geographers consider the factors of language, race, tradition, and independent government, but, at the same time, they insist upon the basic importance of a well-defined environment, more especially if it has a natural center. Moreover, geographers, particularly those who belong to the school of "new geography," are agreed that a multidisciplined approach is of most value in the search for the meaning of the nation. They feel themselves closely allied with the fields of history and sociology.

In this connection the American geographer, Griffith Taylor, has presented a highly original attempt to arrive at a clearer idea of the relative value of factors that have been attributed to the nation. He has shown in a table how such characters were distributed among some of the chief nations of Europe during the past ten centuries. Interpretations of this table may vary, but it sets forth, at least, the viewpoint of the geographer on the significance of environment and natural center (both key terms in the geographer's lexicon) in the meaning of the nation.

All theorists of nationalism, no matter what their field, attribute great significance to territory in the formation and existence of the nation. There is a close and interlocking relationship between territory and nation. Nations were originally formed in a narrow geographical area between natural boundaries. The stimulus was settlement-for-protection in a contiguous territory. The social structure was created by a combination of geographical factors (the configuration of the land, the type of soil, the natural resources, and the climate) and a fundamentally psychological concept (love of homeland). As the population increased, the neophyte nation began to look for wider and more satisfactory natural frontiers, such as oceans, rivers, seas, mountains, and forests. While the nation emerged as a product of geography, the national territory at the same time was affected by the development of the nation. On a map the territory of a nation may appear to be static and unchanging, but actually it undergoes a continuous transformation that is dependent upon the activities of the people who inhabit it.

The fluctuating interactions between nation and territory are especially strong at the natural frontiers, or linear border regions, where the individual nations touch one another. Here the contrast between nationals and aliens is more noticeable. On the other hand, there are more opportunities for the people of one nationality to merge into another, a process facilitated by bilingualism, close cultural ties, and intermarriage. Each nation pays particular attention to its border regions by seeking to inculcate in them a stronger sense of nationalism. The Russian tsars, demanding "one Russia, one Creed, one Tsar," inaugurated a ruthless policy of Russification, making Russian the official language in Finland, prohibiting the native language in Poland,

AN ATTEMPT TO EVALUATE FACTORS IN A NATION [29]

	France	England	Spain	Switzer-land	Italy	Belgium	Germany	Russia	Rumania
Language	Unit	Unit	¾ Unit	4 langs.	Unit	2 langs.	Unit	Unit	Unit
Religion	Unit	Unit	Unit	2 creeds	Unit	Unit	2	Unit	Unit
Race	3 races	2 races	Unit	Unit	2 races	2 races	2 races	Unit	Unit
Tradition	Strong	Strong	Strong	Feeble	Discontinuous	Feeble	Discontinuous	Fair	Fair
Independent Government	10 centuries	9	8	5	10?	1	10?	6	1
Well-defined Environment	Unit	Unit	Unit	Fair	Poor	Poor	Fair	Fair	Poor
Natural Center	Very good	Good	Poor	Fair	Poor	Fair	Fair	Good	Poor

26

[29] Griffith Taylor, *Environment and Nation: Geographical Factors in the Cultural and Political History of Europe* (University of Chicago Press, 1936), p. 22.

and requiring even the favored Balts to speak Russian. Wilhelm II instituted a policy of uncompromising Germanism by suppressing evidences of national sentiment among the Danes in Schleswig, the Alsatians and Lorrainers acquired in 1871, and the Poles taken over by Prussia during the Partitions. Similar policies were adopted by other countries. The border regions are the critical spots, since any threats to their safety menace the entire nation.

Added to the factor of settlement of a territory is the considerably more dynamic factor of population movement. It is possible for the territory of a nation to be changed radically by social mobility, emigration, immigration, and colonization. The composition of a nation may change from homogeneous groupings to mixed nationalities. This process alters the character of what may seem to be a fixed environment. Nations, as well as geography itself, are continually in a state of flux.

Although territory is an essential element in the existence of a nation, it cannot be regarded as the absolute clue to the meaning of the nation. Geography, as a substratum of the historic life of mankind, does not always foreshadow the course of historical development. The spiritual and individual factors in human life may fail to use the existing substratum. The conception of geographical determinists that a territory provides a solid and unchangeable environment, which dominates the destinies of peoples with a blind and ruthless brutality, is a unilateral interpretation that suffers from the same fallacies as Marxian economic determinism. Geography provides a reservoir of possibilities, by no means fixed and unalterable, from which man chooses his course of action. The key factor remains the human selection of possibilities in a given environment. If a trinitarian formula for historical development were sought, it would have to consist of territory, stomach, and mind. Any new approach to the meaning of nationalism must place more and more emphasis upon hitherto neglected psychological factors.

The Historian's Idea of the Nation

It is the aim of the historian to reconstruct as much of the past as he can by re-creating a meaningful image of what has happened based on records which are admittedly incomplete. He is handicapped because to a great extent his historical approach must be subjective, without that experimental method open to the physicist, the geologist, and other natural scientists. Few terms give him more trouble than the word nation, which is, nevertheless, of prime importance in his work. Carlton J. H. Hayes speaks of its "tantalizing ambiguity." [30] Hans Kohn, Ernest Barker, and Edward Krehbiel, as well as many other leading historians, have noted the frequent interchangeability of the terms nation and state.[31] Max Hildebert Boehm points out that the tendency in national development has been to efface the boundaries between nation and state so that at a certain stage in democratic development states automatically become transformed into nations. The national state, he says further, represents a synthesis of nation and state, but there is no clear and unanimous opinion on the exact nature of this synthesis.[32]

As a social science, history embraces all facets of human development—political, social, economic, religious, cultural, and psychological. Historians take into consideration all these factors when discussing the nation, but at the same time they are inclined to give preference, when seeking for its meaning, to its political character. Thus, J. Holland Rose makes this definition: "I use the term 'nation' as a political term, designating a people which has attained to state organization." [33] A nation, in the view of H. A. L. Fisher, "implies a common political sentiment." [34] According to Carlton J. H. Hayes, nation has been employed since the seventeenth century to describe the population of a sovereign political state, regardless of any racial or linguistic unity, and this description still holds general sanction.[35] Hans Kohn designates as the distinguishing characteristic of modern nations the political doctrine of sovereignty.[36] He says further that in the later Middle

---

[30] Carlton J. H. Hayes, *Essays on Nationalism* (New York, 1941), p. 3.
[31] Hans Kohn, *The Idea of Nationalism* (5th printing, New York, 1951), p. 580; Barker, *op. cit.,* pp. 15–16; and Krehbiel, *op. cit.,* p. 1.
[32] Max Hildebert Boehm, "Nationalism: Theoretical Aspects," *Encyclopedia of the Social Sciences* (New York, 1937), XI, pp. 231–32.
[33] J. Holland Rose, *Nationality in Modern History* (New York, 1916), p. vi.
[34] H. A. L. Fisher, *The Commonweal* (London, 1924), p. 196.
[35] Hayes, *op. cit.,* p. 3.
[36] Hans Kohn, *Force or Reason* (Cambridge, Mass., 1937), p. 148.

Ages the word nation often had no political content whatever, but the revolutions of the eighteenth century awakened the masses to political and social activism, with the result that the nation came generally to mean the whole political organization.[37]

Historians recognize, nonetheless, that the term nation has had an etymological development of its own. The Latin *natio* (birth, race) originally signified a social grouping based on real or imaginary ties of blood. Such derivative words as "cognate" or "innate" suggest the idea of birth. In the early Middle Ages *natio villae* was used to describe the kinship group of the village. The barons at Oxford spoke in 1258 of a *natio regni Angliae,* the kinship group of the kingdom of England, as opposed to the foreign followers of Henry III. In the later Middle Ages, the faculty of arts of the Professors' University at Paris was divided into "nations" for voting purposes, according to place of birth.[38]

In the sixteenth and seventeenth centuries the term nation began to be applied to describe the population of a state regardless of racial unity. At the same time, the word began to take on its confusing qualities. Edmund Spenser, in his *Faërie Queen,* spoke of "a nation of birds," and Ben Jonson referred to physicians as "a subtile nation." [39] The term nation was first popularly employed after the Partitions of Poland and the French Revolution during the late eighteenth century. It was then used as synonymous with the word "country," in much the same way as nationalism today is confused with patriotism. Nation began to be used as opposed to "people" (*peuple*). In this sense, it indicated the conscious and active portion of the population, whereas people denoted the politically and socially more passive masses.[40] With the emergence of modern nationalism, the people were integrated

[37] Hans Kohn, *The Idea of Nationalism, op. cit.,* p. 581.

[38] The four most important were: The French nation, including (in addition to the native French) Spaniards, Italians, and Greeks; the Picard nation, composed of those from northwestern France and the Netherlands; the Norman nation, from western France; and a "nation" of students from England, Ireland, Scotland, and the Germanies. Each nation was governed by a procurator. At the University of St. Andrews the "nations" were Britain, Lothian, Fife, and Angus; at the University of Vienna there were Austria, Bohemia, Saxony, and Hungary. (Cf. Hastings Rashdall, *The Universities of Europe in the Middle Ages* [2 vols., Oxford, 1895].)

[39] Hayes, *op. cit.,* p. 3. This tendency carried over into the nineteenth century, when Samuel Butler spoke of lawyers as "too wise a nation t' expose their trade to disputation."

[40] Hans Kohn, *The Idea of Nationalism, op. cit.,* p. 580.

into the nation, which, thenceforth, took on its modern historical meaning.

Despite this narrowing down of the meaning of the nation to its political sense, there has remained among historians a tendency to stress the abstract meaning of the term. Since one cannot see the nation and since it has many members who are separated by a multiplicity of differences, it is often regarded as a mystical reality, whose unity of character must be sensed by faith rather than by sight. Thus, the nation has been defined as "a congeries of wills, acting through centuries," based on the supposition that the individual is a single will acting in the space of a lifetime, while the nation is the sum total of these individuals. The idea of the nation as a "grand solidarity" was expressed by the French critic, Ernest Renan, in his famous definition:

> A nation is a grand solidarity constituted by the sentiment of sacrifices which one has made and those that one is disposed to make again. It supposes a past, it renews itself especially in the present by a tangible deed: the approval, the desire, clearly expressed, to continue the communal life. The existence of a nation is an everyday plebiscite.[41]

According to the British historian, Lord Acton, the change in the meaning of the term nation was due to the work of the French Encyclopedists, who, in the late eighteenth century, made the state of nature the ideal of society, that, in turn, became the basis of the nation.[42] The new definition of nation was borrowed from the material world, and, in order to avoid a loss of territory, it became not only an abstraction but a fiction. The nation was no longer what it had been in the ancient world. It was not now the result of merely physical and material causes, but a moral and political being. It was no longer seen as the creation of physiological or geographical unity, but as a development in the course of history by the action of the state. It was derived from the state, not supreme over it. The nation obtained its rights and its powers from the memory of a former independence.

Lord Acton regarded this new meaning with the greatest misgivings because, in his view, it departed from the lines of tradition

[41] Ernest Renan, *Qu'est-ce qu'une nation?* (Paris, 1882), p. 27.
[42] Baron John Emerich Edward Dalberg Acton, *Essays on Freedom and Power* (Boston, 1948), pp. 173 ff., originally written as *History of Freedom and Other Essays,* ed. by J. N. Figgis and R. V. Laurence (London, 1907).

and historic unity.[43] The new meaning, he said, assumed that a unity existed separate from the idea of representation and the government, wholly independent of the past, and capable at any moment of expressing and changing its mind.

Most historians differ with Lord Acton's contention that the appearance of the modern nation meant a complete departure from the lines of tradition and historic unity. The new unity, they say, was not wholly independent of the past, but, on the contrary, closely tied up with it. In emerging as modern nations during the Reformation, France, Germany, Switzerland, and other nations were giving practical expression to those particularistic tendencies which existed in the past even under the Holy Roman Empire. The vital change that took place represented the dissolution of the medieval polity—a union of *sacerdotium* (church) and *imperium* (state), which formed the nation of the Middle Ages. There is no historical principle which calls for the absolute maintenance of the *status quo*. For example, the emerging German nation combined the diverse trinity of Germano-Roman-Christian characteristics. History is always a process of change and development.[44]

In summary, historians generally agree that a nation is to be distinguished from a race, a state, and a language. It is not the same thing as a church, though it once was, and nations today owe much of their character to religious influences. On the other hand, the occupation of a given territory is important for the existence of a nation, for it is through possession of territory that a nation develops traditions and character. However, the existence of a nation implies a common political sentiment. The following definition by Ernest Barker closely approximates that of most historians on the meaning of the nation:

[43] In understanding Lord Acton's concept of the nation, we should keep in mind the fact that he regarded the Middle Ages with much sympathy, had a strong antipathy to the formation of the ecclesiastical nations of the Reformation, and was opposed to the egalitarian aspects of the French Revolution and modern democracy.

[44] Objection may be entered also against Lord Acton's view that the French people, as a result of the French Revolution, emerged as "an ethnological product rather than an historic unit." (*Ibid.*, p. 173.) We have seen how recent scientists writing on race have demolished this viewpoint. Furthermore, in condemning nationality as "absurd and criminal," Lord Acton was expressing his resentment against the break-up of the medieval polity.

A nation is a body of men, inhabiting a definite territory, who normally are drawn from different races, but possess a common stock of thoughts and feelings acquired and transmitted during the course of a common history; who on the whole and in the main, though more in the past than in the present, include in that common stock a common religious belief; who generally and as a rule use a common language as the vehicle of their thoughts and feelings; and who, besides common thoughts and feelings, also cherish a common will, and accordingly form, or tend to form, a separate State for the expression of that will.[45]

Political Science and the Nation

Modern political science is concerned primarily with problems of government and legislation, political institutions, political power, and the theory of the state and its practical evaluation.[46] Its main interests are in politics,[47] sovereignty,[48] and the state.[49] Often, since it lacks a definitely prescribed methodology, political science overlaps with the field of the historian.

With the exception of those who identify the state with the nation, most political scientists prefer to devote the major part of their attention to the state and leave the concept of the nation to the disciplines of history and sociology. They distinguish a people as a group of individuals who by means of a similar language, folkways, and institutions are able to communicate with each other directly and easily, whereas they regard the state as the formal political and military organization of one of more peoples. A nation is the formal organization of one people. A state need not be a nation. A nation must be a state.[50]

[45] Barker, op. cit., p. 17.
[46] Cf. Ernest Barker, The Study of Political Science and Its Relation to Cognate Studies (Cambridge, England, 1928); and J. R. Seeley, Introduction to Political Science (London, 1896).
[47] For example, H. J. Laski, A Grammar of Politics (London and New Haven, 1925); and Benedetto Croce, Elementi di Politica (Bari, 1925).
[48] For example, H. J. Laski, Studies in the Problem of Sovereignty (New Haven, 1917).
[49] For example, Henry J. Ford, The Natural History of the State (Princeton, 1915); and W. E. Hocking, Man and the State (New Haven, 1926). There has emerged in Germany a discipline closely related to political science, but actually distinct from it, known as "general theory of the state" (Allgemeine Staatslehre or Staatstheorie). The line of demarcation between the two disciplines is not altogether clear. Examples of this work: Franz Oppenheimer, Der Staat (Frankfurt am Main, 1907); and O. Spann, Der wahre Staat (Jena, 1931).
[50] Max Sylvius Handman, "The Sentiment of Nationalism," Political Science Quarterly, XXXVI (1921), p. 104.

Some political scientists persist in confusing the terms nation and race. For example, C. Delisle Burns regarded the nation as primarily a group of men related physically. "It is from physical relationship that nearly all powerful nations have risen. . . . A group of men whose ancestors were divided in interest is now content to subordinate minor purpose to the ambition which they all feel in common. That is the force which we call a nation. . . . We may assert that a nation is, first, a group of men related in blood." [51] Most political scientists reject this conclusion.

In the United States the study of the meaning of the nation was strongly influenced at the middle of the nineteenth century by the German-born scholar, Francis Lieber, who, after 1856, was professor of political science at Columbia University.[52] His definition of nation has been quoted again and again down to the present day:

> What is a nation in the modern sense of the world? The word "nation," in the fullest adaptation of the term, means, in modern times, a numerous and homogeneous population (having long emerged from the hunters and nomadic state), permanently inhabiting and cultivating a coherent territory, with a well-defined geographic outline, and a name of its own,—the inhabitants speaking their own language, having their own literature and common institutions, which distinguish them clearly from other and similar groups of people, being citizens or subjects of a unitary government, however subdivided it may be, and having an organic unity with one another as well as being conscious of a common destiny. Organic, intellectual and political internal unity with proportionate strength and a distinct and obvious demarcation from similar groups, are notable elements of the idea of a modern nation in its fullest sense.[53]

Lieber's definition of the nation is an important one because it removed the earlier emphasis upon the theories of natural rights and social contract and placed it upon the idea of organic growth.

[51] C. Delisle Burns, *The Morality of Nations* (New York, 1916), pp. 7, 9, 12. Burns was influenced by the philosopher, Jellinek, especially by the latter's concept that *"das Wesen der Nation ist dynamischer Natur."*

[52] Shortly after his arrival as a refugee in the United States, Lieber undertook the editorship of the *Encyclopedia Americana,* which helped popularize the German scholarly system of bibliographical references and documentation. While teaching at South Carolina College, he produced the first works in political science by a private American scholar.

[53] Francis Lieber, *Fragments of Political Science on Nationalism and Internationalism* (New York, 1868), pp. 7–8.

In his estimation, the nation did not emerge as a natural right of man, a favorite theory of the rationalists, nor was it a response to the need for a theoretical contract between people and sovereign power. It was an organic unity, the result of organic growth. Lieber felt that some nations were peculiarly fitted for a world mission. A fervent nationalist, he believed that the American nation in particular was an instrument which had been largely successful in solving such problems as the relation of sovereignty to liberty, of local to federal government, and of commonwealth to the family of nations.[54]

Philosophy, Nation, and State

There is a vast philosophic literature on the concept of the state. The prototype for such studies, as well as for consideration of the mechanics of political and legal relations, is Aristotle's *Politics* (Books IV–VI). In the works of Machiavelli, Hegel, Seydel, Jellinek, Bosanquet, and others, we find an intense concern with the theoretical implications of the state, and especially with an ethical justification or denunciation of the coercion which all states practice.[55] Using it as a generic term, philosophers sometimes find that they must define state more or less arbitrarily in correlation with the political philosophy they advocate. Spengler, as an example, goes so far as to call the state "history regarded as at a halt"—which other scholars have labeled "a gratituous confusion."

When they do take up the idea of the nation, philosophers, in common with other scholars, prefer to use the term nation in reference to a unity of culture (common history, language, literature, traditions, and heroes, as well as a sentiment of loyalty). On the other hand, they use state when it is necessary to denote

[54] Cf. Merle Curti, *The Growth of American Thought* (New York, 1943), pp. 482–83.
[55] Philosophic treatment of the nature of the state branches off from the field of the philosopher into the neighboring disciplines of political science and law. In addition to Bernard Bosanquet's *The Philosophical Theory of the State* (London, 1920), the following works may be mentioned: Paul Vinogradoff, *Outlines of Historical Jurisprudence* (2 vols., London, 1920–22); L. T. Hobhouse, *The Metaphysical Theory of the State* (London, 1918); John C. Gray, *The Nature and Sources of the Law* (New York, 1921); Georg Jellinek, *Allgemeine Staatslehre* (Berlin, 1914); and R. M. MacIver, *The Modern State* (Oxford, 1926).

a unity of political and legal authority. Like scholars in other disciplines, they see difficulty in a current belief that the unity of the nation is the proper basis for political authority. They deplore use of the terms state and nation as synonyms. Philosophical discussions of this confusion are on an esoteric and metaphysical plane, but their conclusions are similar to those of other disciplines. Partly because of this and partly because of the paucity of philosophical treatment of the nation, we shall not examine the discipline further.

Sociology and the Nation

Sociology, the study of the structure and functions of society, deals with group behavior, the relationships among men, and the factors entering into and ensuing from these relationships.[56] Its subject matter is variously conceived to be society, culture, race, social institutions, collective behavior, human ecology, and social interaction. Study of the nation, one of the largest and most important groups in human society, is, of course, in the sociologist's province.

The historical concept of the nation concerns the sociologist insofar as it sheds light upon the continuous process of group life. In tracing the origin of the term nation, the sociologist finds himself on common ground with the historian. He sees shifts of meaning with successive types of societies.

The Preliterate (Prehistoric) Tribal Society: Originally *natio* meant a backward, exotic tribe, what we would describe today as natives, which comes from the same root. For example, *nationes ferae* (Sallust), *natio servituti nata* (Cicero), *innumerabiles et ferocissimae nationes* (Hieronymus).

The Ancient World: Here society was divided into units under the sovereignty of either a leader or the people. Great civilized people were called *gens,* and the Roman people as the bearer of sovereignty called itself the *populus.* In the Latin Vulgate, *natio* and *gens* referred to the Gentiles, while the chosen people were called the *populus.*

[56] The term *sociologie* was coined in 1838 by the French positivist philosopher, Auguste Comte, as the name for the comprehensive study of the associated life of man.

The Middle Ages: In the ecclesiastical society of the Middle Ages, nation meant a specific territory within the present boundaries of nations. The most important attributes of the medieval nation were common dialect, traditions, and customs.

Modern Times: Modern society is composed of nations, each with its common and distinct literary culture and its independent organization dedicated to the preservation, growth, and expansion of certain aspects of its culture. Such organizations as the League of Nations and the United Nations represent the union of sovereign nations along international lines, presumably a possible next step in the development of society.[57]

This strictly chronological classification is one with which most sociologists are inclined to agree. However, on the present connotation of nation, there are some differences of opinion. The Italian sociologist, Don Luigi Sturzo, prefers to place the theoretical and practical positings of the modern idea of nation on a national basis. There were, he says, between 1789 and 1848 three great historical affirmations of the idea of nation.

French Affirmation: Nation was taken to mean the country, the state, and the people as a moral and political unit. The nation came to be in opposition to the king. Here the term becomes the assertion of a moral and political personality. The nation "is the popular will organized by the state."

German Affirmation: Beginning in the early nineteenth century with Fichte and his *Letters to the German Nation,* the nation was taken to mean an idea which realizes itself, a spirit that is translated into fact. "The individuals which belong to it are only phenomena of a reality which we think of as collective insofar as we live in and for it." It found its further literary and philosophical fulfillment in the Romantic period, in Hegel's divine-state, and was eventually merged with Bismarck's system of power and force and the materialistic myths of Blood and Soil. From this point of view, the nation becomes "the soul of a people realizing itself through innate virtue."

Italian Affirmation: The third affirmation of nation was the idea of political unity and independence of every nation. While Sturzo does not call this an Italian affirmation, he points out that

[57] Cf. Hertz, *op. cit.,* pp. 6 ff.

Mazzini symbolized this idea. Here the nation becomes an "autonomous and free political personality," such as Italy, Greece, Ireland, and Belgium.[58]

There is much to be said for Sturzo's point of view, and it explains, in part, how the term nation has come to be the subject of so much confusion. In Great Britain nation ordinarily means the totality of citizens in a sovereign state, but even here the Welsh still call themselves a nation, though Wales is not a sovereign state. In France the term has a more inclusive meaning than elsewhere. The French sociologist, S. Sighele, used the terms nation and state interchangeably.[59] The American sociologist, John F. Cuber, designates the political state as a subdivision of the general category of the nation-state.[60] Faced with these difficulties, which seem insurmountable, the American sociologist, Florian Znaniecki, deliberately avoids mention of the word altogether and prefers to use nationality.[61]

The confusion in ancient times in distinguishing between nation and people (*natio* and *populus*) has carried through into the modern era. The German-Argentine sociologist, Rudolf Rocker, sees the distinction as one between a natural and an artificial concept. He defines a people as "the natural result of social union, a mutual association of men brought along by a certain similarity of external conditions of living." This inner relationship cannot be bred artificially nor artificially destroyed. The nation, on the other hand, in Rocker's view, is the artificial result of the struggle for political power. "Belonging to a nation is never determined, as is belonging to a people, by profound natural causes; it is always subject to political considerations and based on those reasons of state behind which the interests of privileged minorities always hide." [62] It follows that nationalism, similarly, is an artificial concept that might be called the political religion of the modern nation.

[58] Don Luigi Sturzo, *Nationalism and Internationalism* (New York, 1948), pp. 10–12.
[59] S. Sighele, *Psychologie des sectes* (Paris, 1898), pp. 42–51, quoted in R. E. Park and E. E. Burgess, *Introduction to the Science of Sociology* (Chicago, 1940), pp. 202–07.
[60] John F. Cuber, *Sociology, A Synopsis of Principles* (New York, 1947), p. 440.
[61] Florian Znaniecki, *Modern Nationalities* (Chicago, 1952), p. 10.
[62] Rudolf Rocker, *Nationalism and Culture*, tr. by Ray E. Chase (New York, 1937), pp. 200–01.

Sociologists believe that a nation is formed only when, besides economic and ecological juxtaposition there is cooperation. Herbert Spencer, one of the fathers of sociology, expressed this basic thought: "Cooperation is made possible by society and makes society possible. It presupposes associative men; and men remain associated only because of the benefits association yields them. But there cannot be concerted actions without agencies by which actions are adjusted in their times, amounts, and kinds; and the actions cannot be different kinds without the cooperators undertaking different duties. That is to say, cooperators must become organized, either voluntarily or involuntarily." [63]

Sociologists, in general, show more interest in the cultural pattern of nations and the structure of societies within national states than in the political nation per se. They feel that their discipline deals more with society than with the nation. Within society they see such great associations as the state, industrial distribution, labor, the church, and so on, and they describe the interplay of forces (cooperation and conflict) within these major groupings. In any one of these structures we find a social process going on, in either the group, in-group, primary and secondary groups, or crowds.

Group: The term group serves as a convenient sociological designation for any number of people, whether small or large, between whom relations are such that they must be thought of together. The term stands for any combination of persons—a family, a mob, a picnic, a trade union, a city precinct, a corporation, a state, or a nation.[64] It may, according to a central position assumed by MacIver, include any number of people having common (rather than like) interests. From this point of view, a nation may be regarded as a relatively large group of people who are united by a common tradition, a common sentiment, and similar cultural traits that set them apart from other groups.[65] The strong bond of the nation is to be found in group memories, in-

[63] Herbert Spencer, *Principles of Sociology* (New York, 1900–01), Section II, *passim.*
[64] Cf. Albion W. Small, *General Sociology* (Chicago, 1905), pp. 495–97.
[65] Robert L. Sutherland and Julian L. Woodward, *Sociology* (New York, 1940), p. 344.

cluding accounts of dead heroes and exploits by representatives of the group.[66]

In-Group: The in-group, of which the nation may be an example, is that to which the individual feels he belongs, tied by loyalty to the group or to some symbols of it.[67] In this sense, an out-group becomes another nation.

Primary and Secondary Groups: The primary group is the growing individual's face-to-face world, the immediate world of security, either his consanguineous group (family) or associational group (peer group). A secondary group, such as a labor union or a religion, may win deep loyalty from the individual, but he reacts to them in the light of earlier group experiences.[68] Some sociologists feel that the generic approach in grouping is an older sociological view and should not be stressed too much within the structural functional analysis.

The Crowd: As used popularly, a crowd is a chance collection of individuals. Such a collectivity becomes a crowd in the sociological sense only when a condition of rapport (mutual responsiveness, contagious excitement, heightened by suggestibility) has been established among the individuals who compose it.[69] In an early sociological view, S. Sighele described the crowd and the nation as two extreme links in the chain of human association, between which lie heteregeneous crowds (street crowds) and homogeneous crowds (sects, classes).[70] The nation becomes here the most perfect type of organization of the crowd, the final and extreme type.[71] Other sociologists refuse to accept this kind of reasoning because it refers to the structural situation as though it had no functional operation. Most sociologists tend to shy away from use of the term crowd in conjunction with nation, and prefer instead to turn their attention to functioning of the "mass," or "public."

[66] Cecil C. North, *Social Differentiation* (Chapel Hill, North Carolina, 1926), p. 43.
[67] Paul A. F. Walter, Jr., *Race and Culture* (New York, 1952), p. 28.
[68] Cf. Gardner Murphy, *Personality: A Biosocial Approach to Origins and Structure* (New York, 1947), p. 842.
[69] Robert Park, "The Crowd and the Public," in Park and Burgess, *op. cit.,* p. 893.
[70] Sighele, *op. cit.,* p. 207.
[71] Sighele then went beyond this "final and supreme type" to speak of another collectivity superior in number and extension, the collectivity formed by "race." (*Ibid.*)

Other sociologists speak of the nation as the largest social unit within which social life has been enduringly ordered as a whole. A distinction is made here between the local social unit, or community, and the larger social unit, or nation, which in turn has many characteristics of the community.[72] This view has been criticized within the discipline as outdated. These sharp differences of opinion are typical. One can understand why Znaniecki has tried in vain to coin a new, compound Greek word to mean a "national culture society," which he uses instead of nation.[73]

In the midst of these conflicting views of the sociologists, there appears to be one common thought—that a nation is formed only when, besides economic and ecological juxtaposition, there are co-operation [74] and association. R. L. Sutherland and J. L. Woodward claim that, in the final analysis, not until the "we-sentiment," or the "feeling of oneness" (the conviction of a group superiority and the awareness and willingness to work to a common objective) has appeared, does a nation really exist.[75] Admitting that such traits as common language, religion, government, and traditions all contribute to the development of a nation, they hold, nevertheless, that the only indispensable factor is the general element of a common tradition supported by a common sentiment —the we-sentiment.

Psychological Views of the Nation

The word psychology is derived from two Greek words which mean the science of the psyche, or soul. Originally, it was a branch of metaphysics concerned with the concept of the soul. Subsequently, with the soul taken out of its religious context and translated to mean mind or self, psychology came to be known as the science of human behavior, treating the mind in all its aspects, systematically investigating the phenomena of consciousness and behavior, and studying the organism and activities in relation to

---

[72] Logan Wilson and William L. Kolb, *Sociological Analysis* (New York, 1949), p. 344.
[73] Znaniecki, *op. cit.*, p. 21.
[74] Cf. Herbert Spencer, *Principles of Sociology* (New York, 1900–01), Section II, *passim*.
[75] Sutherland and Woodward, *op. cit.*, p. 351.

physical and social environment. The field was broken down into an almost bewildering variety of sub-disciplines,[76] from which we can summarize four general approaches: *experimental psychology,* dealing with study of reaction time, transfer of training and maze learning with human and animal subjects, and operant conditioning; *clinical psychology,* investigation of the life history and abilities of the child as a means of improving emotional and social adjustment; *applied psychology,* the attempt to discover to what extent people differ in intelligence, aptitude, and personality, and *social psychology,* the scientific study of the individual as related to other individuals.

It is this latter branch of psychology which is of most concern to us in our quest for the meaning of nationalism. There is a close nexus between sociology and social psychology. But where sociology is concerned primarily with the group, social psychology treats mainly the individual in the group situation. This distinction is often hard to maintain, since social psychologists are becoming increasingly aware of the importance of the group in determining the characteristics of the individual. The process is a continuous one—the individual joins the crowd, the crowd becomes a nation.[77]

Psychologists, like historians and sociologists, recognize "the riddle of the definition of nationhood." [78] Although, on occasion, psychologists use the terms nation and state interchangeably,[79] they are aware of the differences between the two terms. Thus, Wayland F. Vaughan, although admitting that the nation is a cultural configuration and the state a political organization, follows popular usage by employing the terms interchangeably.[80] J. F. Brown finds it desirable to have a word which will stand for the whole paraphernalia of governmental agencies through which the *status quo* is maintained or changed. This he calls the state,

[76] For example, faculty, rational, empirical, existential, functional, structural, Gestalt, self, dynamic, behavioristic, motor, physiological, abnormal, differential, and genetic psychology.
[77] Cf. Otto Klineberg, *Social Psychology* (New York, 1940), pp. 1–5.
[78] William McDougall, *The Group Mind* (New York, 1920), p. 141.
[79] For example, Emory S. Bogardus, *Fundamentals of Social Psychology* (New York, 1924), pp. 301–02.
[80] "Actually, the state and nation would coincide only when all the persons sharing the same culture were organized into one political unit." (Wayland F. Vaughan, *Social Psychology* [New York, 1948], p. 890.)

which he defines as "the pattern of social institutions through which the social organization of the nation is perpetuated." [81] George Malcolm Stratton makes this distinction: "A nation is a sufficiently large body of persons sufficiently united by sympathy and interest to cooperate in the many ways required for a common government, and who are actually organized as an independent state." [82]

Psychologists generally distinguish carefully between race as a biological concept based upon inheritable physical traits and nation as a political concept based upon geographical boundaries. They recognize that the people within a given geographical region are fashioned into a nation primarily by virtue of a common environment and quite apart from the considerable effects of genetic intermixture. One speaks normally of the American nation, which is a melting pot of the so-called white, black, brown, yellow, and red races. If the American people is not to be strictly differentiated as an American race, it does retain its connotation of an American nation. "While a race, as defined in physical terms, on a hereditary basis, is doubtfully distinct, a nation, as a cultural, linguistic, political, and geographic grouping, is very definite." [83]

An important distinction is made by psychologists between the popular and scientific concepts of the nation. The popular version accepts the nation uncritically as a reality projected behind popular symbols and conveyed in the language of metaphor. There are three reasons for the prevalence of the popular concept: emotional habits conditioned in early childhood are carried over into adulthood; this concept is a socially approved method of raising an individual's estimate of himself; and it is an unrecognized manner of attaining, under the guise of patriotism, certain special privileges.[84]

[81] "The state then includes the whole structure of government (legislative, judicial, executive) and the armed forces (police and army) for protecting the existing organization, in fact all the various agencies of government by both force and persuasion." (J. F. Brown, *Psychology and the Social Order* [New York, 1936], p. 123.)
[82] George Malcolm Stratton, *Social Psychology and International Conduct* (New York, 1929), p. 69.
[83] Ellis Freeman, *Principles of General Psychology* (New York, 1939), p. 90.
[84] F. H. Allport, "The Psychology of Nationalism," *Harper's*, CLV (1927), pp. 291–301.

The scientific concept, on the other hand, formulates the nation as existing solely in the behavior of its individuals,[85] and seeks to elicit its meaning in terms of psychological characteristics. Thus, Ralph H. Gundlach believes that any scientific attempt to understand the meaning of the nation must be based on what it involves:

1) Identification with the state, hence *ego-expansion;*

2) Destructive *action* as a substitute for problem solving;

3) *Oversimplification, personalizing and moralizing* the conflict into *Good versus Evil;*

4) Rationalization (*repression and projection*);

5) Shift of responsibility for violence;

6) *Transfer* of fear and hate to pacifists, communists, labor leaders, *et al.*[86]

It is precisely at this point that the psychologist deviates from the main stream in his search for the meaning of the nation. Where historians speak of the traditions of the past and where sociologists stress the activities of the group, psychologists prefer to direct their attention to consciousness and emotion. The British social psychologist, Morris Ginsberg, speaks of "consciousness of kind" as the cement which binds the nation.[87] For Herbert Gurnee the nation "possesses a consciousness and belief in itself as a separate people, and this consciousness and belief help to explain its collective organization."[88] According to the German psychologist, W. Ehrenstein, "the nation is based on the consciousness of bonds with the people to whom the subject is related. The feelings which are experienced towards one's family and closest friends are extended to others."[89] Similarly, psychologists place great stress upon human emotions and the concept of the nation as an ideal center of reference for emotion. W. B. Pillsbury defines the nation as a group of individuals that feels itself one and

[85] "Only insight (recognition of the popular fallacy and acceptance of the scientific concept) can direct the emotional loyalties of individuals to their 'nation' into peaceful channels." (Allport, *op. cit.*)

[86] Ralph H. Gundlach, "The Psychology of Nationalism as a Major Factor in War," *Psychological Bulletin*, XXXVII (1940), p. 590.

[87] Morris Ginsberg, *The Psychology of Society* (New York, 1921), p. 97.

[88] Herbert Gurnee, *Elements of Social Psychology* (New York, 1936), p. 330.

[89] W. Ehrenstein, *"Die Verwurzelung des Nationalismus im Gefühlsleben,"* *Zeitschrift für pädagogischen Psychologie*, XXXV (1934), pp. 16–24.

"has groups of emotions experienced as a whole." [90] Bernard C. Ewer similarly describes a nation as "any group of people which *thinks* it is one," its essential features being a common sentiment of political unity.[91]

Not long ago it was the fashion, influenced, undoubtedly, by Gustave Le Bon, to regard the nation simply as an extension of the crowd and to find all national conduct understandable in the light of crowd psychology. Today, however, psychologists and sociologists call the crowd an "elementary collective group" and distinguish it from a social movement such as nationalism. Le Bon believed in the uniqueness of the crowd and in its distinctness from the individuals of which it is composed:

> Whoever be the individuals that compose it, however like or unlike their mode of life, their occupations, their character, or their intelligence, the fact that they have been transformed into a crowd puts them in possession of a sort of collective mind which makes them feel, think, and act in a manner quite different from that in which each individual of them would feel, think, and act were he in a state of isolation. There are certain ideas and feelings which do not come into being, or do not transform themselves into acts except in the case of individuals forming a crowd.[92]

According to this view, the crowd is motivated by: a feeling of invincible power; contagion, or imitation; and heightened suggestibility. It becomes a single being, less civilized, less intelligent, and more dangerous than its component individuals. This idea was expressed in similar terms by W. D. Scott, who considered the highly emotional crowd at a more primitive level than its individuals; [93] and by E. D. Martin, who described the crowd in terms of psychopathic behavior.[94]

On the more specific subject of the nation, G. E. Partridge sees it as an individual, having personality and self-consciousness and moved by emotions such as those which dominate the individual. "Groups thus endowed with a sense of solidarity and sensitiveness become highly vitalized and persistent personalities which stalk through the pages of history with a tremendous power and

[90] Pillsbury, *op. cit.*, p. 5.
[91] Bernard C. Ewer, *Social Psychology* (New York, 1929), p. 405.
[92] Gustave Le Bon, *The Crowd* (New York, 1896), pp. 29-30.
[93] Cf. W. D. Scott, *The Psychology of Public Speaking* (New York, 1907).
[94] Cf. E. D. Martin, *The Behavior of Crowds* (New York, 1920).

tenacity of purpose." [95] W. B. Pillsbury calls the concept of the nation a reality. "About it the emotions of the members cluster. Increasing [the spirit of loyalty to the nation] gives them emotions of joy, impairing its existence . . . gives sorrow or anger very much as does the waxing or waning of the individual's own ideal self." [96]

Other psychologists reject such analogies between the individual and the group and the concomitant ideas that nations live intensely and in their intense feelings and personal attributes express conscious and unconscious purposes and ideals. They oppose, specifically, the idea that a nation has a group mind or a collective mind. The nation is a psychological entity, they say, merely in the sense that the members think of themselves as belonging together that way. [97] According to F. H. Allport, there is no real difference between the nature of individuals when they are in a crowd or when they are in isolation. "The individual in the crowd behaves just as he would behave alone, *only more so.*" [98] No mind, say these psychologists, can exist without a nervous system.

A compromise position is offered by Klineberg:

> Our compromise position is in agreement with Allport that the crowd is not entirely distinct from the individuals, and that these latter do not entirely lose their identity within it; on the other hand, the phenomena of increased emotionality, heightened suggestibility, and the effect of certain individuals upon others, lend support at least to that part of Le Bon's theory which insists that the group is more than the sum of its parts and that the individual is altered by his presence in it. The notion of a group mind or a corporate consciousness must, however, be definitely rejected. [99]

Recognizing the futility of studying the individual as a self-contained entity, psychologists have turned their researches more and more to the study of the rationale of group forms, functions, changes, and interrelationships. As far as the nation, as an extension of the group, is concerned, social psychologists regard earlier concepts as classificatory and hence Aristotelian, or class-theoretical.

[95] G. E. Partridge, *The Psychology of Nations* (New York, 1919), p. 79.
[96] Pillsbury, *op. cit.*, pp. 222 ff.
[97] For example, Vaughan, *op. cit.*, p. 890. Cf. also F. H. Allport, *Social Psychology* (Boston, 1924), p. 388.
[98] Allport, *ibid.*, p. 388.
[99] Klineberg, *op. cit.*, p. 332.

The new emphasis is upon extension of the horizon. "We are gradually being forced to adapt a field-theoretical rather than a class-theoretical attack on the problems of national psychology." [100]

An indication of the type of work being done in redefining and clarifying the nature of the group is the establishment in 1945 of the Research Center for Group Dynamics at the University of Michigan by the now deceased American psychologist, Kurt Lewin. While not specifically concerned with the nation, the work done here may well throw light on the entire concept of the nation from the psychological point of view. [101]

Psychiatry and the Nation

It would seem upon first thought that psychiatry, the branch of medicine dealing with the causes, symptoms, course, and treatment of disorders and diseases of the mind, would have little to do with the meaning of the nation. However, three revolutionary ideas appeared during the first half of the nineteenth century that irrevocably altered the way psychiatrists think about the nature of mental disorders. [102]

The Swiss-American psychiatrist, Adolf Meyer, made the observation in 1906 that mental illness can be understood only in its biographical setting. It is not, he said, a mere disorder in some mechanism but makes sense only in terms of the patient's attempt at solving a problem in his living. The symbolic operations by the person are to be regarded as more significant than the psychological activity of his neurones.

At approximately the same time, Sigmund Freud, the founder of psychoanalysis, concluded that the symptoms, tastes, attitudes, and types of social action of people represent simultaneously the solutions of intimately personal problems that arose early in childhood, as well as ways of meeting contemporary situations more or less adequately.

[100] Cf. J. F. Brown, *Psychology and the Social Order* (New York, 1936), pp. 124 ff.
[101] Cf. Dorwin Cartwright, *The Research Center for Group Dynamics* (Ann Arbor, Michigan, 1950), for a report of five years' activities of this center. Research at the nation level will be mentioned in Chapter 8.
[102] Alfred H. Stanton and Stewart E. Perry, *Personality and Political Crisis* (Glencoe, Illinois, 1951), pp. 9–11.

Several decades later, the American psychiatrist, Harry Stack Sullivan, made the observation, based upon experimentation, that psychiatry is, in fact, always the study of interpersonal relations, and that mental disorder represents trouble not with the physical universe, but rather with its socially acquired meanings and with other people. Mental health, meaningful only when it refers to interpersonal adjustment, is a balance between physiological, psychobiological, and situational factors.[103]

These developments, placing emphasis upon the crucial conception of personality, brought psychiatry nearer to the social sciences. The value of the psychiatrist in the study of the nation is his technique of observation: by directing his attention upon the individual career line for long periods of time, he can expose the structure of the personality and examine in detail the degree to which a given set of political symbols is integrated with the other features of the total personality.[104] Recognizing this, scholars in other disciplines have begun to work closely with psychiatrists in throwing light upon the special intimacy of the relationships between personality and the social system.[105]

In approaching the problem of the meaning of the nation, psychiatrists bound it up with the thesis that early family life may be used as a key to the understanding of a culturally regular character. Using this as an hypothesis, the psychiatrist examines material on family life, working as a scientist by submitting his hypothesis to the test of specified materials. As a student of human nature in the raw, he is not willing to rely simply upon the physical qualities of the human body but, instead, seeks certain facts about human nature and relationships between human beings.[106] He considers

[103] Cf. Harry Stack Sullivan, "Psychiatry," *Encyclopedia of the Social Sciences* (New York, 1937), XII, p. 579.

[104] Harold D. Lasswell, "What Psychiatrists and Political Scientists Can Learn from One Another," *Psychiatry: Journal of the Biology and the Pathology of Interpersonal Relations,* I (1938), p. 36. "Each symbol [nation, constitution, liberty, duty, law, etc.] which is widely distributed in the vocabularies of political affirmation and negation are symbols which carry multitudes of connotations to the persons exposed to them. The psychiatrist is enabled to explore the unacknowledged associations which are interwoven with these collective symbols in the lives of representative persons." (*Ibid.*)

[105] For example, Harold D. Laswell in political science, Margaret Mead and Ralph Linton in anthropology, Otto Klineberg and Kurt Lewin in social psychology, and others.

[106] Examples of this type of work are to be found in the works of William

childhood environmental conditions, geography, economic situations, common language, as well as what he calls psychic requisites and special psychic welding. This takes him well beyond the old theory that the nation is merely a crowd or a gregarious herd. From the viewpoint of the psychiatrist the nation is made and maintained by an emotionally sustained education in nationhood. He does not forget intelligence quotients, natural selection, differentiated birth rates and the rest, but he must also take into consideration the fact that a nation is a moral as well as a physical achievement. In other words, the modern psychiatrist is quite willing to grant validity to things of the spirit.

Psychiatrists, like psychologists, differ among themselves on whether the nation is an objective reality or whether a new entity arises when individuals constitute a nation. Some refuse to accept the idea of the mind of a nation without any definite organic basis, without any specific brain or nervous system. Others see close parallels between the behavior of the individual and that of the nation. They observe that attitudes and practices which lead inevitably to the breakdown of individuals—to failure, dissatisfaction, insanity—form a design according to which nations have long been living. Behavior patterns of the nation, which statesmen declare to be axiomatic and which the individual finds to be perfectly normal, have been found by psychiatrists to be self-destructive.

> There are parallels between futile, self-defeating attitudes of the individual and the thinking and behavior of nations. The inexorable sequences of reality are not expunged by the bombast of the patient in mania, nor are they circumscribed by categorical assertions of the chauvinistic nationalist. The thinking of both is blatantly wishful, shot through with emotion, markedly unrealistic and contrary to fact.[107]

Psychoanalysis and the Nation

It is a curious fact that new disciplines invariably suffer the ordeal of a period of suspicion and even contempt before winning their way to recognition by other scholars. Economics, sociology, and psychology all underwent this trial. One of the newest of the

Alanson White, *Foundations of Psychiatry* (New York, 1921), and *An Introduction to the Study of the Mind* (Washington, 1924).
[107] K. E. Appel, "Nationalism and Sovereignty: A Psychiatric View," *Journal of Abnormal and Social Psychology*, XL (1945), p. 355.

scholarly disciplines, psychoanalysis, has become both the object of intense faith and the subject of bitter controversy. Since it deals with the submerged part of the human psyche, it is often charged with being a cult instead of a science. Yet, psychoanalytical theory has undergone so much continuous revision and so much progress has been made that no serious scholar can afford to ignore it.

Psychoanalysts grant that the problem of origin of the nation belongs chiefly to the spheres of history, geography, and sociology, but, at the same time, they contend with justification that the meaning of the nation cannot be understood completely until its inner mechanisms are more fully elucidated with psychoanalytical research.[108] While psychoanalysis may have little to do with explaining the phases of industrial development, it can help to clarify the mass impulses of the nation. Having achieved wider recognition, psychoanalysts are now making a more systematic study of the nation and national traits by psychoanalytical methods.

Sigmund Freud originally designated his theory as metapsychology, "a dynamic conception which reduces mental life to the interaction of reciprocally propelling and repelling forces." Since Freud's time, many important variants of his practical and theoretical postulates have arisen.[109] Freudians and non-Freudians alike are using essentially similar methods of diagnosis and research. They consist of bringing to mind feelings, events, and fantasies that had been put out of the mind because they were disagreeable and, in replacing them, as Freud wrote, "with acts of judgment which might result either in the acceptance or rejection of what formerly had been repudiated." [110]

The terminology of psychoanalysis is an abstruse one, and no attempt will be made here to go deeply into either Freudian or variant hypotheses. However, certain key terms may be defined.[111]

---

[108] Cf. Aurel Kolnai, *Psychoanalysis and Sociology* (New York, 1922), p. 97.
[109] Notably Alfred Adler's individual psychology (interpretation of the interactions of the individual with society, stressing such dynamic units as feelings of inferiority and compensations for such inferiorities); Carl Jung's analytical psychology (the flow of the libido considered as the entire stream of psychic energy of which the sexual is only a part); and Harry Stack Sullivan's interpersonal relations (emphasis upon the relationship of personality to the social order).
[110] Horace M. Kallen, "Psychoanalysis," *Encyclopedia of the Social Sciences* (New York, 1937), VI, p. 581.
[111] These definitions, derived from Freud, are based on those by Martin Peck, *The Meaning of Psychoanalysis* (New York, 1950), pp. 223–25.

The Libido: The dynamic expression of the sexual instinct or the energy of that instinct which deals with all that is included in the word "love" (sexual love, self-love, filial love, friendship, love for humanity, attachments to concrete objects and abstract ideals).

The Unconscious: A postulated region of the psyche, the repository of repressed concepts (urges, or wishes, invested with energy).

The Id: The impersonality of the psyche apart from its ego; the true unconscious. It is dominated by the pleasure principle and blind impulsive thinking.

The Ego: That part of the id which has been modified by the direct influence of the external world through the senses, which has become imbued with consciousness and whose function is the testing of reality.

The Super-Ego: That part of the mental apparatus which criticizes the ego and causes pain to it whenever it tends to accept impulses emanating from the id. It is a sort of inner monitor synonymous with conscience.

In his *Massenpsychologie und Ich-Analyse,* published in 1922, Freud inferred that the group sentiment typical of the nation is the product of the libido focused on a leader. The reasoning here is a basic one in psychology: in much the same way as all other responses, the canalized and conditioned responses transfer to persons similar to those with whom the first associations are formed. Thus, the deeper and constantly reinforced responses to parents and to brothers and sisters become the matrix from which the field of attachments and hostilities grows. Freud emphasized two major social aggregates: the church (attachments to the parish priest, "father"); and the army ("my buddy").[112] The nation is the largest of those social aggregates to which the individual attaches his loyalty.

Since Freud's original contributions, other psychoanalysts have tended to examine the nation in its relation to the super-ego and the unconscious, both basic Freudian concepts. Ernst Simmel defines the nation as an external representation of the super-ego, the

---

[112] Cf. Gardner Murphy, *Personality: A Biosocial Approach to Origins and Structure* (New York, 1947), pp. 842–43.

inner, subconscious censor.[113] In a nation newly emerged under a leader, the conditions favoring group formation exist to a striking degree; moreover, the leader becomes a part of the super-ego of the individual. The group, as Freud phrased it, "replaces its ego ideal by the object." [114] Contradictory elements in the character of various nations may be explained as an alloy of the various traditional elements in the super-ego.[115]

The emphasis upon the super-ego and other parts of the unconscious seems to be basic in the psychoanalytic interpretation of the nation. The process by which the individual becomes absorbed in the nation may be explained as follows: the child forms a highly imaginary picture of his parents, brothers, and sisters, a more or less distorted version of reality which persists in his unconscious fantasy throughout his life. This picture always reflects both good parents, whom the child imitates, follows, and looks to for security, and bad parents, against whom he must be protected. This pattern is decisive in the child's behavior in facing the external world. As he grows older, the child finds common symbols in his environment for the elements of this unconscious pattern. He gravitates unconsciously to the nation, for he now has common values to defend—common traditions, common heroes, a common leader or leaders, common standards of behavior, and common enemies.[116] Thus, attachment to the family, the original psychological agent of society,[117] is the basis for loyalty to the nation.

The ambivalence conflict, common in most families, is repeated in the nation. The simultaneous attractiveness and repulsiveness of mother, father, sisters, and brothers, a painful state of consciousness resulting from the inability to renounce one course of satisfaction to gain another, is well known to psychoanalytical psychology. Once past the stage of childhood, the individual unconsciously

---

[113] Ernst Simmel, "War Tensions," in *Psychoanalysis Today,* ed. by Sandor Lorand (New York, 1944), p. 231.

[114] Henry Lowenfeld, "Freud's *Moses* and Bismarck," in *Psychoanalysis and the Social Sciences,* ed. by Géza Róheim (New York, 1950), II, p. 281.

[115] *Ibid.,* p. 290.

[116] Roger Money-Kyrle, "Varieties in Group Formation," in Róheim, *op. cit.,* II, p. 329.

[117] Gertrud M. Kurth, "Hitler's Germanies: A Sidelight on Nationalism," in Róheim, *op. cit.,* II, pp. 293–312.

brings other symbols into his conditioned ambivalence conflicts. More often than not, the nation becomes to him "an unambiguously maternal symbol." [118] He does not regard the nation objectively as a sovereign, self-governing people, but rather as a maternal symbol which becomes the object of his impassioned, somewhat hysterical, and highly emotional worship.

Like sociologists and psychologists, psychoanalysts differ on socio-individual parallelisms,[119] that is, on the problem of the relationships of the individual and society as expressed in the nation. Ernst Simmel states flatly that "the nation represents the collective character of the individual." [120] Roger Money-Kyrle goes so far as to say that a nation, like an individual, may be either pathological or sane. He states further:

> If the individuals who compose it [the nation] have severe internal conflicts they are apt to create enemies for themselves by suspecting enmity where none at first existed or to become depressed if they fail to get fanatical leadership they need. Or they may relieve their inner tension by a character formation corresponding to a neurotic group-ideal. But if, as a result of a favorable environment in early life, or of later treatment, the individuals who compose a group are at peace with themselves, the group itself, whatever its form, will certainly be sane.[121]

Richard Brickner [122] and Bertram Schaffner [123] described the Germans as an authoritarian nation whose character resulted from the dominant position of the father in the German family. In Brickner's view, the Germans are a pathological nation.[124]

---

[118] *Ibid.,* p. 305. The author quotes her indebtedness to Dr. Ludwig Jekels for pointing out the implied meaning of the word "fatherland": it is, indeed, the mother who is of the "father's land"!

[119] Aurel Kolnai believes that it is precisely at this point that psychoanalysis can be most fruitful in its research: "As far as concerns socio-individual parallelism, the main result of psychoanalysis may be summed up as follows: whereas, hitherto, the idea of a mechanical solidarity based upon similarity has been a somewhat anaemic schema, and liable to misunderstanding, psychoanalysis has now filled in the outline with a living psychological intent." (Kolnai, *op. cit.,* p. 33.)

[120] Simmel, *op. cit.,* p. 230.

[121] Roger Money-Kyrle, "Varieties of Group Formation," in Róheim, *op. cit.,* II, p. 329.

[122] Richard Brickner, *Is Germany Incurable?* (Philadelphia, 1943).

[123] Bertram Schaffner, *Father Land, A Study of Authoritarianism in the German Family* (New York, 1948).

[124] There is, of course, strong criticism of this extreme position. We shall see later that anthropologists, who are interested in describing the nation in terms of

The view that the nation is a collective entity functioning like the individual is by no means universal among psychoanalysts and psychiatrists. Critics of this view hold that it leads to the use of a concept like nation anthropomorphically, as an entity that believes as an organic unit; this is permissible only in a metaphoric sense. They believe that society and the nation are not organisms, because in them will be found no automatic regulation of the individual parts to one another. The American psychiatrist, Abram Kardiner, says that once we tie the concept of history to a psychological base, we also destroy the age-old assumption that society can be treated as if it were an organism or a machine of many parts. "There is no such thing as a *social homeostasis*—to use Cannon's physiological term, a being made up of individuals who are potentially alike. . . . The harmonious or unharmonious relations of members of society to each other depend on the same voluntary cooperation or resistance of each human unit in the society." [125]

The continuing contributions of psychoanalysis to the understanding of the nation hinge on the clarification of "psychic tendencies" as addenda to the historical and sociological concepts of the nation. If the nation be defined as "the unlimited ruler of one's interests," [126] only those things can be acknowledged as desirable that further the interests of the nation, whereas all things that might react to the nation's disadvantage are considered to be undesirable. We shall examine these psychic tendencies in more detail in a subsequent chapter on the sentiment of nationalism.

its cultural heritage, use psychoanalytic terms in stating their case. The English anthropologist, Geoffrey Gorer, explains the Japanese adult characteristics as at least partly the result of the strict toilet training of the Japanese child, leading to a kind of obsessive, compulsive personality; (Geoffrey Gorer, "Themes in Japanese Culture," *Transactions of the New York Academy of Sciences*, V [1943], pp. 106–24). The Russian nation can be understood, in part at least, from the tight swaddling of the Russian infant, which tends to develop frustration, aggression, and concomitant guilt feelings and inhibitions; (Geoffrey Gorer and John Rickman, *The Peoples of Great Russia* [New York, 1950]). Certain similarities in child rearing in the American nation lead to rejection of the father, of authority in general, and of the European heritage; (Geoffrey Gorer, *The American People* [New York, 1949]). Such views, defended and attacked heatedly, await further scientific investigation.

[125] Abram Kardiner, *The Psychological Frontiers of Society* (New York, 1945), p. 415.

[126] L. Fessler, "The Psychology of Nationalism," *Psychoanalytical Review*, XXVIII (1941), p. 374.

Conclusions and Summary

The consensus of opinion among all disciplines is that the term nation is tantalizingly ambiguous and that much additional study is necessary to clarify its definition. There are many differences of opinion within each discipline. The preponderant point of view holds that the nation is not a race, nor is it a state. Language, religion, and territory are important factors in the nation, but none of them is the exclusive determinant of the nation.

Geographers point to the basic significance of natural center and environment. Historians regard the nation as the population of a sovereign political state, living within a definite territory, and possessing a common stock of thoughts and feelings that are acquired and transmitted during the course of a common history by a common will. The meaning of the nation is itself subject to historical change. Political scientists see the nation as the formal organization of one people and as an organic unity, the result of organic growth. Philosophers sometimes regard it as a unity of culture, with common history, language, literature, traditions, heroes, and sense of loyalty. Sociologists regard the nation as one of the largest and most important collectivities in human society, but prefer to use such terms as group, in-group, secondary group, and social unit instead of the more controversial word nation. They hold that the one indispensable factor in the nation is the "we-sentiment," or the feeling of oneness.

Psychologists base the existence of the nation primarily on the behavior of its individuals and seek its meaning in terms of psychological characteristics. Consciousness and emotion, they say, form the cement that binds the nation. They have differing views on the existence of a group mind, a collective mind, or a corporate consciousness within the nation. Psychiatrists, who are now more and more concerned with the intimacy of the relationships between personality and the social system, see the nation as made and maintained by an emotionally sustained education in nationhood, beginning with the crucial factor of family life and extended later to the large collectivity. Psychoanalysts describe the nation as the largest of the social aggregates to which the individual ordinarily attaches his loyalty, and as the external representation of the super-ego (the inner, unconscious censor). Some psychoanalysts believe that nations are subject to the same tensions (neurotic group ideals) as the individual, but, like sociologists, psychologists, and psychiatrists, they differ among themselves on the existence of parallels between the individual and society.

III

The Meaning of Nationality

A portion of mankind may be said to constitute a nationality if they are united among themselves by common sympathies, which do not exist between them and any others, which make them coöperate more willingly than with other people, desire to be under the same government, and desire that it should be government by themselves, or a portion of themselves exclusively.   —JOHN STUART MILL *

Complexity of the Idea

"[Nationality] cannot be tested or analyzed by formulae, such as the German professors love." [1] This comment by Ramsay Muir reveals that, once again, we are faced with a term of the utmost complexity, an elusive idea that defies exact definition. Even able scholars find it difficult to distinguish between nation and nationality. [2]

The factors of a common country, language, and tradition have been used in defining nationality. But, as Arnold J. Toynbee has pointed out, it is impossible to argue a priori for the presence of one or a combination of these factors in the existence of a nationality. "They may have been there for ages and kindled no response. And

---

* *Considerations on Representative Government* (1861).

[1] Ramsay Muir, *Nationalism and Internationalism: The Culmination of Modern History* (Boston, 1916), p. 51.

[2] Some scholars contend that the definition of a nation should be more properly that of nationality. Thus, although Sydney Herbert defines a nation as "a social group bound together by a consciousness of kind which springs from the tradition evoked by the group's historic past and is directly related to a definite home country," Bernard Joseph contends that this definition would be more appropriately applied to a nationality. (Sydney Herbert, *Nationality and Its Problems* [London, 1920], p. 37; Bernard Joseph, *Nationality, Its Nature and Problems* [New Haven, 1929], p. 21.)

it is impossible to argue from one case to another—precisely the same group of factors may produce nationality here, and there have no effect." [3] In other words, nationality is a general term which does not always cover adequately the various possible combinations of its specific factors.

To add to the puzzle, nationality is often used in a concrete sense but may on occasion be applied in an abstract or ideal sense. When used concretely, it refers to a group of persons bound together by certain common attributes, or may designate an undeveloped and nonindependent national group that has not yet attained national sovereignty. When it is used abstractly, it refers to an aspiration to united existence; in the ideal sense, it means the idea of the grouping of persons in nations or the quality of uniting the people of the same nation.

Nationality may also have either a political or a cultural connotation. According to the political concept of nationality, there is a definite Swiss nationality based on membership in the Swiss state; yet, from the cultural point of view, a German, French, or Italian nationality attaches to every Swiss individual.

How did the term nationality arise? It was partly to atone for abuse of the word nation, in the early part of the nineteenth century, that nationality was coined and speedily incorporated into most European languages.[4] From this time on, a major distinction was made between the three terms—nation, nationality, and nationalism. Nation continued to be used to describe the citizens of a sovereign political state; nationality was used more exactly to refer to a group of persons speaking the same language and observing the same customs; and nationalism began to be used as a descriptive term for a sentiment of a social movement. Though there have been many variations from this basic pattern of meanings,[5] the above simple, provisional definitions convey the distinguishing marks of the three words.

[3] Arnold J. Toynbee, *Nationality and the War* (London, 1915), p. 13.
[4] Carlton J. H. Hayes, *Essays on Nationalism* (New York, 1926), p. 4.
[5] We shall note many variations, but an example is Bernard Joseph's contention that the sentiment that forms the basis of nationality should be designated as the sentiment of nationality and not as nationalism. (Cf. Joseph, *op. cit.*, p. 28.)

False or Inadequate Explanations

Let us seek the meaning of nationality by eliminating at the outset certain demonstrably false ideas. This method of exclusion may not be completely satisfactory, but it will serve at least to clear away some mistaken concepts.

Nationality does not depend upon race. Both nation and nationality, in their concrete senses, are groups of people. What has been said in the previous chapter on the confusion of nation and race holds true for nationality and race. The idea that blood (or race) exists forever, carries an unchangeable inheritance, and forms the basis of nationality is a mythical concept without scientific validation. The mixture of races, especially in Europe, has been so widespread that the identification of nationality and race becomes a simple fallacy.[6]

Nationality does not depend exclusively upon language. Language may be an important component in the existence of a nationality, but by no means is it the *sine qua non.* The people of Switzerland speak German, French, or Italian, or various subsidiary dialects, and there is no commonly accepted Swiss language for the Swiss nationality. The Belgians speak French and Flemish; there is no Belgian tongue. The idea that German-speaking minorities throughout the world, whether in the Baltic States, the Netherlands, Denmark, the Balkans, Brazil, or the United States, remain parts of the German nationality, may be dismissed as the propaganda of Pan-Germans [7] and Nazis.[8] The view that people speak-

[6] To a certain extent, nationality in many parts of the world, especially among anti-Semites and Jewish nationalists, is considered to be *eine Angelegenheit des Blutes,* a matter of blood. Racialists insist vehemently upon the identification of nationality and race. The greatest living Jewish philosopher, Martin Buber, devoted the whole of his *Rede über das Judentum* to the argument that the Jews are a community by blood and race, and the poet, Richard Beer-Hofmann, in his *Schlaflied,* said that the determining factor in every single Jew is his Jewish blood.

[7] An organization formed in 1891 assumed in 1894 the name of the Pan-German League, which was dedicated to "a quickening of national sentiment of Germans and in particular to awaken and foster the racial and cultural homogeneity of all sections of the German people." It sought to Germanize Poles, Danes, and Alsace-Lorrainers within the borders of the German Reich and also called for the preservation of the German *Volkstum* throughout Europe and overseas. Cf. Mildred S. Wertheimer, *The Pan-German League, 1890–1914* (New York, 1924), pp. 23–48.

[8] In the 1937 Congress of Germans Domiciled Abroad, held at Stuttgart, some

ing the same, or almost the same language form one nationality, appears natural to fervent nationalists in all countries, and it is not shared by others. According to Frederick Hertz, "the identification of a nation with a language group is untenable. It conflicts with both the legal and sociological concept of a nation. The groups constituted by sentiment, citizenship and language very often do not coincide but overlap. In many cases, peoples of different tongues are citizens of the same state, and sometimes also regard one another as members of the same nation. On the other hand, many different nations in both senses speak the same language." [9]

Nationality and state are not synonymous terms. A national state is always based on nationality, but a nationality may exist without a national state. An example is that of the Polish nationality. After the three Partitions of Poland in 1772, 1793, and 1795, there remained no territorial Polish state; it was not recreated until 1919 with the Treaty of Versailles. But all during that period the Polish nationality continued to exist.

The idea that nationality is a "folk spirit" (Volksgeist) *is fictitious.* This myth sees the "folk spirit" as the ever-welling source of nationality and its manifestations. It has been demolished by Hans Kohn: "This theory offers no real explanation of the rise and the rôle of nationality; it refers us to mystical pre-historical pseudo-realities. Rather, it must be taken as a characteristic element of thought in the age of nationalism, and is subject itself to analysis by the historian of nationalism." [10]

Nationality is not an emanation of the "World-Spirit." Hegel, in his *Philosophy of History* (1837) projected a theory assuming that "a world-force visited the peoples in a predetermined order and endowed them with exceptional vitality for some special task. While they performed the task they were moral, virtuous, vigorous." [11] The ordinary scholar, limited in his access to this "World-

---

10,000 Germans from foreign countries heard Foreign Minister von Neurath challenge the right of other countries to interfere with Germans living abroad. "We will certainly not permit Germans living abroad to be subjected by special rulings by foreign governments because of their National Socialist faith." (New York *Times,* Sept. 5, 1937.)

[9] Frederick Hertz, *Nationality in History and Politics* (3rd ed., London, Routledge and Kegan Paul, 1951), pp. 95–96.
[10] Hans Kohn, *The Idea of Nationalism* (5th printing, New York, 1951), p. 13.
[11] Cf. J. Holland Rose, *Nationality in Modern History* (New York, 1916), p. 143.

Spirit," would have some difficulty in either proving or disproving this interesting theory.[12] In the meantime, it would be far more realistic to regard nationality as a man-made concept that emerged as one means of regulating the social order.

That nationality and citizenship are one and the same thing is erroneous and contrary to fact. The reasoning of the average man is as follows: the welfare of the state requires that all persons permanently residing in it be citizens; nationality is the same as citizenship; and a state, therefore, can be composed of only one nationality, for any other condition would be abnormal and undesirable.[13] In a significant comment, Carlton J. H. Hayes attributed this corruption of the term to jurists, who have done their best to add confusion to the new word nationality, just as they have corrupted the old term nation. "They have utilized nationality to indicate citizenship. For example, they speak of a person of British nationality though thereby they mean any subject of King George V, a subject mayhap who, in a non-legal sense, belongs to the Boer nationality of South Africa or to the French-Canadian nationality of North America." [14]

The legal code on nationality is explicit. Nationality is defined in Article I of the Code on the Law of Nationality as "the status of a natural person who is attached to a state by the tie of allegiance." [15] Thus, legally, nationality is a reciprocal relationship, involving claims of the national upon the state as well as obligations of the national to the state.[16] This use of nationality as synonymous with citizenship has caused much mischief, since citizens are included in the general term "nationals," but not all such "nationals" are citizens.

[12] Ideas like this one led critics of Hegelianism to point to its dangerous abstractness, idealism, and formality. John Dewey stated flatly that Hegel produced a series of abstractions and absolute ideas, which, far from being innocuous playthings of the intellect, came to serve as a cloak and justification for political absolutism and fanaticism. (John Dewey, *German Philosophy and Politics* [New York, 1915], pp. 30 ff.)

[13] Joseph, *op. cit.,* p. 19.

[14] Hayes, *op. cit.,* p. 4.

[15] Harvard University, *Research in International Law: Nationality* (Cambridge, Mass., 1929).

[16] Richard W. Flournoy, "Nationality," *Encyclopedia of the Social Sciences* (New York, 1937), VI, p. 249. "Although not necessarily dissoluble, the allegiance of a national to his state is said to be permanent, as distinguished from the temporary allegiance or obligation or obedience owed by an alien resident or visitor." (*Ibid.*)

Historians on the Origins and Characteristics of Nationality

Historians regard nationality as a product of the development of society and, therefore, as an historical force of the utmost importance. It is not identical with the clan, the tribe, or the folk–group— bodies of men united by actual or supposed common descent or by a common homeland. Hans Kohn points out that ethnographic groups like these existed throughout history, yet they have not formed nationalities; they are nothing but "ethnographic material." [17]

Nationality is of recent origin, stemming out of the French Revolution; it is clothed with all the complexity of the great forces emerging at that time. It did not spring full-blown, but was rather the result of an evolutionary process. J. Holland Rose set a precise date for its emergence to maturity—the famous sitting of the National Assembly of August 4, 1789, when Lorraine, youngest of the French provinces, expressed her desire to join intimately in the life of "this family." [18] Lord Acton placed the date a bit earlier: "The Partition of Poland, this famous measure, the most revolutionary act (1771) [19] of the old absolutism, awakened the theory of nationality in Europe, converting a dormant right into an aspiration." [20] A third British historian, Lord Morley, felt that there was nothing new in the sentiment of nationality. It was one of the main keys of Luther's Reformation. "What is new is the transformation of the sentiment into a political idea." [21]

[17] Kohn, *op. cit.*, p. 13. "Even if a nationality rises, it may disappear again, absorbed into a larger or new nationality. Nationalities are products of the living forces of history, and therefore are always fluctuating, never rigid." (*Ibid.*)
[18] Rose, *op. cit.*, p. 147. Rose finds the time element significant—nationality appeared at a time when the National Assembly (representing the nation) was having disputes with the king (symbol of the old absolutism).
[19] Lord Acton made a minor slip here. The first treaty partitioning Poland was signed at St. Petersburg between Russia and Prussia on February 6–17, 1772; the second, admitting Austria to a share, on August 5–16 of the same year. Great Britain adopted the Gregorian Calendar in 1752.
[20] Baron John Emerich Edward Dalberg Acton, *Essays on Freedom and Power* (Boston, 1948), p. 169. "Thenceforward, there was a nation demanding to be united in a state—a soul, as it were, wandering in search of a body." (*Ibid.*)
[21] Viscount John Morley Morley, *Politics and History* (New York and London, 1914), p. 72.

The course of the concept of nationality closely reflected historical developments after the French Revolution. Since the late eighteenth century there have been three successive waves of attacks upon the existing order—upon the aristocracy (power), the middle class (property), and sovereignty (territory). These attacks were inspired, respectively, by theories of equality (Rousseau), communism (Babeuf), and nationality (Mazzini).[22] All three sprang from a common origin, possessed many links, and opposed what they felt to be identical evils. Nationality, like equality and communism, went through several stages as it grew into an urgent and dominating force. First, as an instinct for security and survival, it inflamed the minds of individuals who rebelled against governmental failure, political persecution, intolerable economic conditions, and wars. Then the masses became infected with the rigid idea that it was always the "foreigner" who was responsible for their misery. "Nationality went through all the stages. From instinct it became idea; from idea abstract principles; then fervid prepossession; ending where it is today, in dogma, whether accepted or evaded." [23]

There is some difference of opinion among historians on whether nationality in its concrete sense is primarily political, cultural, or a combination of both. Lord Acton regarded nationality as essentially the basis of political capacity.[24] Carlton J. H. Hayes believes that nationality is primarily cultural and only incidentally political.[25] He comes to this conclusion because a nationality may exist without political unity, without a state of its own, and vice-versa, while a political state may embrace several nationalities. This point of view holds that nationality signifies adherence to a people rather than a state. Hans Kohn takes the position that in recent history man has begun to regard nationality as the center of both his political and cultural activity and life.[26]

The Kohn compromise position is substantiated by the British scholar, John Oakesmith, who constructed a formula for the defini-

[22] Acton, op. cit., p. 169.
[23] Morley, op. cit., p. 72.
[24] Acton, op. cit., p. 192.
[25] Hayes, op. cit., p. 5.
[26] Kohn, op. cit., p. 13.

tion of nationality by utilizing three terms which required preliminary definition: *interest; continuity of interest;* and *organic.* He defined *interest,* not in the purely personal or selfish sense, but as the common interests of a group of people in their common material, intellectual, moral, and artistic possessions, a community of interest in a wide and general sense. *Continuity of interest* implies an historical moulding, since every generation is the inheritor of the social tradition and culture of its predecessor. In that it is *organic,* nationality, like all evolutionary organisms, has developed machinery for entering into relationships with its environment, and, being a human organism, it is endowed, as part of that machinery, with intelligence, the last product of natural evolution. Nationality, then, becomes the organic continuity of common interest. It is "a community of interest developed in course of time into a characteristically traditional culture, which gradually creates for itself machinery, legislative, administrative, and other, for effecting its ends in the world of human action." [27]

At the same time, historians recognize the abstract, or ideal, sense of the meaning of nationality. Some are more inclined than others to place major emphasis upon this abstract sense. According to Arnold J. Toynbee, nationality, "like all great forces in human life, is nothing material or mechanical, but a subjective psychological feeling in living people." [28] Sydney Herbert sees nationality as a form of consciousness of kind which binds men together irrespective of their political allegiances or opinions, religious beliefs, and economic interests. [29] J. Holland Rose regards nationality as "a spiritual conception." [30] He finds it impossible to define this "instinct" exactly, but he describes it as something "unconquerable and indestructible." The French scholar, Robert Michels, believes that nationality does not consist necessarily in either language or religion or a common past, but in an essential, single element—

[27] John Oakesmith, *Race and Nationality: An Inquiry into the Origin and Growth of Patriotism* (London, 1919), p. ix.
[28] Arnold J. Toynbee, *Nationality and the War* (London, 1915), p. 13. On another occasion, Toynbee defined nationality as "a present-will to cooperate in a political organization"; (Arnold J. Toynbee, *The New Europe* [London, 1916], p. 16).
[29] Sydney Herbert, *Nationality and Its Problems* (London, 1920), p. 20.
[30] Rose, *op. cit.,* p. 153.

the will of a people; the expression of this will is found in a synthesis of some or all of the constitutive elements generally attributed to nationality (common homeland, language, traditions, etc.).[31]

Historians thus recognize the fact that nationality connotes something more than a political or social contract or a cultural phenomenon: in addition, a mysterious kind of instinct, consciousness, or will that leads to a union of hearts. In recounting the course of historical development, some historians see evidence of this binding, abstract instinct in early kinship groups, for which family life was a matter of self-preservation. They observe further how, in a glow of wider enthusiasms, but still motivated by the search for security, the larger groups formed nations. The earlier instinct became a consciousness or will for unity. Political organizations were founded on a natural basis, and the peoples of a nation began to recognize as kinsmen those who once were regarded as strangers. In its modern form, the cohesive cement which binds the group together has become this feeling of nationality. The historian quite properly leaves the scientific investigation of these abstract qualities of nationality to the psychologist.

Though it is not ordinarily the function of the historian to pass judgment on historical phenomena, Lord Acton considered nationality a deleterious force in modern civilization. He denounced it in no uncertain terms, while admitting the importance of its mission: "Although the theory of nationality is more absurd and criminal than the theory of socialism, it has an important mission in the world, and marks the final conflict, and therefore the end, of two forces which are the worst enemies of civil freedom—the absolute monarchy and the revolution." [32] To Lord Acton the greatest adversary of the rights of nationality is the modern theory of nationality itself, because it makes the state and nation commensurate with each other in theory and reduces practically to a subject condition all other nationalities that may be within the boundaries.

The historian, Karl W. Deutsch, expresses dissatisfaction with the conventional definition of nationality as a term that may be applied to a people "among whom there exists a significant move-

[31] Robert Michels, *Notes sur les moyens de constater la nationalité* (The Hague, 1917), p. 1, as quoted in Kohn, *op. cit.*, p. 582.
[32] Acton, *op. cit.*, p. 195.

ment toward political, economic, or cultural autonomy, that is to say, toward a political organization; or a market area, or an area of literary or cultural exchange, within which the personnel and the characteristics of this people will predominate." [33] All these notions, he says, involve difficulties, since some of the most frequently cited objective characteristics of a people do not seem to be essential to its unity—language, common or contiguous territory, a common condition or experience, community of character, community of values. Deutsch proposes instead a functional definition of nationality. What counts, he believes, is not the presence of any single factor, but merely the presence of sufficient communication facilities with enough complementarity to produce the overall result. Deutsch regards membership in a people as consisting essentially in the ability to communicate more effectively, and over a wider range of subjects, with members of one large group than with outsiders. He, therefore, defines nationality, in the political and social struggles of the modern age, as "an alignment of large numbers of individuals from the middle and lower classes linked to regional centers and leading social groups by channels of social communication and economic intercourse, both indirectly from link to link and with the center." This function of nationality differs from other attempts to specify nationality in terms of some particular ingredient. As a result, nationality and nationalism are opened to "performance tests," based on detailed analysis of the functions carried out, to measurement, and even to prediction. We shall discuss the Deutsch formula in a later chapter.

Political Science and Nationality

Political scientists and historians differ little in their attitudes toward the meaning, origin, and characteristics of nationality. The special contribution of political scientists to the meaning of nationality is the emphasis they place upon its exclusive and separatist character. In his classic definition of the nation, Francis Lieber, founder of political science in the United States, stated that "a nation is a

[33] Karl W. Deutsch, *Nationalism and Social Communication: An Inquiry into the Foundations of Nationality* (New York, 1953), pp. 3–4. See also pp. 70–80.

nation only when there is but one nationality; and the attempt at establishing a nationality within a nationality is more inconsistent and mischievous than the establishment of an 'empire within an empire.' " [34] Similarly, the German-Swiss political theorist, Johann Kaspar Bluntschi, defined nationality as "a union of masses of men of different occupations and social strata of hereditary society, of common spirit, feeling and race bound together especially by language and customs in a common civilization which gives them a sense of unity and distinction from all foreigners quite apart from the union of the state." [35] Harold J. Laski, also called attention to this exclusive nature of nationality: "Members of the national unit recognize their likeness and emphasize their difference from other men. . . . The fact of nationality is urgently separatist in character. . . . It is exclusive and it promotes a loyalty which may often, like family affection, live its life independent of right and truth." [36]

Though political scientists are concerned primarily with the study of all aspects of political power, by no means do they insist upon the exclusively political character of nationality. The British political scientist, Sir Alfred E. Zimmern, pointed out the abstract quality of nationality: "Nationality to me is not a political question at all—not a question of sovereign governments, armies, frontiers, and foreign policy. . . . It is primarily and essentially a spiritual question, and, in part, an educational question." [37] Zimmern's fellow countrymen, Israel Zangwill and C. Delisle Burns, agreed. According to Zangwill, nationality is "a state of mind corresponding to a political fact," [38] while Burns stated: "I use nationality to mean the quality uniting men and women of the same nation." [39] Typical of similar reactions by American political scientists is that of Max Sylvius Handman: "Nationality is the attitude towards one's people

[34] Francis Lieber, *Fragments of Political Science on Nationalism and Internationalism* (New York, 1838), p. 8.
[35] Johann Kaspar Bluntschi, *Theory of the State* (Oxford, 1892), p. 90. A native of Zurich, Bluntschi was trained and influenced at Berlin by Savigny, from whom he absorbed the methods of the historical school. His major work, *Allgemeines Staatsrecht,* was written and published in Munich (2 vols., 1851–52). From the point of view of present-day political science, Bluntschi's definition of nationality shows an insufficient perception of its character, especially in the plainly erroneous reference to hereditary and racial factors.
[36] Harold J. Laski, *A Grammar of Politics* (London and New Haven, 1925), p. 221.
[37] Alfred E. Zimmern, *Nationality and Government* (London, 1918), p. 65.
[38] Quoted in Adam de Hegedus, *Patriotism or Peace?* (New York, 1947), p. 17.
[39] C. Delisle Burns, *The Morality of Nations* (New York, 1916), p. 12, footnote 1.

engendered by having ideas concerning its welfare, its honor, and its position among other peoples." [40] Here again, political scientists, as do historians, give due recognition to the psychological implications of nationality.

Sociology and the Group-Emphasis

Sociology regards nationality as primarily a social category, and gives weight, in its definition, to such sociological terms as people, collectivity, and group. Max Wirth defines nationality as "a people, who, because of their belief in their common descent and their mission in the world, by virtue of their common cultural heritage and historical career, aspire to sovereignty over a territory or seek to maintain or enlarge their political or cultural influence in the face of opposition." [41] Similarly, Florian Znaniecki looks upon nationality as "a collectivity of people with certain common and distinctive cultural characteristics." [42] Logan Wilson and William L. Kolb point out that since the vast majority of all social relations and social systems are to be found within communities and societies, nationality is "a social unit which has been enduringly ordered as a whole." [43]

Some sociologists prefer to stress the term group when speaking of nationality. Emile Durkheim, the French sociologist, defines nationality as "a group whose members wish to live under the same laws and form a state." [44] In an additional definition, Wirth describes nationality as "sociologically a conflict group." [45] There is, however, a fine distinction in meaning between the two terms nationality and group. Nationality is to a social group what personality is to an individual. Moreover, there is a very real difference between the terms national group and nationality. Both have similar attributes, such as common territory, traditions, and culture, but

[40] Max Sylvius Handman, "The Sentiment of Nationalism," *Political Science Quarterly*, XXXVI (1921), p. 104, footnote 1.
[41] Max Wirth, "Types of Nationalism," *American Journal of Sociology*, XLI (1936), p. 723.
[42] Florian Znaniecki, *Modern Nationalities* (Chicago, 1952), p. xiii.
[43] Logan Wilson and William L. Kolb, *Sociological Analysis* (New York, 1949), p. 344.
[44] Quoted in George P. Gooch, *Nationalism* (London and New York, 1920), p. 8.
[45] Wirth, *op. cit.*, p. 724.

these possessions are less clearly marked in a national group than in a nationality. In the former the specific "will to live" as a nation is lacking: this will must exist at one time or another if a national group is to become a nationality.

Sociologists, like scholars of other disciplines, see one of the main difficulties in defining nationality in the fact that the term may be used in either a concrete or abstract sense. They use different terms, however, for these two basic senses: the concrete becomes objective, or external facts (national language, territory, state, civilization, and history), while the abstract is referred to as subjective, or internal facts (national consciousness or sentiment).[46] It is far easier to ascertain the external facts than the internal. In the words of Frederick Hertz:

> One can explore the growth and the rules of a national language or the institutions of a national State with considerable exactness, and without interrogating members of that nation which may be an extinct one as the old Romans or Greeks. National consciousness or national sentiment, however, is an exceedingly elusive thing. Its manifestations can be studied in political literature, public speeches, or national institutions, but the interpretations of such documents or objects in regard to the underlying national spirit is always more or less insecure. . . . Legal nationality, cultural nationality, and the status of a people according to international practice can easily be ascertained. But political nationality is a very complicated matter as it depends on a sufficient degree of national consciousness which cannot be observed and measured by exact methods.[47]

The important conclusion is that nationality is always a combination of both concrete and abstract senses. Luther Lee Bernard is quite willing to admit that the chief elements of nationality are a common language, a common culture, including a common history during at least a part of its career, common traditions, customs, conventions, and religions, but he adds that they are all "united through a collective psychological group consciousness." [48]

Though they speak of legal nationality, sociologists take the same position as historians and political scientists in rejecting the idea that nationality is synonymous with citizenship in a sovereign state.

[46] Hertz, *op. cit.*, p. 9.
[47] *Ibid.*
[48] L. L. Bernard, *An Introduction to Social Psychology* (New York, 1926), p. 240.

They say, furthermore, that nationality is often wrongly identified with ideas of racial unity.[49] They believe that religion may or may not be an attribute of nationality. Since the spirit of nationality can be understood only against the background of civilization, and since religion often has national implications, religion may be regarded as a social force and, on occasion, as a symbol of nationality.[50]

The practical problem of developing an objective theory of nationality is an exceedingly complex one for the sociologist because there are many varieties of social structure that cannot be restricted to any one time and people but must include many eras and many peoples.[51] Close study of the considerably wider field of history is indicated before sociological generalizations can be made. At the same time, the structure of nationality itself cannot be determined without the assistance of the psychologist, who, in his turn, is dependent upon the historian. Only a multidisciplined approach can break this vicious circle.

Psychology and the Subjectivist Approach

Psychologists leave the concrete, or objective, sense of nationality to historians, political scientists, and sociologists, and concern themselves primarily with the abstract, or subjective, sense. Nationality is for them, like religion, subjective, psychological, a condition of mind, a spiritual possession, a way of thinking, feeling, and living. Although closely bound up with the questions of corporate life, corporate growth, and corporate self-respect, nationality remains in their view essentially a psychological question. It is a form of con-

[49] Cf. Paul A. F. Walter, *Race and Culture Relations* (New York, 1952), pp. 92–93. This false identification is understandable from the sociological point of view, since nationality is the focal point of the strongest individual and group loyalties, and, as such, it tends to subordinate other cultural and institutional attachments. Sociologists are willing to admit the importance of classes and states as human aggregates in searching for the meaning of nationality, but they, quite properly, reject the idea of crowds determined by race as of decisive significance.

[50] Cf. Hertz, *op. cit.*, pp. 98–145.

[51] One of the most promising attempts made thus far by sociologists to develop an objective theory of nationality was made by the Belgian ethnologist and sociologist, Arnold Van Gennep, under the title, *Traité comparatif des nationalités*. Three volumes were planned: (I) *Les éléments exterieurs de la nationalité;* (II) *La formation des nationalités;* and (III) *La vie des nationalités.* Unfortunately, the author died soon after publication of the first volume (Paris, 1922). The work has not been continued.

sciousness of kind that binds men together despite varieties of political allegiances, religious beliefs, and economic interests.

When the psychologist defines nationality, he tends to favor the use of the terms instinct, consciousness, mental state, and spirit. In other words, he sees the emotional factors as dominant. According to W. B. Pillsbury, nationality is the personification of the unity of the nation, "the mental state, or the community in behavior." [52] To discover what nationality an individual belongs to, the simplest way is to ask him, and while his answer cannot always be trusted, but must be interpreted in terms of his general behavior, it is, if he speaks the truth, a better criterion than history, or racial descent, or physical measurement.[53] William McDougall describes nationality as "an extension of the self-regarding sentiment typical of the members of the nation." [54] Morris Ginsberg attributes nationality to "the consciousness on the part of members of a group that they belong to that group and the gathering of a large number of different emotional dispositions round that group as their object or nucleus." [55] Wayland F. Vaughan defines nationality as "a configuration of citizens each of whom regards himself as belonging to the whole." [56] In discussing nationality, F. H. Allport speaks of the "exaltation of self-consciousness through identification with the nation." [57] In all these definitions it is the emotional sentiment that makes of nationality a psychological entity.

On the ground that nationality is primarily cultural while race is biological in meaning, most psychologists hold that nationality should not be confused with race; with some rare exceptions, they make a careful distinction.[58] The dominant view is expressed by

[52] W. B. Pillsbury, *The Psychology of Nationality and Internationalism* (New York, 1919), p. 5.
[53] *Ibid.*
[54] William McDougall, quoted in F. H. Allport, *Social Psychology* (Boston, 1924), p. 388.
[55] Morris Ginsberg, *The Psychology of Society* (New York, 1921), p. 97.
[56] Wayland F. Vaughan, *Social Psychology* (New York, 1948), p. 890.
[57] F. H. Allport, *Social Psychology* (Boston, 1924), p. 388.
[58] For example, Herbert Gurnee defines nationality as "the character which members of a race possess"; (Herbert Gurnee, *Elements of Social Psychology* [New York, 1936], p. 330). George Malcolm Stratton defines it as "a considerable body of people with ties of blood and the sympathy and sense of spiritual union which go with a common culture, but who have not necessarily attained political independence and statehood"; (George Malcolm Stratton, *Social Psychology and International Conduct* [New York, 1929], p. 70).

Allport, who contends that nationality transcends the bounds of racial and geographic origin and even of language, though he admits that homogeneity in these respects naturally favors its development.

Psychologists, then, see nationality as clearly consisting of a complex of emotional dispositions with their nucleus, or object, the group as a whole. How can these complex emotional dispositions be measured? And is it possible to explain such elusive things as the individual's feeling of oneness, his willingness to sacrifice himself, as well as group emotions, in terms of inborn instincts? Can psychological experimentation and formulae furnish the master key? The answers to these questions are important because it is exactly at this point that the historian, the political scientist, and the sociologist defer to the psychologist and await the tangible results of his research.

The problem hinges on the very nature of the social sciences. Some scholars believe that the physical and social sciences can never meet, but others contend that the scientific methods of the chemist or physicist can be used by the psychologist, even by the sociologist or the historian. Natural scientists hold that, since the social sciences deal with man, it is not easy to make controlled experiments to test the validity of psychological hypotheses.

It is a tribute to the perspicacity of psychologists that they are not disheartened by this pessimism. Many of them feel that complex emotional dispositions can be measured by anthropometry, the science of measuring the human body, its parts, and its functional capacities.[59] In conjunction with experimental biologists, ethnologists, and anthropologists, they are conducting experiments in group intellectual testing and are investigating agglutinative reactions of the red corpuscles, body temperatures, respiration, susceptibility to disease, basal metabolism, the time and effects of puberty and menopause, color vision, reaction of the endocrine glands, constitutional types, brain size and structure, mental types, speed of nerve conduction, nature of the sense of smell, body odors,

[59] By no means is there any unanimity on this point. Pillsbury, for example, contends that only indirectly can nationality be determined by anthropometry or even by history. (Pillsbury, *op. cit.,* p. 20.) There has been much progress since his time. See Chapter 8 for further discussion of the quantitative approach for ascertaining national character.

etc. It is believed that this inductive approach will build up a vast body of knowledge of group behavior that will be used by social scientists to determine the true nature of nationality. It is a long-time project, and patience is indicated.

Conclusions and Summary

A term of the utmost complexity, nationality defies exact definition. It may be used in a concrete (objective, or external) sense (national language, territory, state, civilization, and history), or in an abstract (subjective, internal, or ideal) sense (national consciousness, or sentiment). Nationality does not depend on race, nor exclusively on language. Nationality and state are not synonymous terms. Nationality is not a "folk-spirit," nor is it an emanation of the "World-Spirit." The commonly accepted idea that nationality and citizenship are one and the same thing is erroneous.

A preliminary distinction between the three terms nation, nationality, and nationalism is roughly as follows: A nation refers to the citizens of a sovereign political state; nationality is used more exactly to describe a group of persons speaking the same language and observing the same customs; and nationalism is a descriptive term for the sentiment of a social movement.

To historians, nationality is a concept of recent origin, stemming out of the French Revolution, but after undergoing a preliminary evolution from instinct to idea, to abstract principle, to dogma. In its concrete sense it may be either political, cultural, or a combination of both. Historians also recognize the abstract sense of nationality as a subjective psychological feeling. Political scientists place emphasis on the exclusive and separatist character of nationality. They do not maintain that it is entirely political in character, and they give due recognition to its psychological implications.

Sociologists regard nationality as a primarily social category, and in defining it they give weight to such terms as people, collectivity, social unit, and group. They see it as a combination of external and internal facts (concrete and abstract senses). They admit the impossibility of developing an objective theory of nationality without the assistance of the historian and the psychologist. To psychologists, nationality is a subjective and psychological condition of mind, a spiritual possession, a way of thinking, feeling, and living. They believe that more attention should be given to emotional factors. They are seeking currently to measure these complex emotional dispositions at a group level.

Perhaps the most satisfactory simple definition of nationality is that projected by Frederick Hertz, who calls it "a community formed by the will to be a nation." [60] This definition combines the main interests of several disciplines—the community (sociology and anthropology), the will (psychology, psychiatry, and psychoanalysis), and a nation (history and political science). Hertz's definition rejects as inadequate objectivist theories (holding that the decisive criteria are objective factors, i.e., factors independent of the will of individuals), and proclaims the essential correctness of the subjectivist view. At the same time, he says that this definition needs a careful formulation, and urges that the subjectivist theory not be stretched so far as to obliterate the significance of the objective factors. Convinced that no static definition can explain completely such partly concrete, historical, and dynamic phenomena like nationality, he recommends careful examination of the general characteristics of nationality as the best means of ascertaining its meaning.

[60] Hertz, *op. cit.*, p. 12.

IV

The Sentiment of Nationalism

By nationalism I mean first of all the habit of assuming that human beings can be classified like insects and that whole blocks of millions or tens of millions of people can be confidently labelled "good" or "bad." But secondly—and this is much more important—I mean the habit of identifying oneself with a single nation or other unit, placing it beyond good or evil and recognizing no other duty than that of advancing its interests. —George Orwell *

The central fact of modern history, most observers agree, is the existence of the sovereign nation-state as the unit of political organization. Nationalism is a powerful emotion that has dominated the political thought and actions of most peoples since the time of the French Revolution. It is not a natural, but an historic phenomenon, that has emerged as a response to special political, economic, and social conditions.

Thus far, the tendency has been to search in history for clues to the meaning of nationalism; and the historian, therefore, has played a vital rôle in investigating the nature of nationalism. It has become increasingly obvious, however, that the study of nationalism has passed beyond the frame of reference ordinarily reserved for the historian. The historian, from his essentially objectivist position, is well equipped to describe the course of nationalism and its leading apostles. But to explain the meaning of nationalism he will have to take into account the work being done in other fields, especially by social psychologists, psychiatrists, and psychoanalysts.

* Such, Such Were the Joys (New York, 1953), pp. 73–74.

74

The Sinister Suffix "-ism"

The addition of the suffix "-ism" to a noun or adjective evidences some kind of excess over the original conception. It may indicate a theory, an organized activity, or a collective sentiment,[1] characterized by a strong, ordinarily one-sided, or militant, emphasis of a principle. Socialism is a specific kind of organization of society; Communism is not the same as communal enterprises; militarism means more than a mere interest in military matters; and pacifism does not denote simply a pacific disposition.

Similarly, the addition of the suffix "-ism" to national has altered profoundly the original meaning of the nation. The nation was originally conceived to be a community of people organized on the basis of common geographical area, history, language, traditions, and culture, but the new "-ism" endowed it with new, excessive traits which changed the entire concept. Nationalism makes more of the nation than a mere political or cultural community. Its realization becomes the supreme ethical goal of human beings on earth; it is depicted categorically as the most important thing in life; it becomes the be-all and end-all of man in his search for security. The concept is superimposed upon the natural order and is interpreted as the final cause and the final goal of the community. Thus, we are faced at the outset with a fallacious and perverted idea capable of causing untold mischief.[2]

[1] "The '-ism' was accepted to mean either a theory founded upon those principles or qualities (according to the particular viewpoints), or an organized activity which, adopted by some special interpretation of the principle, built up to a theoretico-practical system; or, finally, a collective sentiment favoring in any way the tendency represented by the 'ism' in question." (Don Luigi Sturzo, *Nationalism and Internationalism* [New York, 1946], p. 1.)

[2] Once the term nationalism was accepted, linguistic logic called for still other words closely related to the new meaning. From nationalism came nationalistic, an adjective denoting the advocacy of, or belief in, nationalism. The verb nationalize began to be used to describe the process of making national; to make a nation of; and to endow with the character of a nation, or the peculiar sentiments and attachments of the people of a nation. The noun nationalization means the act of nationalizing, or the state of being nationalized. The noun nationalist, meaning generally an advocate, or believer in nationalism, means either an advocate of national unity and independence, as in Ireland, Turkey, or China; or one who favors nationalization or state control or ownership of an industry or a public utility; a collectivist; or a person who belongs to the Nationalist party. All these terms are tinged with the same fallacy lurking in the term nationalism.

The Historian's Understanding of Nationalism

We have seen that historians feel that they are the specialists to be consulted first in the study of nationalism.[3] Projecting nationalism against the background of total historical development, they conclude that it is the most pregnant fact of modern times and is the most important sentiment in the life of contemporary civilized peoples. Not the least significant clue to its power is the fact that the very writing of history is infected with nationalism. Nationalism has been the dominant, although almost invariably unconscious, creed of many historians.[4] "It has had the support of governments not so much by their direct encouragement of national historians as by the development since the French Revolution of national support of national archives, national libraries, national historical societies, and national historical periodicals— in all of which major attention is generally given to the national history." [5]

In their search for the meaning of nationalism, historians think immediately of its many connotations. Carlton J. H. Hayes distinguishes four shades of meaning:

Nationalism is an actual historical process. Here nationalism stands for the actual historical process of establishing nationalities as political units, of building out of tribes and empires the modern institution of the national state.

Nationalism is a theory. From this point of view, nationalism indicates the theory, principle, or ideal implicit in the actual historical process.

Nationalism concerns political activities. Nationalism may mean the activities of a particular political party, combining the historical process and a political theory (Irish nationalism; Chinese nationalism).

Nationalism is a sentiment. Nationalism may describe a con-

[3] Cf. Herbert Adams Gibbons, *Nationalism and Internationalism* (New York, 1930), p. 2.
[4] A roll call of nationalist historians by country would include such distinguished names as: *France:* Michelet, Michaud, Mignet, Lamartine, Guizot, Thiers; *England:* Freeman, Stubbs, Froude, Carlyle, Macaulay; *Germany:* Dahlmann, Droysen, Sybel, Treitschke, Giesebrecht; *United States:* Bancroft, Fiske.
[5] Louis Gottschalk, *Understanding History* (New York, 1950), p. 218.

dition of mind among members of a nationality, in which loyalty to the ideal or to the fact of one's national state becomes superior to all other loyalties, and in which pride is exhibited in the intrinsic excellence and in the mission of one's national state.[6]

Max Hildebert Boehm distinguishes between a broad and a narrow meaning. Nationalism in its broader sense refers to the attitude that ascribes to national individuality a high place (similar to that of patriotism) in the hierarchy of values. On the other hand, nationalism in the narrow sense also connotes a tendency to place a particularly excessive, exaggerated, and exclusive emphasis on the value of the nation at the expense of other values, resulting in a vain overestimation of one's own nation and the criticism of others. "Nationalism of this sort stands in the same relation to national consciousness as does chauvinism to genuine patriotism. Although it represents but one aspect of national movements, this narrower kind of nationalism, espoused by militant groups and often by mass parties, exercises an enormous political influence." [7]

Other historians make the same distinction as they do for nationality, i.e., nationalism may have either a concrete or abstract meaning. Herbert Adams Gibbons believes that nationalism in the concrete sense may be taken to mean some paricular ways of manifesting national spirit (history, tradition, language); in the abstract sense the ideas controlling the life and actions of a nation would be its nationalism (consciousness of solidarity).[8]

After due deliberation on these various approaches to the meaning of nationalism, Hans Kohn entitled his major work on the subject *The Idea of Nationalism.* He feels that nationalism is "first and foremost a state of mind, an act of consciousness." He reasons that men are subject to both ego- and group-consciousness; with the growing complexity of civilization, the number of groups, unfixed and changing, increases. Within these pluralistic kinds of group-consciousness, there is generally one recognized by man as the supreme and most important. Kohn shows here a keen understanding of the importance of social psychology:

[6] Carlton J. H. Hayes, *Essays on Nationalism* (New York, 1926), pp. 5–6.
[7] Max Hildebert Boehm, "Nationalism: Political," *Encyclopedia of the Social Sciences* (New York, 1937), XI, pp. 231–32.
[8] Gibbons, *op. cit.,* p. 2.

The mental life of man is as much dominated by ego-consciousness as it is by group consciousness. Both are complex states of mind at which we arrive through experiences of differentiation and opposition, of the ego and the surrounding world, of the we-group and those outside the group. The collective or group consciousness can center around entirely different groups, of which some have a permanent character—the family, the class, the clan, the caste, the village, the sect, the religion, etc. . . . In each case, varying with its permanence, this group-consciousness will strive towards achieving homogeneity within the group, a conformity and like-mindedness which will lead to and facilitate common action.[9]

It is an encouraging fact that other students of intellectual history are gradually beginning to use the phraseology of social psychology in defining nationalism. Thus, Crane Brinton says that "nationalism is at bottom no more than the important form the sense of belonging to an in-group has taken in our modern Western culture." He describes it as one of the facts of life, one of the observed facts no scientist can neglect. "It is most usefully studied by the social psychologist, who is as yet no more than at the beginning of his scientific work of building cumulative knowledge." [10] Nationalism becomes a form of consciousness by which the individual proclaims his supreme loyalty to the nation.

This point of view, expressed also by Hayes in his fourth shade of meaning of nationalism, and intimated by Boehm in his description of the narrow meaning, enjoys most support among historians. Herbert Adams Gibbons gives the "logical definition of nationalism" as "consciousness of a solidarity of privileges and obligations with all others living under the same political unit." [11] George P. Gooch also defines nationalism as "the self-consciousness of a nation." [12] "Nationalism denotes the resolve of a group of human beings to share their fortunes, and to exercise exclusive control over their own actions." [13] J. Holland Rose goes even

[9] Hans Kohn, *The Idea of Nationalism* (5th printing, New York, 1951), pp. 10–11.
[10] Crane Brinton, *The Shaping of the Modern Mind* (New York, 1953), pp. 151, 221.
[11] Gibbons, *op. cit.*, p. 1.
[12] George P. Gooch, *Nationalism* (London and New York, 1920), p. 6.
[13] "Where such a conscious determination exists there should be a state, and there will be no abiding peace until there is a state. Where there is a soul there should be a body in which it may dwell. Here is the master-key to the political history of the nineteenth century." (Gooch, *op. cit.*, p. 8.)

further by describing this self-consciousness as "an intolerant and aggressive instinct." [14]

Although most historians are in accord that nationalism is primarily a state of mind and that it is a psychological and social fact, they are aware that it is an idea superimposed upon the natural order and endowed with a questionable personality. "Each state," says Edward Krehbiel, "is supposed to stand for something *sui generis:* to have a personality and qualities peculiar to it and not attainable by other peoples; and its ideas for *Kultur* are supposed to be incompatible with others and to lead to conflict." [15] Nationalism is not chiefly a product of physical geography, but "rests on traditions of politics, religion, language, war, invasion, conquests, economics, and society, which have been fashioned by peculiar and often fortuitous circumstances and which have been preserved and synthesized by great writers and other intellectuals." [16] The motivating desire is always to increase as far as possible the consciousness of power of the dominating nationality.[17]

From the historical vantage point this supreme group consciousness, or condition of mind, or will of forming, or attitude, or sentiment, was not a spontaneous exhalation of spiritual qualities of an exalted order. The community of sentiment could be created only through the trials of historic circumstance. Although a perversion of the original word nation, nationalism has had its own peculiar historical development. Not the least significant factor in its rise was the tendency of the group, from the small group to the community of the nation, to act in common. H. A. L. Fisher

[14] J. Holland Rose, *Nationality in Modern History* (New York, 1916), p. vi.
[15] Edward Krehbiel, *Nationalism, War and Society* (New York, 1916), p. 8.
[16] Carlton J. H. Hayes, *France, A Nation of Patriots* (New York, 1930), p. 16.
[17] Not all historians give primacy to the idea of consciousness in the definition of nationalism. Edward Krehbiel defines nationalism simply as "the political system of co-existing sovereign states." Nationalism then becomes the absolute sovereignty of the state. The reasoning behind this is as follows: at present each nation (used synonymously with state) is theoretically sovereign, i.e., independent of every other state; current philosophy of the state accepts the nation as the best and highest development; each nation regards its civilization as superior; believes it has a peculiarly important mission to perform; is certain that its citizens show a superior bravery and fighting quality; believes that its aspirations and policies are righteous; and feels that its highest duty is to survive. The idea of consciousness is thus relegated to the third stage of the process. (Cf. Krehbiel, *op. cit.*, pp. 1–8, *passim*.)

believes that an understanding of nationalism hinges upon this word, common. "What is essential," he says, "to the growth of the national spirit is a common history—common sufferings, common triumphs, common achievements, common memories, and, it may be added, common aspirations." [18]

The historical evolution of nationalism is similar to that we have already discussed in the preceding chapter on nationality. Among primitive peoples ancient tribal instincts centered on fear of and hostility to the stranger. In the Middle Ages this same sentiment of suspicion of the outsider existed in the small, localized communities. But nationalism as we know it today was unknown to the ancient and medieval worlds. Certain of its elements appeared during the Renaissance and were strengthened during the Reformation.

Modern nationalism, however, was the product of the late eighteenth-century revolutionary era, "a child of the French Revolution." [19] The state of nature, the new ideal of society, was made the basis of the nation. The earlier provincialism was revived on a grand scale, this time with the nation demanding the supreme loyalty of men. All men, not merely certain individuals or classes, were drawn into the new common loyalty, into the new supreme group-consciousness. Inspired by the cry of *fraternité*, the revolutionists arose as a nation in arms to defend their newly won liberties against the Old Régime. "By the French idea of *fraternité* every European country was soon affected, so that formerly latent sympathies were galvanized into a most lively sentiment, and theorists from the domain of history or philosophy or even of economics could find popular approval for their solemn pronouncements that 'people speaking the same language and sharing the same general customs should be politically united as nations.'" [20] Formerly Louis XIV could say, it has been asserted, without challenge, *"L'état, c'est moi!"* but now the new powerful bourgeoisie was insisting that the French nation had an existence quite apart from the king.

The revolutionary sentiment of nationalism was diffused from

[18] H. A. L. Fisher, *The Common Weal* (London, 1924), p. 195.
[19] George P. Gooch, *Studies in Modern History* (London, 1931), p. 217.
[20] Carlton J. H. Hayes, "The War of the Nations," *Political Science Quarterly*, XXIX (1914), pp. 687–88.

France to other parts of Europe from 1792 to 1815, and some countries saw a transformation from autocratic rule to a more popular form. This may be attributed not so much to the French Revolution itself as to a kind of defense reaction against the conquests of Napoleon.

> The French Revolution began, it is true, in a period of philosophic cosmopolitanism, since that was the tradition of the *philosophes,* and the French armies undertook to liberate other peoples from their tyrants in the name of the rights of *man,* not of *nations.* But Napoleon, in a somewhat incidental and left-handed fashion, did so much to promote the progress of both democratic institutions and of nationality in Western Europe that he may, in a sense, be regarded as the putative father of them both. His plebiscites were empty things in practice, but they loudly acknowledged the rights of people to decide on vital matters. He was a friend of constitutions—so long as he himself made them. . . . He is the founder of modern Germany.[21]

Following these initial impulses came the profound stimulus of the Industrial Revolution. From England to all corners of the world, the new means of transportation and communication (the steamship, the railroad) eliminated the old isolation and made possible a new psychic unity within each nation. Huge quantities of printed matter appeared, national armies were raised, great systems of free schools arose, all concomitant with the new economic nationalism.[22] The old blind and unreasoning attitudes of love for the nation and hatred for the outsider were solidified on a national scale. The implications were dangerous, for the new nationalism was subject to sudden and hysterical explosion.

Since technological advances were no more favorable to one than to the other, either nationalism or internationalism might have won dominance in the new machine age. It is a fact, however, that such technological advances have been used primarily for nationalistic ends. Economic developments of recent times seem to have stimulated nationalistic development, rather than the reverse.[23] The internationalism of Europe's crowned heads and

[21] James Harvey Robinson, "What is National Spirit?" *Century Magazine,* XCIII (1916), p. 61.

[22] See Chapter 6 for a discussion of economic nationalism.

[23] Cf. E. M. Patterson, "The World Trend Towards Nationalism," *Annals of the American Academy of Political and Social Science,* CLXXIV (1934), pp. 1–149; also, Commission of Inquiry into National Policy of International Relations, *International Economic Relations* (Minneapolis, 1934).

liberal parties, which had been so conspicuous in the 1850's, began to fade rather quickly. The national revolutions and social transformations of the mid-century placed the continued existence of the Concert of Europe in jeopardy, "a precarious equilibrium which was restored in the period between 1871 and 1890." [24] But nationalism persisted as a major historical force, the most powerful in modern times. After both World Wars it took on increasing strength and vigor.

Sociological Views of Nationalism

We have seen that sociologists regard the nation and nationality within the framework of social categories, as "great collectivities," or "human aggregates," or "in- and out-groups." They trace the evolution of society as it has banded itself together for mutual protection and prosperity. For some sociologists nationalism becomes a social movement which characterizes the behavior of nationalities. Max Wirth defines nationalism as "the social movements of nationalities striving to acquire, maintain, or enhance their position in a world where they are confronted by opposition or conflict." [25]

From this point of view, a key factor in the existence of nationalism is the group. In the animal world the gregarious instinct persists among herds, whose members associate only with their own kind and rigidly exclude the outsider. [26] There is a parallel within human groups, although the instinctive factor must not be exaggerated. One of the best-known results of sociological research is the discovery that organized groups of humans are more powerful socially than unorganized masses of peoples. [27] The formation of groups follows a well-recognized pattern. The experiences which the individual has with the group into which he is born or in which he lives are either good or bad experiences because he is a member of the group. From the group the individual imbibes traditions

[24] Hajo Holborn, *The Political Collapse of Europe* (New York, 1951), pp. 37, 50.
[25] Max Wirth, "Types of Nationalism," *American Journal of Sociology*, XLI (1936), p. 723.
[26] F. Alverdes, *Social Life in the Animal World* (New York and London, 1927), p. 107.
[27] Florian Znaniecki, *Modern Nationalities* (Chicago, 1952), p. xvi.

(patterns of behavior from the collective heritage, regardless of utility, beauty, or supernatural sanction), interests (aims useful to the existence and well-being of the group), and ideals (aims which are not the direct interests of individuals).[28] These experiences, solidified through the process of education, eventually become organized into a system with the group as the central object. When the group becomes large and takes on a deep and zealous concern for its own honor and prestige, it becomes subject to the sentiment of nationalism.

Some sociologists place emphasis upon the group itself as the first and motivating factor in nationalism, but others prefer to direct attention to the sentiment itself as the more important component. An example of this approach is the simple definition of nationalism by R. L. Sutherland and J. L. Woodward as "regard for and loyalty to a nation."[29] Paul A. F. Walter uses the term ethnocentrism as synonymous with nationalism and defines it as "loyalty to one group, reinforced by a corollary disdain or hostility toward other groups."[30] In other words, the sentiment of nationalism brings to the fore all those specific emotions that are serviceable to its end and rejects those that have no apparent use.

Not all sociologists accept the concept of the we-sentiment, which is sometimes given as the acid test of nationalism. Harry M. Shulman points out that the we-sentiment appears usually in times of stress. Nationalism, says Dr. Shulman, is not a we-sentiment but "a form of homeostasis, the equilibration of opposed vested interests within a series of specialized interdependent functional systems."[31]

Sociologists, like scholars of other disciplines, make the familiar distinction between concrete and ideal senses of nationalism. One group of sociologists holds that concrete factors in nationalism

[28] Frederick Hertz, *Nationality in History and Politics* (3rd ed., London, 1951), pp. 18–19. These motives are always gregarious in nature. Rabindranath Tagore, the Hindu poet and author, defines nationalism as "a gregarious demand for the exclusive enjoyment of the good things of the earth"; (quoted in R. Mookerjli, *Nationalism in Hindu Culture* [London, 1921], p. 26).
[29] Robert L. Sutherland and Julian L. Woodward, *Sociology* (New York, 1940), p. 345.
[30] Paul A. F. Walter, Jr., *Race and Culture Relations* (New York, 1952), p. 28.
[31] Prof. Harry M. Shulman, in an interview with the author.

(language, customs, tradition, territory, citizenship of the large in-group—the nation) can be observed and defined easily, though theorists may disagree on their relative importance. But ideal factors, according to other sociologists, must be investigated psychologically and left to social psychologists and collective psychologists.

Though interested primarily in the social aspects of nationalism and secondarily in its psychological character, sociologists do not ignore its cultural and political qualities. Florian Znaniecki considers the cultural side of nationalism so important that he defines nationalism as "the active solidarity of a national culture society." [32] He regards the latter phrase as the fourth and culminating chronological stage beyond the old pre-literate tribal society, the political society or state, and the ecclesiastical society. The national culture society, his synonym for nationalism,[33] has "a common and distinct literary culture and an independent organization functioning for the preservation, growth, and expansion of the future." [34] Luther Lee Bernard agrees that in its milder and more normal form nationalism is primarily cultural, but feels that at the point when consciousness of a common nationality becomes so strong in a group that its members are likely to desire unity, nationalism becomes political.[35]

There is some difference of opinion among sociologists as to whether nationalism is a survival of primitive barbarism or the product of modern society. [36] Representatives of the survival school believe that nationalism is an assertion of the cave man within us. It arose, they say, in response to the conditions of primitive times and has been preserved in the communal mind, which exists independent of the individual mind, as well as outside the nervous system and body of the individual. In support, they cite numerous instances of close parallels between the behavior of primitive tribes and modern human beings, such as rejection of reason, exaltation

[32] Znaniecki, op. cit., p. 21.
[33] "We would prefer a simpler term to denote this fourth group, but none can be devised in English, and we have tried in vain to coin a new compound Greek term." (Ibid.)
[34] Ibid.
[35] L. L. Bernard, War and Its Causes (New York, 1944), p. 378.
[36] This carries over into the field of anthropology. See the next section for a continued discussion on this difference of opinion.

of instinct, and irrational emotions (belief in "the mystic mass soul" and "the voice of the blood").

This theory of the survival school has been criticized by Hertz and other sociologists, who contend that nationalism cannot be explained simply by a harking back to or revival of primitive barbarism and its instincts, since, in this case, such instincts would be equally strong at all times and in all members of the species. There must be social factors that account for its variations according to time, nation, and class. Merely because a parallel seems to exist between the nervous excitement and motoric intoxication of primitive societies and the irrational behavior associated with nationalism does not mean that the latter is an outgrowth of the former. Nationalism is an independent sentiment which has arisen as a response to the peculiarities of modern mass society. Not only adolescent schoolboys but also intellectuals are taken in by the intensification of nationalism.[37]

Further progress in explaining nationalism from the sociological point of view awaits more fruitful study of the complex nature of contemporary society. Karl Mannheim, in his study of modern mass society, traces the growth of national aggressiveness to social disintegration.[38] When we know more about the character of social change, we shall be able better to understand the meaning and nature of nationalism as a sentiment reflecting community behavior.

Anthropological Views of Nationalism as an Instinct or a Persistent Mode of Behavior

Anthropology, the study of human beings as creatures of society, focuses its attention "upon those physical characteristics and industrial techniques and values, which distinguish one com-

[37] Hertz, *op. cit.*, pp. 270 ff. "[Modern nationalism] contains also much of the misused intellectualism and utilizes the results of intellectual progress. . . . Certain classes of intellectuals form an important element in many nationalist movements. . . . The disposition of nationalism is largely the product of the spirit of the times and, therefore, more or less permeates all classes, but it depends on the particular conditions of a nation how far this disposition is actualized." (*Ibid.*, pp. 272–74, *passim*.)
[38] Karl Mannheim, *Man and Society in an Age of Reconstruction*, tr. by Edward Shils (New York, 1940), pp. 126 ff.

munity from all others that belong to a different tradition." [39] It includes in its area of research other societies than our own. The anthropologist is interested in human behavior, not only as it has been shaped by one tradition, i.e., our own, but as it has been shaped by any tradition. Nationalism, as a social sentiment, falls within this category. We shall consider in succeeding chapters the work of anthropologists on national character and patriotism, but let us at this point look into some anthropological views of nationalism itself.

Sir Arthur Keith, the British anthropologist, believes that there is a striking lack of harmony between the ancient structure of our minds and modern environments. [40] The mental machinery of man was evolved for the specific purpose of binding small groups into social units as a means of achieving security. The sentiment of nationalism, the contemporary means of achieving security, is but another form of an inherited tribal instinct. [41] Modern man inherited this tribal instinct, but it is in conflict with his present condition of life.

The instinct theory has fallen into disrepute because it is said to describe something mystical and intangible. E. Hanbury Hankins, another British scholar, uses a different phraseology in expressing a similar idea. Hankins believes that a clue to the nature of nationalism may be found by study of persistent customs and modes of thought to which a large part of the human race is or has been addicted. These customs—blood-drinking, cannibalism, restricted cannibalism, mutilation of teeth, change of rulers, human sacrifice, and hatred of strangers—are all apparently useless, despite the fact that the strongest emotions must have been concerned in their origin. They are not instincts, although they are maintained by impulses that resemble instincts in certain respects.

> [Each] is not a product of reasoning by the individual; it comes from the past; it may give rise to frenzied conduct as great as or even more than that produced by recognized instincts. The impulse differs from

---

[39] Ruth Benedict, *Patterns of Culture* (9th printing, New York, 1952), p. 1.
[40] Sir Arthur Keith here elaborates upon the theory of Metchnikoff, the Russian biologist, that there is a marked lack of harmony between the ancient structure of our body and modern environments. (Cf. L. S. Greenberg, *Nationalism in a Changing World* [New York, 1937], pp. 28–29.)
[41] See the next section on psychology for a discussion of the instinct theory.

an instinct in that it is useless; it has been waning throughout the historical period, and it may affect only a small portion of the community. Thus it appears highly improbable that the impulse, coming from the past, is inherited in the same way as are recognized instincts.[42]

Hankins then undertakes a detailed anthropological study of these persistent customs among peoples all over the world, from the Persians and Hindus to the Eskimos of the Mackenzie River and the Red Indians of British Columbia. The survival of primitive tribes was dependent upon the possession of lands from which they drew their subsistence. Trespass or even the threat of trespass caused resentment or alarm. Moreover, there was a sense of satisfaction in the undisputed ownership of tribal territory as well as the acquisition of new territory, with its prospective additions to food resources. These impulses, says Hankins, are a likely basis for the sporadic appearance of national feeling in the historic period.

There are other feelings which carry over from the primitive era:

> As an example we may quote the blood-feud impulse. Sporadic instances of its occurrence are not infrequently reported in the newspapers of countries in which this custom has otherwise been extinct for centuries. The impulses by which such customs are perpetuated resemble in many ways the impulses concerned in national feeling. Thus the knowledge of these customs that we owe to the labor of anthropologists acquires an unexpected importance in throwing a light on the nature of our political feelings.[43]

Hankins' main point is that these persistent modes of behavior are typical of what he calls the communal mind. He admits that it is not easy to learn much about it because of the complicated nature of human life, but he claims to prove its existence outside the nervous system and body of the individual by the route-finding faculty shown by migrating animals, and by the changes that have taken place in the course of ages in various substitutes for human sacrifice. He calls upon psychologists and sociologists for support of his thesis.[44]

[42] E. Hanbury Hankins, *Nationalism and the Communal Mind* (London, 1937), p. 4.
[43] *Ibid.*, p. vii.
[44] For example, William McDougall, the American psychologist, was the first to

88 THE MEANING OF NATIONALISM

Nationalism, then, in Hankins' view, is a persistent mode of behavior of the communal mind. Unlike an instinct, it is a sentiment that may have remained latent for centuries and, suddenly, on an appropriate stimulus, burst into full activity. It has arisen with threats to the security and dignity of a nation. Analogues for nationalism may be found in persistent customs that once were prevalent among our ancestors and survive today among the "lower races" of mankind.

This ingenious explanation of the nature of nationalism succeeds in warding off much of the criticism that has been made of the instinct theory. Nevertheless, Hankins still assumes the existence of underlying common-human characteristics. Whether they are called instincts or persistent modes of behavior, there is still no explanation for their variations in time and in nations. Other anthropologists would say that animal, primitive, and civilized behaviors illustrate varieties, not stages. Hankins' emphasis upon route-finding by migrating animals does not necessarily mean that the human species possesses this same mysterious ability. Most historians, sociologists, and psychologists would agree that patriotism, as love of country, might possibly fall within the category of a persistent mode of behavior, but nationalism is a considerably more complicated mass phenomenon, which was called into being in relatively recent times to meet the new and complex demands of modern society. They would say that nationalism, far from being an innate, biological trait, equally strong at all times in all nations, is rather an invention designed to meet the problems of the modern nation. The behavior pattern is persistent only to the extent that the human animal naturally gravitates to those sentiments which he believes are vital in the process of attaining good and warding off evil.

---

make the suggestion that there exists some kind of collective unconscious, and he expressed the hope that it could be shown eventually that "great mass movements, emigrations, religious or political uprisings and so forth do occur, for which no adequate explanation is to be found in the mental processes of individuals." (William McDougall, *The Group Mind* [Cambridge, England, 1920], p. 33.) Émile Durkheim, the French sociologist, similarly concluded that conceptions when once formed might occasionally continue to exist independently, to some extent, of the nerve centers. (Émile Durkheim, *Sociologie et philosophie* [Paris, 1924], p. 32.)

Psychology and Nationalism

Among psychologists, too, there has been a strong difference of opinion as to whether or not nationalism comes within the category of instincts. The psychological theory of instincts in its modern form was introduced in 1908 by William McDougall, who described them as innate movers of all human activity and as the forces shaping the life of individuals and society.[45] Other psychologists, notably E. L. Thorndike [46] and H. C. Warren,[47] accepted this hypothesis but presented varying lists of instincts. In explaining how group behavior develops out of individual behavior, W. D. Trotter assumed that group consciousness, or gregariousness, is one of the four major human instincts (gregariousness, self-preservation, nutrition, and sex). The mind of man, he said, functions most satisfactorily in the herd, which is the source of his opinions, beliefs, power, and weakness.[48] Therefore, he concluded, some types of behavior in the crowd, such as the impulse to imitate actions of the masses, liability to suggestion, and pugnacity, are instinctive in nature.

This theory of instincts was criticized by other psychologists on the ground that it was based on simple reflex patterns of behavior of animals, primitives, and children, rather than on the complex patterns of men. The contention that nationalism is merely an instinct may be rejected as unscientific, mystical, and unprovable. Granted that the gregarious instinct exists as a specific innate tendency common to animals and men, and granted that the instinct of imitation, a stabilizing and conservative agency which preserves traditions, may play a rôle in the formation of human groups, it would be rash to presume that these instincts include the sentiment of nationalism. Biologically determined, instincts exist

[45] William McDougall, *Introduction to Social Psychology* (New York, 1908). McDougall listed thirteen major instincts (including curiosity, self-assertion, food-seeking, mating, acquisitiveness) and six minor instincts (sneezing, coughing, laughing, etc.).
[46] E. L. Thorndike, *Educational Psychology* (3 vols., New York, 1913).
[47] H. C. Warren, *Human Psychology* (Boston, 1919).
[48] W. D. Trotter, *Instincts of the Herd in Peace and War* (London and New York, 1919), pp. 47 ff.

in the nervous systems of the individual and are passed on from generation to generation by a biological process. Nationalism, on the other hand, is a sentiment which is re-created in each generation by acculturation and is transmitted from mind to mind by education. Instincts are innate; nationalism is implanted in each new generation. Instincts belong to the whole human species, not specifically to the nation. Specific innate tendencies of the mind are common to all members of the human race, but it is impossible to isolate any specific national instincts. There is little doubt that the gregarious and imitative instincts assist in the formation of national traditions, but they play an auxiliary and not a definitive rôle. Certainly the gregarious instinct helps to bind nations together, while the imitative instinct assists them in maintaining their traditions, but together they do not present the complete picture of nationalism. Each nation develops its own character and traditions in its own way, utilizing supranational instincts in the process, but gearing its actions to its own purely national ideas. Nationalism cannot be explained merely on the basis of reflex action, since among all peoples there exists a reservoir of thought and will that lies outside the range of instincts.

In discussing the many underlying motives in behavior common to human beings many psychologists have sought to steer away from the theory of instincts. They have devised new terms that they consider less objectionable than instinct: "drives" (Holt),[49] "desires" (Dunlap),[50] "motives" (Gurnee),[51] "dependable motives" (Woodworth),[52] and "needs" (Murray).[53] As a substitute for the instinct hypothesis, the late Kurt Lewin developed his "field theory," holding that human behavior is due not so much to the nature of the individual as to his relationship to the environment in which his behavior occurs.[54] Building upon Lewin's field theory, J. F. Brown concludes there is no such thing as human nature independent of the social field.[55]

[49] E. B. Holt, *Animal Drives and the Learning Process* (New York, 1931).
[50] K. Dunlap, *Civilized Life* (Baltimore, 1934).
[51] H. Gurnee, *Elements of Social Psychology* (New York, 1936).
[52] R. S. Woodworth, *Psychology* (New York, 1929).
[53] H. A. Murray, *Explorations in Personality* (New York and London, 1939).
[54] K. Lewin, *Principles of Topological Psychology* (New York and London, 1936).
[55] J. F. Brown, *Psychology and the Social Order* (New York, 1936). Later versions of the field theory give more credit to biological characteristics of man as an im-

Closely associated with the theory of instincts is the theory of sentiments, which some psychologists regard as more complex systems of behavior constructed on an instinctive basis.[56] Others regard sentiments as "systems the character and function of which is to organize certain of the lesser emotions by imposing upon them a common end and subjecting them to a common cause." [57] From both these points of view, nationalism can be regarded as a sentiment, since the nation, the largest of the groups, is subject to latent emotions, such as increase of suggestibility, impulsiveness, and inhibitions.

From the psychological point of view, the relationship between the individual and the collective mentality is a key factor in understanding nationalism. Some psychologists hold that the mass mind is an integration of individual minds functioning as a unit. It may be synthetic, but it nevertheless exists.[58] A motive of identification arises because the individual's thought processes are not checked at all points by the realities of the physical world; hence, he tends to transcend the boundaries of his self by his imagination. In his mind he becomes part of a greater world, a process known as "expansion of the ego." In the words of Daniel Katz, "In thus identifying himself with the nation-group, the individual is able better to satisfy his material needs, build up a psychic reserve income, feel at one with his familiar group, and project his hatreds and hostilities upon the foreigner, the 'out-group.'" [59] According to G. M. Gilbert, psychodynamics and social forces represent two

_____

portant aspect of the total field. The weight given, respectively, to heredity and environment remains one of the most disputed problems in biology, psychology, and medicine.

[56] In his treatment of the instinct theory, Otto Klineberg suggests that the criticism that McDougall's instinct theory did not deal with social phenomena is not quite fair, since he used his theory of sentiments in treating group behavior. (Cf. Otto Klineberg, *Social Psychology* [New York, 1940], p. 57.)

[57] A. F. Shand, *The Foundations of Character* (London, 1914), pp. 49–50. Shand bases this conclusion upon the idea that mental activity tends to produce and to sustain organization. "Every sentiment tends to include in its system all those emotions that are of service to its end, and to exclude all those emotions which are useless or antagonistic." (*Ibid.,* p. 62.)

[58] "The mass mind is a synthetic mind, an artificial mind, a mind which thinks in common, believes in common, feels in common—and in an age of dictators and demagogues is far too often fooled in common." (From a speech by Archibald MacLeish, quoted in *American Writer,* I [1953], pp. 14–15.)

[59] Daniel Katz, "The Psychology of Nationalism," in *Fields of Psychology,* ed. by J. P. Guilford (New York, 1940), p. 164.

levels of explanation, though there is necessarily interaction between the two. "Some of the concepts of psychodynamics and psychopathology (like paranoid sequences) cannot be applied directly to the body politic without making necessary distinctions in the phenomenology at the two levels. Other clinical concepts (like frustration and aggression) may come into play on the group level by social facilitation, though they may emerge with additional manifestations." [60]

Nationalism, then, becomes a form of the psychologically recognized phenomenon of individuals identifying themselves with symbols which stand for the mass. It is not a mystical entity hovering over the individuals that constitute a nation but, according to some psychologists, a measurable totality of psychical characteristics.[61] Nationalism is a response to the widespread need for security in a dangerous and hostile world. Just as the individual holds to his family relationships to achieve security in the small group, so does he identify himself with its extensity, the nation, against the real or imagined dangers from other nations.

In defining nationalism, psychologists show preference for terms dealing with central emotional qualities, such as consciousness, feeling, state of mind, and psychic characteristics. F. H. Allport defines nationalism as "the consciousness which the individual has of his nation as a whole, consisting of imagery of a vast number of people, of awareness of traditions which he supports in common with all the rest, and of present interests and ideals toward which all are disposed in the same manner as he." [62] W. Ehrenstein holds that nationalism "is based upon the consciousness of bonds with the people to whom the subject is related; the feelings which are experienced toward one's family and closest friends are extended to others." [63] According to Bernard C. Ewer, nationalism is "a state of mind, which in the individual tends to exalt the importance of the state, its opposition to other states, and its superiority to the individual." [64] The British social psychol-

[60] G. M. Gilbert, *The Psychology of Dictatorship* (New York, 1950), p. 287.
[61] Morris Ginsberg, *The Psychology of Society* (New York, 1921), p. 102.
[62] F. H. Allport, *Social Psychology* (Boston, 1924), p. 388.
[63] W. Ehrenstein, "Die Verwurzelung des Nationalismus im Gefühlsleben," *Zeitschrift für pädagogsichen Psychologie*, XXXV (1934), pp. 16–24.
[64] Bernard C. Ewer, *Social Psychology* (New York, 1929), p. 405.

ogist, Morris Ginsberg, defines it as "the totality of certain fundamental psychical characteristics peculiar to and widespread in a certain people, influencing their behavior, and manifested with greater or less continuity in a succession of generations." [65]

Some psychologists contend that there is a close analogy between the emotional qualities of nationalism and religion. On the premise that the modern nation-state contains within itself many of the characteristics of religion, Steuart Henderson Britt defines nationalism as "the religion of the state." [66] Nationalism, like religion, has its hymns of praise, its days of feasting, and its altars. The quality of self-sacrifice demanded from the people of a nation at times takes on religious aspects. The people are urged to be pious; they are conditioned to adore national heroes and martyrs. Nationalism is famous for its missionary spirit and, in effect, represents the cult of the nation. According to Kimball Young, the national state is for the modern man the largest in-group that calls for his reverence, deference, and sense of belonging, replacing the church as the center of affection, social solidarity, and security, as the core of basic in-group attitudes and values. [67]

Psychologists who reject the instinct theory agree with historians, political scientists, and sociologists that nationalism is a modern phenomenon stemming out of the period of the French Revolution. There are certain parallels with previous forms of group solidarity (primitive totemism, medieval feudal loyalty), but modern nationalism is the result of exposure to considerably more complex socio-cultural and economic factors. Psychologists also accept the conclusion of historians that modern nationalism is subject to variations in time and place and that it becomes necessary to understand the individual situation of a given nation at a given time. Daniel Katz believes that early nationalism owed its tremendous motivating force to the fact that it represented an integration between man's bread-and-butter drives and his egoistic wishes. "Today's nationalism no longer represents a fusion of psychic and material satisfaction. Instead, it furnishes a compensatory psychic income for individuals whose material income has

[65] Ginsberg, *op. cit.,* p. 103.
[66] Steuart Henderson Britt, *Social Psychology in Modern Life* (New York, 1949), p. 557.
[67] Kimball Young, *Social Psychology* (New York, 1947), p. 379.

been reduced. European peoples accept nationalism today because they find solace in group-indentification for their frustration in everyday life." [68]

Psychologists feel that it is their task to find and measure the new master symbols which attract the emotional attachment of peoples in current society. There is a considerable body of psychological as well as anthropological literature which seeks to describe and measure personality norms. The assumption here is that there is a fairly close correlation between the common denominator of the values and attitudes of a nation's population and a personality norm. The existence of this correlation among small, culturally homogeneous, primitive societies appears to be well established. It seems probable that these same measurements can be applied to the study of culturally homogeneous societies within modern nations, but the development of objective techniques has barely begun.[69] Psychologists hope that some day, with a greater fund of knowledge on common value-attitudes, they may be able to throw more light on the various aspects of nationalism.

Psychiatry and Nationalism

Psychiatry, among the medical disciplines, corresponds to social psychology among the social sciences. Unlike social psychology, psychiatry approaches the understanding of human life by way of the aberrant processes, or mental disorders,[70] which may be somatic, psychical, or social. Man, the animal, is born with individual variations in an astounding potentiality for living. He can never be explained adequately in terms of biology alone, since, as a growing organism, he is subjected to continuing acculturation by his environment.

We need not discuss these aberrant processes in detail as this would lead too far from our immediate subject. To understand

[68] Katz, op. cit., p. 175.
[69] Cf. Ralph Linton, "The Concept of National Character," in Personality and Political Crisis, ed. by Alfred H. Stanton and Stewart E. Perry (Glencoe, Illinois, 1951), p. 144.
[70] Harry Stack Sullivan, "Psychiatric Aspects of Morale," in Personality and Political Crisis, op. cit., p. 44. "This is its approach; but its field proves to be coterminous with that of social psychology—in fact, rather wider than the field of some social psychologists." (Ibid.)

the psychiatric approach to nationalism, however, it will be necessary to define briefly several basic psychiatric terms, keeping in mind the fact that these classifications are not hard and fast.

Neurosis: a functional nervous disorder, without demonstrable physical lesion, such as neurasthenia (attributed to emotional conflict, feelings of inferiority, and worry), and anxiety neurosis. Psychoneurosis, commonly used synonymously with neurosis, is mental (psychogenic) rather than physical in origin (examples—hysteria and compulsion).

Psychosis: any serious mental derangement, such as paranoia (systematized delusional insanity); schizophrenia (loss of contact with the environment and disintegration of the personality); manic depressive insanity (alternating periods of stupor and activity); and megalomania (grandiose delusions).

Although psychiatrists have worked out procedures for treating mental disorders on an individual basis, they seem to find it difficult to apply such procedures to extensive groups like the nation. There is no neat, simple formula that can explain the integration of the individual with the social system. According to Harry Stack Sullivan, as personality expands, it becomes more and more completely inaccessible to the instrumentalities of the natural sciences, progressing to a complexity that defies meaningful statistical approach and ceases to be a suitable object for scientific method.[71] A complicating factor is the variability of the constitutional composition of a population. Talcott Parsons, the sociologist, points out that it is quite impossible, under the circumstances of human society, for the distribution of the genes in the population to correspond in any close way with the distribution of the statuses in society. "The mechanisms for personality analysis cannot be directly identified with the mechanisms of social process analysis because of the different empirical focus that is used." [72]

In spite of these obstacles to the study of abnormal psychology on a group basis, psychiatrists feel that the logic they use in the analysis of individual mental health can be applied to the social system as a whole. They feel, however, that this approach should

[71] *Ibid.,* p. 45.
[72] Talcott Parsons, "Personality and Social Structure," in Stanton and Perry, *op. cit.,* pp. 65, 74–75.

go beyond the theories of personality and should take into account the complexities of social interrelations. Personality, they feel, may be treated as a hypothetical entity useful in explaining such phenomena as nationalism.

Some psychiatrists, as well as some social scientists, believe that mental disorders should be regarded as diseases of society rather than of the individuals in it. In his *Psychosocial Medicine: A Study of the Sick Society,* James Lorimer Halliday contends that society as well as the individual may be sick.[73] L. K. Frank projects the idea of "society as the patient": "Instead of thinking in terms of a multiplicity of so-called social problems, each demanding special attention and a different remedy, we can view all of them as different symptoms of the same disease." [74]

The analogy must not be pressed too far, but there are in fact some striking similarities between the well-recognized neurotic and psychotic behavior of individuals and the behavior patterns of the group implicit in nationalism. Caroline E. Playne, the British scholar, devoted several books to the study of nationalism "as a social neurosis caused by the stress and strain of modern life." [75] She denies the contention of Hankins and the survival school that modern nationalism is an atavistic return to primitive barbarism and, instead, labels it a neurosis caused by the wear and tear on man's nervous make-up from the increased pressure, complications, and the fullness of life generally.

Three of the major characteristics that psychiatrists find in neurosis are present in the group sentiment of nationalism: anxiety, sense of inferiority, and instability. In each case these are symptoms of emotional conflict.

Anxiety: Nationalism is in part a psychological response to grave threats of insecurity. A national group which finds itself endangered by a hostile nation and, therefore, deprived of a feeling of security rapidly becomes demoralized and subject to anxiety. Groups do not understand what is taking place, and, as one rebuff

---

[73] James Lorimer Halliday, *Psychosocial Medicine: A Study of the Sick Society* (New York, 1948).
[74] L. K. Frank, "Society as the Patient," *American Journal of Sociology,* XLII (1936), p. 336.
[75] Caroline E. Playne, *The Neuroses of the Nations: The Neuroses of Germany and France before the War* (London, 1925); *The Pre-War Mind in Britain* (London, 1928); and *Society at War* (London, 1930).

after another occurs, they take refuge in the symbols of nationalism. However irrational, these symbols offer some measure of security. The mental state of anxiety becomes automatic; a kind of numbness takes place; there is little rational thinking; and what there is consists of ideas that have been entertained many times before.[76]

Sense of Inferiority: In thought, talking, and writing, all nationalists exaggerate the superiority of their own power unit. The most inconsequential slur upon a nation's honor and prestige calls for heated replies. Nationalists automatically insist upon the superiority of their own art, language, literature, climate, political virtue, even cooking. The Olympic Games, ostensibly dedicated to international good-will and aiming at friendly competition, are widely regarded as tests of national physical superiority. The Soviet claim to priority in inventions actually made elsewhere is an indication of this overpowering desire for national recognition. All this is actually psychological overcompensation for feelings of inferiority, the consequence of which may be neurosis.[77]

Instability: Nationalism is characterized by a neurotic predisposition to instability. According to George Orwell, nationalism is a transferable sentiment, which, on occasion, may be fastened upon a country by another. Transferred nationalism is common among intellectuals; Lafcadio Hearn shifted his allegiance to Japan and Houston Stewart Chamberlain to Germany. Many great national leaders changed their allegiance from one country to another, including Napoleon, Beaverbrook, de Valera, and Hitler. Orwell sees in nationalism an emotional irregularity that is symptomatic of neurotic behavior, whether on an individual or a mass basis.[78]

On the considerably more serious matter of psychotic behavior, some psychiatrists show an understandable reluctance to label

[76] Sullivan, *op. cit.,* p. 48.

[77] This pattern is the group analogue to Alfred Adler's individual psychology, the dynamic units of which are "feelings of inferiority" and "compensations for such inferiority." Feelings of inferiority initiate compensating movements of self-assertion, such as irrational demand for attention. Self-centered and self-gratifying, these demands call for a will to power, regardless of the social order. (Cf. Alfred Adler, *Über den nervösen Charakter* [4th ed., Munich, 1928], tr. by Bernard Glueck and J. E. Lind as *The Neurotic Constitution* [New York, 1917], and *Praxis und Theorie der Individualpsychologie* [4th ed., Munich, 1930], tr. by Paul Radin [rev. ed., London, 1920].)

[78] Cf. George Orwell, *Such, Such Were the Joys* (New York, 1953), pp. 81–82.

whole nations as mentally diseased. Rather than consider nationalism a disease process, Dr. Nathaniel Breckir describes it as "a reaction type," a fusing together of many diverse morbid elements such as hereditary or genetic, environmental, and psychically developed factors.[79] The emphasis here, as in most advanced psychiatric thinking, is placed upon the importance of acculturation processes without omitting altogether the significant factor of heredity.

There are, indeed, parallels between the futile, self-defeating attitudes of the psychotic individual and the thinking and behavior of nations. The bombast of the patient in mania and the irrational actions of whole nations in war periods have much in common. In both cases there exist emotions completely unrealistic and contrary to fact.

Megalomaniac-Paranoid Trend: Ruth Benedict, the anthropologist, points out that there are a number of societies in which the usual pattern of behavior may be regarded as abnormal. She found a megalomaniac-paranoid trend among the Kwakiutl Indians of British Columbia. All the motivations of the Kwakiutl society—their social organization, their economic institutions, their religion, birth, and death—center on the will to superiority. The triumphant publicly heap ridicule and scorn upon their opponents. The behavior required of the chief is arrogant and tyrannical ("I am the great chief who makes people ashamed"). According to Benedict, these delusions of grandeur as well as delusions of reference (interpreting accidents as deliberate "insults" directed from somewhere in the universe) are plainly paranoid in nature.[80]

We have seen that Dr. Richard Brickner, although criticized by other psychiatrists, sees a similar pattern of abnormal behavior in the nationalism of Nazi Germany.[81] K. E. Appel, finds the concept of absolute and unlimited and irresistible power (typical in

[79] Dr. Nathaniel Breckir, in an interview with the author.
[80] Ruth Benedict, *Patterns of Culture* (9th printing, New York, 1952), pp. 160–205, *passim*. Similar manifestations of abnormal social behavior may be found in the intricate system of taboos in Polynesia, trance and ecstasy among the shamans of many California tribes, cataleptic seizures among the Siberian shamans, continual and excessive fear among the Dobuans of Melanesia, and the homosexual practices of many American Indian and Siberian communities. (Cf. Klineberg, *op. cit.*, pp. 507 ff.)
[81] Richard Brickner, *Is Germany Incurable?* (Philadelphia, 1943).

the totalitarian state) reminiscent of the vocabulary and delusions of the manic patient and the paretic. "They recall the phantasies of magic and power so frequent in children's dreams and fairy tales. Yet statesmen, senators, and journalists talk in the same complacent, self-satisfied, grandiloquent vein." [82]

Schizophrenic Behavior: The late brilliant British novelist and critic, George Orwell, stated that some nationalists are "not far" from schizophrenic behavior, living quite happily amid dreams of power and conquest that have no connection with the physical world. All nationalists, in Orwell's estimation, are alike in that they do not see resemblances between similar sets of facts. The British Tory will defend self-determination in Europe and oppose it in India with no feeling of inconsistency. Actions are held as good or bad, not on their own merits, but according to who does them. Almost any kind of outrage—bombings, assassinations, imprisonments, deportations—is acceptable as long as it is sponsored by "our side." Indifference to objective truth is encouraged by sealing off one part of the world from another. Although endlessly brooding on victory, power, defeat, and revenge, the nationalist is often little interested in what is happening in the real world. He wants to feel that his own country is getting the better of some other country.[83]

The rapid development in recent years of group psychotherapy indicates a new awareness of the nature of mental disorders. In group therapy there is a more objective experience, a more clearcut demonstration of social standards and the social conscience.[84] Whether or not a meaningful approach can be extended beyond the small group to the complexities of the "sick" nation is problematical. An interesting case was the effort made by American Occupation authorities to re-educate Germany after World War II.

[82] K. E. Appel, "Nationalism and Sovereignty: A Psychiatric View," *Journal of Abnormal and Social Psychology,* XL (1945), pp. 359 ff.
[83] Orwell, *op. cit.,* p. 82.
[84] J. W. Klapman, *Group Psychotherapy: Theory and Practice* (New York, 1946), p. 45. Cf. also N. S. Ackerman, "Dynamic Patterns in Group Psychotherapy," *Psychiatry,* V (1944), pp. 341–48; L. K. Frank, "Society and the Patient," *American Journal of Sociology,* XLII (1936), pp. 335–44; L. C. Marsh, "Group Treatment of the Psychoses by the Psychological Equivalent of Revival," *Mental Hygiene,* XV (1931), pp. 328–49; E. W. Snowden, "Mass Psychotherapy," *Lancet,* II (1940), pp. 769–70; and L. Wender, "Group Psychotherapy: Application," *Psychiatric Quarterly,* XIV (1940), pp. 708–18.

Psychoanalysis and Nationalism

What can the psychoanalyst offer to an understanding of the meaning of nationalism? The answer lies in the twin facts that nationalism is a form of human behavior, and psychoanalysis, the psychology of the unconscious mind, is dedicated to clarifying the motivations of such behavior. The revolutionary contribution of psychoanalysis is the discovery that of the total mind only a small upper layer is in the realm of the conscious; the great mass lies beyond the reach of self-awareness or introspection.

Let us for a moment, in somewhat oversimplified terms, discuss the characteristics of the conscious and the unconscious minds. Prehistoric man attributed what went on in the world around him to the actions of fickle, supernatural gods. In the historic period, man was gradually liberated from prejudice and bias. By using his conscious intellect—the logical thought processes of his mind—he was able to gather a tremendous fund of objective knowledge about the external world and to utilize it for his own needs. With his highly perfected conscious thinking he was able to come to grips with his outer universe and make progress in moulding it to suit his purposes.

The inner universe of the unconscious mind of man is something else. From the beginning of his abstract thought, man has sought to apply his reason and will power to explain and clarify the working of his conscious mind. This effort has been rewarded with but little success. The responsibility for his failure may be attributed to the fact that the unconscious mind has little connection with logical thought. The inner mentality, we know today, is only to a small degree affected by the intellect. On the contrary, it is controlled by emotions, impulses, feelings, and desires not directly related to intellect, and it is resistant to exploration, measurement, or direction. It is wrong to assume that only primitive impulses reside in the unconscious mind. Here are located a reservoir of passions and prejudices that should be differentiated from the ethical and moral standards of the conscious mind. The motivating power for the conscious mind comes from the unconscious, and it propels human beings on waves of emotions that they do not comprehend.

How does this concern our discussion of the meaning of nationalism? It is becoming increasingly obvious that this great phenomenon of human behavior is a product of the inner universe of the unconscious. Nationalism is neither wholly logical nor rational. Its roots lie in the illogical, irrational, and fantastic world of the unconscious. Unconscious fears, anxieties, and cravings are projected into the conscious mind, where they seek symbols to satisfy the need for security—one of the basic needs of human beings. The individual substitutes his nation or his church for his parents, not by a careful reasoning process, but primarily because he unwittingly seeks something familiar and because he automatically gravitates to the traditional and the authoritative. The nation becomes his father or mother; he will love it, hate it, or disregard it, depending upon his childhood patterns of behavior.

From the psychoanalytical point of view, then, nationalism is determined more by the emotional factors within human beings than by any question of its merit as a form of human behavior. It is more a product of infantile fears and antagonisms carried over from the unconscious to the conscious than a mature response to a given set of social conditions. If objective scientists were given the opportunity to use the conscious intellect to create the best of all possible worlds, it is questionable whether they would accept the idea of a society of mutually antagonistic national states as a logical form of social organization. They would not object, of course, to the healthy manifestations of cultural nationalism.

Psychoanalysts, like psychologists and psychiatrists, regard nationalism as a psychical phenomenon and as an important expression of applied psychology. By directing attention to the psychical processes, psychoanalysts help us to understand how nationalism attained its terrifying expansion.[85] The analytic investigation of significant experiences of a people can contribute to an understanding of character development and of the character traits typical of a people in a national group.[86] The expansion of psychoanalytical study helps to show how particular impulsive trends are dominant in certain nations, how and to what extent symbols are used, and

[85] L. Fessler, "Psychology of Nationalism," *Psychoanalytic Review,* XXVIII (1941), p. 383.

[86] Cf. Henry Lowenfeld, "Freud's *Moses* and Bismarck," in *Psychoanalysis and the Social Sciences,* ed. by Géza Róheim (New York, 1950), II, p. 289.

what kind of manifestations are exhibited in individual nations.[87]

Some psychoanalysts believe that, since the urges of the individual develop in a social setting, the social structure of a collective group, such as a nation, inevitably repeats the motivations of the individuals who compose it.[88] The individual is ever in relation to or in possible conflict with social sanctions. The manner of accepting adaptation to the social structure is a decisive factor in normality or abnormality. Forms of social control are subject to their own types of neuroses and maladaptations. According to Freud, a certain amount of neurotic disturbance has necessarily accompanied the growth of civilization, and the higher cultures have more completely succeeded in repressing the instinctive urges.[89]

Critics of Freud agree with him on the existence of social neuroses but take exception to his theory of instincts. Eric Fromm sees man's problems just beginning with his needs for food, drink, and sex. "He strives for power, or for love, or for destruction, he risks his life for religious, for political, for humanistic ideals, and these strivings are what constitutes and characterizes the peculiarity of human life." [90] Karen Horney pointed out that the particular needs that are relevant to understanding the personality are not intellectual in character but are created by the entirety of conditions under which we live.[91]

Some psychoanalysts, in seeking for the meaning of nationalism, attach great significance to its close relation to mythology and religion.[92] Freud believed that man by nature has certain instincts that inherently are socially destructive and which, for the sake of social welfare, must be repressed.[93] Mythology and religion perform the social function of diverting these strong repressed instincts toward gratification in phantasy only. They offer compromises be-

---

[87] Cf. Aurel Kolnai, *Psychoanalysis and Sociology* (New York, 1922), p. 96.
[88] "The herd control appears as the Freudian censor, a concept made more truly sociological by Rivers." (Joseph Jastrow, *Freud: His Dream and Sex Theories* [New York, 1948], p. 125.)
[89] Cf. Sigmund Freud, *Civilization and Its Discontents,* tr. by Joan Riviere (London, 1939). Freud's theory of instincts as a constant and inescapable force has been attacked as an elaborate and unnecessary intellectual construction built up in order to account for certain observed facts.
[90] Eric Fromm, *Man for Himself* (New York, 1947), p. 46.
[91] Karen Horney, *New Ways in Psychoanalysis* (New York, 1939), p. 78.
[92] Sigmund Freud, *The Future of an Illusion* (London, 1943), p. 9.
[93] *Ibid.*

tween the unconscious and the processes of repression. Religion opens the way to civilization but at times may permit things hostile to civilization.

Other psychoanalysts offer varying interpretations of the rôles of religion and nationalism in society. J. C. Flugel believes that nationalism may be, in part, a substitute for religion as an answer to psychic needs. "In actual practice, to judge from recent tendencies, when traditional religious belief is abandoned, an emotional substitute is now most likely to be found. . . . In obedience to the state or party, man finds an alternative to obedience to God, while *Mein Kampf* or *Das Kapital* replaces the Bible." [94] One of Freud's critics, Carl G. Jung, differed with him on the rôle of religion, on the ground that it is a psychic attitude of inestimable importance. Jung defined religion as more than dogma or a creed, rather as an outlook satisfying faith, hope, and love.[95] On the other hand, Karen Horney said that religion, which in the past has offered the possibility for individuals to find a satisfactory outlet for their introvert tendencies, has lost its appeal for the majority.[96]

To these varied opinions it might be added that nationalism differs from religion in that the latter is addressed to mankind, while nationalism concerns certain groups. Moreover, religion, as a spiritual concept, seeks the blessings of peace, but nationalism, as a psychical concept, emphasizes superiority and inferiority and leads to conflict. Religions, in their dogma at least, preach tolerance, but nationalism rewards hostility and aggression.

It would be best, perhaps, to abandon these inconclusive arguments and turn our attention to the dominant themes concerning the nature of nationalism that are gradually emerging in psychoanalytic literature:

Nationalism is a response to the individual's need for security. The individual gravitates towards the group because he is convinced that in union there is strength.[97] He may doubt his own

[94] J. C. Flugel, *Man, Morals and Society: A Psychoanalytical Study* (New York, 1945), p. 294.
[95] Carl G. Jung, *Modern Man in Search of a Soul*, tr. by W. S. Dill and Cary F. Baynes (New York, 1943), p. 140.
[96] Karen Horney, *The Neurotic Personality of Our Time* (New York, 1937), p. 278.
[97] See Sigmund Freud, *Group Psychology and Analysis of the Ego*, tr. by James Strachey (New York, n.d.).

capacities, but never those of the group. Nationalism frees his psychic energy and channels it into a common stream, where he finds a sense of belonging and a feeling that his superiority is unchallenged. This urge is unconscious and unrecognized, and is subject to irrational motivation. In his conscious mind the individual may well understand the dangers and fallacies of nationalism, but he is conditioned by his environment to eliminate any rational or intellectual effort, to lower his critical attitudes, and to give nationalism his absolute confidence. Nationalism suppresses his own principles of conscience and morality, but it relieves him of the conscious, rational, and intellectual efforts to assure his own security and, at the same time, alleviates his countless fears in favor of a feeling of strength.

The psychoanalyst, Dr. Edmund Ziman, regards nationalism as a part of the acculturation process by which the adult seeks satisfaction for his dependency needs acquired in infancy.[98] The infant, a helpless creature, is dependent upon his mother for food, protection, and love. This dependency need should be satisfied in the infant before he proceeds to the next stages of his life—childhood, puberty, adolescence, and adulthood. If the need is not satisfied in childhood, there is a tendency to search for it in succeeding stages, even in adulthood. The goal is emotional maturity, which has to be acquired mostly by learning. This process, familiar in individual cases, is also typical of the group, in which it becomes socially acceptable to transfer the early need for dependency from the mother to other people or to the nation. The nation and its symbols provide a perfect substitute. In Dr. Ziman's view, the degree of nationalism in any given country may be explained by the extent of what might be called "national emotional maturity."

Nationalism may be in part a carry-over of parent and family fixation. Some psychoanalysts believe that nationalism grows partly out of the basic authoritarian system of the family, with its hierarchy, and the father's use of the family group relationships as a means of keeping his authority. In early life the individual attributes unlimited power to the father; in later life, as a member of the group, he identifies the state childishly with the omniscient,

[98] Edmund Ziman, *Jealousy in Children* (New York and London, 1949), pp. 29–30, 39.

omnipotent father.[99] The unconscious, symbolic relationship to the parent-figures of infancy is transferred to the nation.[100] Freud went so far as to claim that the masses possess an innate need to submit and actually have a "mania for authority." "One might say," Freud went on, "that the great man is the authority for whose sake the effort is made, and since the great man achieves this because he is a father-substitute, we need not be surprised if he is allotted the rôle of super-ego in mass psychology." [101]

Other psychoanalysts see nationalism as the direct continuation of family attachment, but believe that it is attributable to an unconscious, deeply anchored mother fixation. The theory is that this cannot be explained biologically, since the mother fixation itself is a *social* product.[102]

We need not concern ourselves here with the bitter interprofessional quarrels about Freud's outline of the nature of the Oedipus complex and myth,[103] except to say that some psychoanalysts see in modern nationalism a new symbolism similar to parent fixations. Most psychoanalysts believe that fundamental child-parent relationships are centuries old, change very slowly, and have a decisive effect upon the events of human history, the interactions between human nature, and cultural development.[104]

Nationalism expresses deep-seated fear and hostility. Psychologists believe that lack of maturity may be responsible to some extent

[99] Appel, *op. cit.,* p. 359.

[100] "As psychoanalysts have insisted, our state or country makes a great appeal to the unconscious, inasmuch as it stands in a symbolic relationship to the parent-figures of our infancy, as is revealed in the very words 'patriotism,' 'motherland,' 'fatherland,' etc. . . . Our earlier loyalty and obedience to the parents are thus very easily transferred to the state." (Flugel, *op. cit.,* p. 290.)

[101] Sigmund Freud, *Moses and Monotheism,* tr. by Katherine Jones (New York, 1939), p. 185. A biographer of Freud, Helen Walker Puner, says that Freud, in his later career, abandoned his original theory of instincts; (Helen Walker Puner, *Freud: His Life and His Mind* [New York, 1947], p. 209). The quotations above, however, are from one of his late works.

[102] An extension of this theory holds that the mother fixation is perpetuated socially and becomes the basis for nationalist feeling in the adult. Reactionary social forces, especially Fascism, it is said, may be due in part to this process.

[103] King Oedipus slew his father Laius and wedded his mother Jocasta in response to the wish-fulfillment of childhood. Patrick Mullahy considers this myth so important that in presenting a comprehensive exposition of psychoanalytic theory, he combined it with a thoroughgoing treatment of the Oedipus complex and myth. (Cf. Patrick Mullahy, *Oedipus Myth and Complex: A Review of Psychoanalytic Theory* [New York, 1948].)

[104] C. P. Oberndorf, "Child-Parent Relationship," in *Psychoanalysis Today,* ed. by Sandor Lorand (New York, 1944), p. 87.

for the existence of fear and hostility at the adult level. Here, again, the Freudian emphasis upon response to parents becomes the matrix from which fears and hostilities grow.[105] In the healthy solution of the Oedipus conflict, hatred for the father gives way to a more friendly relationship, and the love attachment for the mother foregoes its sexual aim.[106] In many other cases, as the child becomes adjusted to its environment, his hostility towards his father becomes successively directed upon various substitute objects. According to P. Hopkins, "in some cases the sublimation may be carried on until at last the hatred becomes directed upon an object that the whole community agrees in disliking. What more likely object is there than 'the enemy,' who thus fulfills the extremely important function of providing intense expression for the repressed father-hate of childhood? The desire to 'punish' the enemy then becomes a consuming passion, and a harmless citizen becomes a fanatical supporter of a ruthless war policy." [107] Franz Alexander expresses the view that fear of the parents becomes embodied in the fear of one's own conscience.[108]

Nationalism, according to Gertrud M. Kurth, involves a regressive ambivalence conflict—the father becomes the anvil of infantile fears and hostilities and the mother becomes identified with the nation.[109] Some psychoanalysts see nationalism as representing in part a dramatization at the group level of the fears and hostilities that arose originally in the child's relations to his parents. Not all psychoanalysts, however, hold this view. Karen Horney, Eric Fromm, and others lay less emphasis upon the innateness and inevitability of hostile behavior and more upon conflicts that are socially conditioned.[110]

Nationalism is an outlet for aggression. The Freudians believe that there is in all of us an unmistakable, though latent, aggressive-

105 This idea is a basic theme in Freud's *Group Psychology and Analysis of the Ego, op. cit.*
106 Sandor Lorand, "Character Formation," in *Psychoanalysis Today, op. cit.,* p. 211.
107 P. Hopkins, *The Psychology of Social Movements* (New York, 1939), p. 129.
108 Franz Alexander, "Development of the Ego-Psychology," in *Psychoanalysis Today, op. cit.,* p. 143.
109 Gertrud M. Kurth, "Hitler's Germanies: A Sidelight on Nationalism," in *Psychoanalysis and the Social Sciences, op. cit.,* II, p. 393.
110 Cf. Karen Horney, *New Ways in Psychoanalysis, op. cit.,* and Abram Kardiner, *The Individual and His Society* (New York, 1939).

ness. We are all born as little cannibals,'they say. Through the realities of environment the child learns gradually to conquer his antisocial, libidinal, and aggressive instinctual demands. The superego is built up in children by the suppression of aggressive energies against the parents.[111] However, the controls set up by society limiting aggressiveness actually stimulate it and arouse a desire to "get even." In war time, this spirit of aggressiveness is socially approved.

This idea of *latent* aggressiveness has been attacked as another fallacy in Freud's theory of instincts. Otto Klineberg says that aggressiveness, whether overt or latent, is apparently far from universal and must be stimulated, even in war time, by every artificial means at the disposal of governments and army staffs and propaganda experts.[112]

Talcott Parsons, a member of the William Alanson White School, which places greater stress upon the significance of interpersonal relations than upon Freudian sexuality and theory of instincts, explains how aggression is channeled into national antagonisms by the environment.

> The immense reservoir of aggression in Western society is sharply inhibited from direct expression within the smaller groups in which it is primarily generated. The structure of the society in which it is produced contains a strong predisposition for it to be channeled into group antagonisms. The significance of the nation state is, however, such that there is a strong pressure to internal unity within each such unit and therefore a tendency to focus aggression on the potential conflicts between nation-state units.[113]

Nationalism is in part an expression of anxiety at the group-level. Psychoanalysts believe that one of the most troubling neuroses of mankind is anxiety—constant doubts, hesitations, unrest, and frustrations. The stresses and strains of living, encountered by the individual in the basic training ground of the family, are repeated in the group. "Nationalism . . . eventually arouses opposing elements. Principles of conscience and morality cannot be suppressed

[111] Ernest Simmel, "War Neurosis," in *Psychoanalysis Today, op. cit.,* p. 231.
[112] See Otto Klineberg, *Social Psychology* (New York, 1940), p. 88.
[113] Talcott Parsons, "Sources and Patterns of Aggression," in *A Study of Interpersonal Relations: New Contributions to Society,* ed. by Patrick Mullahy (New York, 1949), p. 293.

permanently, and through them we approach an abatement on the real scourge of mankind—anxiety.[114]

Nationalism may reflect a sense of inferiority. The Adlerian theory of individual inferiority complex is considered by some psychoanalysts to be applicable to the national group level.[115] Each nation, it is said, is strongly ambivalent about the superiority-inferiority problem. It is conditioned to believe in its own superiority and in a corresponding rejection of the claims of other nations. It insists that in its historical episodes it has been treated unfairly and that other nations lie in wait to pounce upon the superior people. It is certain of its historical mission, and it regards with suspicion similar motives of other peoples. Talcott Parsons points out the danger of this nationalistic point of view: "The 'jungle philosophy'—which corresponds to a larger element in the real sentiments of all of us than can readily be admitted, even to ourselves—tends to be projected into the relation of nation-states at precisely the point where, under the technological and organizational situation of the modern world, it can do the most harm." [116]

To these varying conceptions of the meaning of nationalism might be added the unique definition proposed by F. H. Allen: "Nationalism in its narrower and more intense manifestation might well be described as cultural homosexuality." [117] Homosexuality, Allen believes, is an individual reaction to difference, and nationalism is a cultural response, having its roots in "racial" difference. The two phenomena, he says, spring from a feeling of insecurity and represent attempts to find a way of living. In both cases, paranoid sequences often follow.

This interesting theory awaits further clarification and study. On a strictly unscientific level, the German Emperor, Wilhelm II, claimed that not only individuals, but races are endowed with sex. Races inhabiting valleys are inclined to be feminine, while those from the highlands foster masculine attributes. The French are a feminine race, the Germans are a masculine race. He concluded

[114] Fessler, *op. cit.*, p. 383.
[115] e.g., W. Wegener, "Zur Frage des Würzeln völkischen Geschehens," *Internationale Zeitschrift für Individualpsychologie,* VI (1931), pp. 438–77.
[116] Parsons, *op. cit.*, p. 293.
[117] F. H. Allen, "Homosexuality in Relation to the Problems of Human Differences," *American Journal of Orthopsychiatry,* X (1940), pp. 129–36.

that the reasons for Franco-German enmity were not political but anthropological.[118]

Conclusions and Summary

Historians readily admit that nationalism, in its ideal sense, is a psychological fact, but they see it as a community of sentiment created only through the trials of historic circumstance. Sociologists believe the key factor in nationalism to be the group, from which the individual imbibes traditions, ideals, and interests. Various schools of sociology hold different opinions on whether nationalism is a survival of primitive barbarism or the product of modern society. Similarly, anthropologists do not agree on the question of whether or not nationalism is a vestige of instinctual behavior. Some anthropologists call nationalism an instinct; others define it as a persistent mode of behavior. All three disciplines agree that nationalism is a superimposed, perverted sentiment that has often tended to become the final cause of the community.

Psychologists tend to shy away from using the term instinct in describing nationalism; they have devised several substitute terms for instinct in their definitions, including drives, desires, motives, and needs. Most psychologists regard the relationship between individual and collective mentalities as vital in the search for the meaning of nationalism. They see nationalism as a form of the psychologically recognized phenomenon of individuals identifying themselves with symbols that stand for the mass. It is the task of psychology, they say, to find and measure the new master symbols.

From the psychiatric point of view, nationalism is a defense mechanism, working on a large, in-group scale, by which the group seeks to assure security in a hostile world. Nationalism may appear on a rationalistic level, but it is subject, like the individual, to deviant forms of expression. Psychiatrists find three elements of neurosis in nationalism: anxiety, a sense of inferiority, and instability. Some psychiatrists see evidences in nationalism of psychotic behavior along schizophrenic and megalomaniac-paranoid lines. They recognize that the relationship between individual and social

[118] Cf. George Sylvester Viereck, *The Kaiser on Trial* (New York, 1937), pp. 240–42.

behavior is exceedingly complex because of the different empirical focus that is used.

Psychoanalysts direct attention to the psychical processes of nationalism. Some psychoanalysts believe that the social structure inevitably repeats the motivations of the individuals who compose it. Nationalism, they say, may be in part a substitute for religion as an answer to psychic needs, or it may be in part a carry-over of parent and family fixation, since group formations, by and large, appear to depend on early mechanisms. In any event, nationalism offers a response to the individual's need for security and protection. As a group sentiment, nationalism may express deep-seated fear and hostility; it may be an outlet for aggression; it may express anxiety at the group level; or it may reflect a sense of inferiority.

What is the consensus of opinion among the various disciplines? Nationalism has two major senses: concrete (geographical, linguistic, political, social, economic, and cultural); and ideal (psychological). It is not an innate instinct, but rather a socially conditioned, synthetic sentiment. It is a socially approved symbol in modern society and acts as a response to the group's need for security and protection. Its realization seems to have become the supreme ethical goal of peoples on earth. It is a persistent but not necessarily a permanent mode of behavior.

Nationalism has taken so many forms and expressions and permeates so many different activities of man that it is almost impossible to arrive at an exact definition that would satisfy everyone. There are always exceptions, no matter what the definition. Among the many complicating factors is the fact that by the second quarter of the twentieth century, the nature of nationalism had undergone an unexpected and fundamental transformation in Central and Eastern Europe and Asia. The nation-state of the West had meant an open society of free citizens based on laws, but the new nationalism stressed the collective power of a closed society. An additional factor causing confusion in defining nationalism is that the same generic term is customarily used to describe both beneficial and harmful nationalism, and the line of demarcation between the two is left to antagonistic ideologies or interests.

The problem is essentially linguistic in nature. Unfortunately, there exists no world ecumenical linguistic council which could meet regularly to consider the changing meanings of key historical terms. Perhaps a world community of scholars might some day initiate a campaign to clarify the definitions of words like nationalism and democracy. In the last several decades, the scholars of many disciplines have performed a valuable service in clearing up the meaning of the term race. This scientific scrutiny, accompanied by highly successful popularization, has consigned the word race to its proper sphere—biology.

A similar campaign to formulate more clearly the meaning of nationalism might help to contribute to a practical solution of the desperate political problems of our times. A possible first step would be a tacit agreement among scholars never to use the word nationalism without a qualifying adjective indicating what form of nationalism is meant (liberal nationalism, integral nationalism, xenophobic nationalism). This habit might eventually seep into popular usage. The German custom of forming compound words to obtain more precise meanings has much to recommend it, though few other languages present this possibility. It is reasonable to hope that, in an age of unprecedented expansion of political knowledge, more deliberate and effective efforts will be made to clarify a phenomenon that is among the most powerful forces of modern life.

V

Classifications of Nationalism

Nationalism! Of all the evils I hate I think I hate nationalism most. Nationalism—national egoism, thinking in terms of one's nation rather than in terms of humanity—nationalism is evil because it concentrates on comparative inessentials (where a man lives, what sort of language he speaks, the type of his culture, the character of his "blood") and ignores the essential, which is simply that he is a man. It pursues a spurious and abstract "national glory," which is devoid of any actual existence, and has nothing whatever to do with the glory, or with the daily and hourly happiness and well-being of the nationals in question. It is partly an invention of ambitious and unscrupulous politicians, and partly a drug from which the populace derives, not individual peace of mind, but a kind of bogus and vicarious satisfaction. It makes one set of people hate another set that they haven't the smallest real occasion for hating: it leads to jealousy, expansionism, oppression, strife and eventually war.   —Victor Gollancz *

The Historian's Concept of the Genesis and Development of Nationalism

Nationalism in its modern form is by no means a new phenomenon, but rather a revival and fusion of older trends. It existed in the cruder form of tribalism among the primitive peoples before the dawn of recorded history. Each primitive tribe had its distinctive speech, religion, traditions, and social organization. Throughout the period of recorded history, from the time of the Egyptian and Mesopotamian civilizations to the eighteenth century, tribal nationalism in its primitive form was submerged in metropolitanism or localism. Metropolitanism here refers to attachment to a city-state

* *My Dear Timothy* (New York, Simon and Schuster, 1953), p. 292.

or cultural center; it may be defined as a sort of localized cosmopolitanism. Localism means attachment to the local village or region; it is akin to modern ruralism or regionalism. Some elements of nationalism existed during the ancient and medieval periods among peoples with kindred languages, customs, and traditions, but, on the whole, the sentiment of group cohesion in those times was more closely related to primitive localism than to modern nationalism.

Modern nationalism appeared in Western Europe between the fourteenth and eighteenth centuries. The new nationalism was similar to previous forms in its accent upon a community of language, customs, and historic traditions, but it differed in that it encompassed a relatively large group of persons professing different religions and possessing different economic interests. Moreover, it was now a cultivated sentiment, whereas, before, group sentiment had arisen naturally as the expression of loyalty to tribes, classes, or masses.

Virtually all the major historical movements of the early modern period favored the development of nationalism. Among these may be included such diverse factors as the disruption of the medieval church and the establishment of national churches, the appearance of vernacular literatures, the rise of national armies, the development of mercantilism, the emergence of the middle class, the rise of individualism as manifested in the Renaissance, the increasing rivalry of one people with another in the drive to capture the world's markets, and the growth of capitalism. For the national monarch, who desired an intensification of nationalism to improve the position of his dynasty, and for the bourgeoisie, which wanted above all the extension of its own politico-economic powers, nationalism became the spirit of a new order.

These historical developments took place more fully in England by the eighteenth century than elsewhere. It was in England that nationalism in its modern form first appeared. On the Continent, which lagged behind in this respect, nationalism received a powerful impetus in the French Revolution and in the Napoleonic era, both of which helped to intensify the nationalistic ambitions of European states. The ideal of nationalism persisted—peoples became united by strong ties of community interests; their flag symbolized national glory and prestige; and they came to believe that their particular culture and way of life were superior to those of other nations. Previously, the individual had given his paramount loyalty to the church, to his feudal lord, his guild, or his university; now he gave his primary allegiance to the national state.

Since historians are interested primarily in the processes of development, they are prone to classify the stages of nationalism along chronological lines and assign to each stage a specific character.

Integrative Nationalism (1815-1871): During the period from 1815 to 1871, nationalism was a unifying force in the sense that it helped to consolidate the states that most quickly outgrew their feudal divisions, and to unify others that had been long split into hostile factions. For example, both Germany and Italy, which throughout the medieval period had been "geographical expressions," achieved unification on the basis of nationalism. When it became apparent in these countries that liberalism was not dynamic enough to inspire national unification, liberalism was superseded in popularity by nationalism. Bismarck's famous dictum revealed the character of the movement: "Not by parliamentary resolutions are the great questions of the day settled . . . , but by iron and blood."

Disruptive Nationalism (1871-1890): The success of nationalism as a powerful force for the unification of Germany and Italy aroused the enthusiasm of subject nationalities in other countries. For example, the minority nationalities in Austria-Hungary, Turkey, and other conglomerate states called for independence based on geographic unity, common language, interests, culture, traditions, customs, and even upon the ground of a nonexistent common "race."

Aggressive Nationalism (1900-1945): Toward the end of the nineteenth century and at the beginning of the twentieth, international hatreds flared up, as nations struggled for markets, raw materials, and capital in a world too small to satisfy the desires of all. In the popular mind nationalism became virtually identical with aggressive imperialism. Super-patriots claimed it as their "mission" to bring civilization to the more backward peoples of the earth. The collision of opposing national interests came with explosive impact in the two World Wars.

Contemporary Nationalism (1945-1954): Hardly had World

War II come to an end when the colonial peoples of the world began to seethe with unrest. In the Far East, the Middle East, and Africa, political nationalism asserted itself in the form of widespread revolts against European masters. The movement had already begun during World War I, when Woodrow Wilson proclaimed the idea of self-determination. Native peoples who demanded the right to independence and self-government were for a time appeased by the offer of autonomy within the framework of empire. But now these peoples demanded nothing less than complete independence. The Javanese, for example, publicized their determination by inscribing on their banners the words, "*Merdeka* [independence] or death." [1] It is a further indication of the power of nationalism that communism, which Marx and Lenin had conceived of as an international movement, in its Stalinist form took on the trappings of nationalism in the Soviet Union.

The Hayes Formula

A valuable classification of the types of nationalism is that originated by Carlton J. H. Hayes. [2] The Hayes formula ingeniously strikes a mean between chronology and description.

Humanitarian Nationalism: The first systematic doctrine of modern nationalism was expounded in the eighteenth century during the Enlightenment. As the name implies, humanitarian nationalism had strictly humanitarian objectives: tolerance and regard for the rights of other nationalities. It had three main proponents. Henry St. John Bolingbroke, a conservative English politician, conceived of an aristocratic form of nationalism tinged with humanitarianism. The French philosopher, Jean-Jacques Rousseau, advocated a democratic form of nationalism, humanitarian in spirit. Johann Gottfried von Herder, a German philosopher, unlike Bolingbroke and Rousseau, saw nationalism as a cultural rather than as a political phenomenon. The humanitarian nationalists believed that every nationality was entitled to its own development consonant with its own particular genius. Each nation, they said,

[1] Robert R. Ergang, *Europe in Our Time* (Boston, 1953), p. 758.
[2] The précis of the Hayes formula is based on Carlton J. H. Hayes, *Essays on Nationalism* (New York, 1928), and *The Historial Evolution of Modern Nationalism* (New York, 1931).

should attend to the business of its own national development and should have only the kindest and most understanding sentiment towards other nations striving for similar ends.

Jacobin Nationalism: Under the impact of the French Revolution, the earlier nationalism, which had not yet crystallized into a dogma, separated into several distinct types. The democratic, humanitarian nationalism of Rousseau became known as Jacobin nationalism, after the Jacobins, a revolutionary political club dedicated to the achievement of republicanism and democracy. Jacobin nationalism sought to safeguard and extend the liberty, equality, and fraternity that had been asserted and partially established under humanitarian auspices in the early days of the Revolution. The Jacobin nationalists, intolerant of opposition, relying upon force to achieve their ends, fanatical in their determination to succeed, and characterized by missionary zeal, gave to the present form of nationalism many of its basic qualities.

Traditional Nationalism: The aristocratic, humanitarian nationalism of Bolingbroke emerged after the reactionary period as traditional nationalism. The conservative and reactionary critics of the Jacobins were quite certain that the quiet happiness of humanity could be assured less by the masses than by the classes. Being opposed to revolution and reason as factors in national development, they turned to history and tradition. In effect, this type of nationalism was a counter-movement to the forces set in motion by the French Revolution; nevertheless, it claimed the same humanitarian motives as the Jacobins. Among the traditional nationalists may be included Edmund Burke, Louis Gabriel Ambroise, and Friedrich von Schlegel.

Liberal Nationalism: Midway between Jacobin and traditional nationalism was liberal nationalism, a type neither democratic nor aristocratic, but with some of the characteristics of each. Supported vigorously by an English lawyer, Jeremy Bentham, liberal nationalism rose in England, the country of perpetual compromise and of acute national consciousness, towards the end of the eighteenth century, and later spread to the Continent. It emphasized the absolute sovereignty of the national state but at the same time stressed the principle of individual liberty. It held all national states responsible for the establishment and maintenance of international peace. Liberal nationalism looked to the day when all nations would enjoy opportunities for independent development.

Integral Nationalism: Liberal nationalism persisted throughout the greater part of the nineteenth century. However, with the sharpening of rivalries between national states, with the emergence of modern imperialism, nationalism assumed a form decidedly hostile to liberalism and humanitarianism. Integral nationalism rejected sympathy for and cooperation with other nations, promoted jingoism, militarism, and imperialism, and opposed all personal liberties when they interfered with the aims of the state. Loyalty to the national state was elevated above all other loyalties, and all social, cultural, economic, and even religious considerations were subordinated to the ends of nationalism.

Economic Nationalism: In its early stages, dominantly political considerations lay behind nationalism, but the later tendency became to regard the state as an economic as well as a political unit. The desire of modern states to achieve economic self-sufficiency led to the erection of tariff barriers between nations, and to an intensified struggle for control of markets, raw materials, and fields for the investment of capital. Economic nationalism merged with imperialism to become one of the most important and powerful forces in contemporary civilization. We shall discuss these developments in more detail in the next chapter.

The Kohn Dichotomy

The historian, Hans Kohn, sees a different fundamental division among nationalisms. In his view, the meaning, origins, characteristics, and development of nationalism in any given area are the fruits of a long historical process. Nationalism and nationalism may not be the same thing, always depending upon the historical traditions and the political climate in which each arises. Kohn sees a fundamental distinction between two basic types of nationalism in the world: 1) nationalism in the Western world (England, the British colonies, the Netherlands, and Switzerland); and 2) nationalism outside the Western world (in Central and Eastern Europe and in Asia). These two concepts of nationalism are the poles around which the new age with its multiplicity of shadings and transitions revolves. The existence of both types of nationalism indicates a kind of dichotomy of meaning within the recent historical process.

The Kohn classification is considered to be so important and so fundamental by historians that we shall present its details in outline form. Developed consistently over the years and presented in a series of notable books,[3] Kohn's fundamental division has withstood the challenge of recent historical developments. The difference in meaning between the two types of nationalism emerges upon a close scrutiny of origins, characteristics, and development.

Western World: England, British Dominions, France, Netherlands, Switzerland	*Central and Eastern Europe and in Asia*

Origins

Predominantly political occurrence: The rise of nationalism was preceded by the formation of the future national state, or, as in the case of the United States, coincided with it.

Original impulse from cultural contact: Nationalism arose here not only later, but also generally at a more backward socio-political stage. The frontiers of an existing state and of a rising nationality rarely coincided. Nationalism emerged as a protest against the existing state pattern. Each new nationalism received its original stimulus from cultural contacts with some older nationalism, and then began to extol the heritage of its own past.

Historical motivations: The Renaissance and the Reformation resulted in the creation of a new society in which the secularized bourgeoisie, gaining political power, abandoned in fact and in theory the universal, imperial concept of the medieval world. In the West there

Persistence of medieval idea of world - empire: The Renaissance and Reformation had not deeply changed the socio-political order in Germany, where they were essentially scholarly and theological events. Russia and the Near East remained untouched, thus deepening

[3] Hans Kohn, *The Idea of Nationalism* (5th printing, New York, 1951), pp. 329 ff., 349 ff., and 573 ff.; *Prophets and Peoples* (New York, 1946), *passim;* and *The Twentieth Century* (New York, 1949), pp. 19–32. A similar point of view is presented in Kohn's analysis of the recent course of world history in an article "Is the Free West in Decline?", *Commentary,* XVI (1953), p. 8.

were vital changes in the political and social order. Nationalism here was a product of apparently indigenous forces.

the old cleavage between the Western and Eastern Empire. A politically ephemeral universalism persisted. Nationalism here was a product of cultural contact and an erroneous interpretation of the past.

Characteristics

Pluralistic and open society: The nation-state in the West was born out of the struggle by the people for liberty, constitutionalism, tolerance, and a society of free citizens based on laws.

The authoritarian, closed society: The tendency was to an authoritarian uniformity of state and faith. Here nationalism meant either: 1) collective power and national unity; 2) independence from foreign domination, rather than liberty at home; or 3) the necessity of expansion for the "superior" nation.

Debt to the Enlightenment: Nationalism in the West was closely connected with and strongly influenced by the concepts of individual liberty and rational cosmopolitanism current in the eighteenth century Age of Reason. It was born in a generous wave of enthusiasm for the cause of mankind.

Opposition to outside influences: Originally influenced by the West as teacher and model, the native educated classes soon began to develop their own form of nationalism, ending in strong opposition to the "alien" example of rationalism and liberalism. The goals were narrow, self-centered, antagonistic.

The political reality: Nationalism in the West was a response to the challenge of building a nation in the political reality and in the struggles of the present without too much regard for the past. The nation was accepted as valid, existing, realistic. There was a strong belief in political integration round a rational goal, as well as a belief in rational political ends.

The ideal fatherland: Nationalism was concerned, in many cases, with myths of the past and dreams of the future, devoid of immediate connection with the present. The "ideal" fatherland was the goal, long before it became a political reality. The nascent nation held a wistful image of itself and of its "mission." It harked back to the past, to non-political and more emotional, history-conditioned factors.

Concept of nation: It was felt in the West that nations grew up as unions of citizens, by the will of individuals expressed in contracts, covenants, and plebiscites. Integration was almost always around a

Concept of nation: The nation is a political unit centering around the irrational, pre-civilized folk concept. Unable to find a rallying point in society or in the free and rational order, nationalism here found it in political idea, a common future achieved by common effort. Emphasis was laid on universal similarities of nations.

the folk-community, which was elevated to the dignity of an ideal or mystery. Stress was placed on the diversity and self-sufficiency of nations.

Citizenship: The West accepted a legal and rational concept of citizenship. Appealed to individual rights. All men are fundamentally alike as individuals, regardless of social class or historical nationality.

Citizenship: Here the idea of folk was an infinitely vaguer concept, which lent itself more easily to the exaggerations of imagination and the excitations of emotion. Appealed to collective rights. Peculiarities of race or class were emphasized.

Attitude to nationalism: The rationalists' optimism concerning the political possibilities of natural law was reflected in the self-assurance of Western nationalism.

Attitude to nationalism: Not rooted in socio-political reality, this type lacked self-assurance. Its inferiority complex was often compensated by overemphasis and overconfidence. It regarded itself as deeper, richer, and more valuable than Western nationalism.

Chief support: The politically and economically powerful and educated middle class, and, with a shift in emphasis, the social-democratically organized labor movements.

Chief support: The aristocracy and the masses.

Development

The course of Western nationalism: With reliance on the autonomy of the individual and voluntary association, with a rationalistic and humanitarian regard for one's fellow man, Western nationalism, with exceptions of course, gradually asserted itself as an outgrowth of the Enlightenment. The secularized Stoic-Christian tradition lived on: in England in its Protestant form, in France in its Catholic form. The growth to nationhood was, to a large extent, a process of internal or immanent forces.

The course of non-Western nationalism: Originally impelled by and dependent upon outside forces, non-Western nationalism grew into two opposing branches. One accepted the Western form, with its implications (British parliamentary institutions; the French middle-class republic; the Industrial Revolution). The second branch stressed national peculiarities and uniqueness and set itself outside the influence of cultural contact with alien civilizations. Spellbound by the past, fascinated by the mysteries of ancient times, re-creating tribal solidarity, and tending towards isolation, non-Western nationalism utilized history for national ends.

The value of the Kohn division lies in its clarification of the many inconsistencies and contradictions that surround the meaning of nationalism. It explains the variations in definitions by directing attention always to the climate of opinion at certain times and in places where nationalism functions. It shows how the meaning of linguistic terms depends upon the historical milieu. Much of the difficulty now encountered in use of the generic term "nationalism" could be dispelled by qualifying its use according to the Kohn formula of Western nationalism and non-Western nationalism.

Several examples may be noted of how the Kohn classification operates. There have been many explanations of why German and Russian nationalism took on a different quality from that of the West. Kohn shows the original acceptance of the Enlightenment by a small group of German and Russian intellectuals and its later rejection as alien by policy-shaping enemies of the liberal-democratic tradition. Discarding the Western idea of nationalism, Germany and Russia geared themselves to the type of authoritarianism they found traditional in their own historical development.

In addition, the Kohn formula explains, on a strictly historical basis, the puzzling phenomenon by which both Herder and Bismarck have been classified as German nationalists. Conceding that Herder was an eighteenth-century liberal, Kohn points out that the nationalism which goes back to Herder, especially the nationalism of the German Romantics and the Russian Slavophiles, is not a liberal nationalism in the meaning of the word as he uses it. Though Herder unconsciously prepared the way for folk nationalism, which rose in revolt against Western and universal civilization, the responsibility does not rest upon him. Steeped in universal civilization, he, of all people, would have rejected the "organic-heroic mentality" which was later superimposed upon his thought, in much the same way as the meaning of Nietzsche's philosophy was perverted by nationalists. Herder, as scholar and poet, unsupported by public opinion, was influenced by the opening stages of Western influence, but his venture in Western education and propaganda disappeared almost completely in the new policy of blood-and-iron nationalism.

The Kohn formula further encompasses the process of cultural influence and resistance in non-European areas. For too many years the appearance of nationalism in non-European areas has been regarded as a kind of spasmodic, accidental phenomenon. Kohn shows here again how the idea of nationalism may be communicated by cultural diffusion, but its particular meaning and form will in most cases take on characteristics dictated by the aims and aspirations of each people concerned. India is a good case in point. Through cultural contact with England, several generations of Indian intellectuals were imbued with British ideas of freedom and self-government. Soon the Indian desire for nationhood, entirely a product of British influence, was awakened by the Indian National Movement. The new Indian nationalists objected not only to British political but also cultural domination. Indian nationalism had to be different from that of England. The emphasis now was not on British constitutional liberalism, but on Indian national customs, India's superior metaphysical profundity, India's religiosity, India's unique destiny in the service of mankind, and India's mission to Aryanize the entire world. Nationalism in the Slavic countries, in the Near East, the Far East, and in Africa is currently undergoing a similar development. A dominantly Western idea is transformed into a moral obligation to protect the nation from foreign and alien influence. A new mission, grounded in legends and dreams of the past and guaranteeing heavenly bliss and redemption, is discovered and hailed as a beacon for a darkened world.

The Kohn formula has served a generation of historians well, and there have been no significant attempts to alter or modify it. It has many of the advantages of a multidisciplinary approach, since it takes into account political, social, cultural, economic, and psychological factors. In this sense it is good history, for the aim of the historian is over-all awareness.

Classification by the Political Scientist, Handman

In other disciplines the classification of the types of nationalism generally follows the main interests of the particular discipline. In political science, for example, the emphasis is on the political nature of nationalism. The following classification of the types of nationalism by the political scientist Max Sylvius Handman may be taken as typical of this discipline.[4]

[4] Max Sylvius Handman, "The Sentiment of Nationalism," *Political Science Quarterly*, XXXVI (1921), pp. 107–14.

Oppression Nationalism: This type of nationalism concerns the system of reactions found to prevail in a group whose members are exposed to a definite and clear-cut régime of disabilities and special subordination. Examples are the Poles in Germany and Russia, the Greeks and Armenians in the Turkish Empire, the Jews, and the Irish.

Irredentist Nationalism: This form of nationalism has arisen among such peoples as Italians, Rumanians, Serbs, and Bulgars, who demand the liberation of their people from the domination of others.

Precaution Nationalism: This type responds to the stimulus presented by the competitive organization of the modern state-system as well as by the identification of commercial expansion with the interests of national security and of general national well-being. On occasion, it is difficult to distinguish precaution nationalism from imperialism. Its striking characteristic is an agitated concern for the life and honor of the group.

Prestige Nationalism: Here the stimulus is to be found in the attitude of contempt or of insufficient esteem with which the nation is regarded, especially when, from its own point of view, its glorious history of the past or its present and future possibilities entitle it to greater respect or consideration. The *Action Française* in France and Sir Oswald Mosley's Fascists in England are examples of those who pursue the idea of prestige nationalism.

While this classification works toward an accurate description of the political side of nationalism, especially in its description of predominantly negative qualities, it does not stress strongly the cultural and social aspects of nationalism, nor does it, as does the Hayes formula, account for the chronological sequence of types of nationalism. In concentrating upon political forms, it gives one side of a many-faceted phenomenon.

Typology by Sociologists

From the sociological point of view, nationality is a conflict group. Nationalism in its various types must conform to the types of relations of opposition and conflict which characterize the relations between groups. This can be understood, since the primary aim of the sociologist is to analyze the concept of society as organism. Political scientists are interested mainly in the political aspects of nationalism; sociologists regard it as a sentiment reflecting group behavior. Some scholars, more than others, do recognize the dependence of social phenomena on specific historical factors. Thus, Quincy Wright, in distinguishing a number of types of nationalism, follows the historical pattern of chronology and gives them in order as: medieval; monarchical; revolutionary; liberal; and totalitarian, each with its own particular pattern of relationship to war.[5]

Perhaps the most fruitful classification of the types of nationalism from the sociological point of view is that of Max Wirth, who sees the forms of nationalism distinguished by group power struggles.[6] The vital factor is a profound social conditioning reflecting the aims and aspirations of groups.

Hegemony Nationalism: Wirth describes the series of movements of national unification in the nineteenth century as hegemony nationalism. The familiar examples are the drives for unification of Italy and Germany. The national group is motivated by the urge to derive advantage from consolidating smaller principalities into larger and more dynamic units. The tendency of the national group after attaining its unification is to extend its hegemony by developing ever more aggressive imperialistic aims.

Particularistic Nationalism: This type of nationalism is based upon the secessionist demand for national autonomy. The first aim is divisive in character, to be followed by union with a more satisfactory group. Particularistic nationalism begins with strivings for cultural autonomy or toleration, and then, as the movement makes headway, it takes on political significance. Examples are to be found among the potential nationalities of the Austro-Hungarian Empire, Germany, Russia, and the Turkish Empire before World War I. The sentiment exists also among Jews and Negroes, in the latter case in incipient and utopian form.

Marginal Nationalism: This form of nationalism refers to the nationalistic movements of marginal people, the population in the frontier regions between two states, who generally have a mixed

---

[5] Quincy Wright, *A Study of War* (Chicago, 1942), pp. 996–99.
[6] Max Wirth, "Types of Nationalism," *American Journal of Sociology,* XLI (1936), pp. 723–37.

culture. Marginal people are likely to cling to traditions of their motherland with the utmost tenacity. Included in this category would be such border territories and populations as Alsace, Lorraine, Silesia, Schleswig, the Saar, Rhineland, the Italo-Austrian border, and the Swiss frontier. Wirth notes that the Germans of the border territory were more German than those of Berlin.

Nationalism of the Minorities: Minority groups, universal and possessing apparently insoluble problems, have their own type of nationalism. Showing the ethnic and cultural penetration of the peoples of Europe, they strive for recognition of their own traditional nationality and seek zealously to maintain their own culture within another nationality.

The Italian scholar, Don Luigi Sturzo, as a means of supporting his definition of nationalism,[7] tries to find its verification in the characteristics of nationalisms as they have developed in their historical objectivity and as they have been theorized by their chief propounders. He feels that since nationalism takes on so broad a variety of colors, it is necessary to classify its present types on a geographical basis by countries.

German Nationalism: The anti-Catholic *Kulturkampf* immediately following the formation of the Bismarckian Empire had its nationalistic motive. Bismarck failed in the undertaking, but the idea of national *Kulturkampf* persisted and spread, Heinrich von Treitschke being its chief theorizer. The idea of the homogeneity of the Reich's population (Germanism or German nationalism, the same thing) was not an end in itself but was conceived as a means of strengthening the state's power and of uniting the nation. The spurious Aryan theories of Arthur de Gobineau and Houston Stewart Chamberlain, a Frenchman and an Englishman, lent themselves admirably to Treitschke's nationalism and were well received by Germans. Thus, the "scientific apparatus" of the nineteenth century was utilized in Germany to give nationalism substance.

French Nationalism: After the establishment of the Third Re-

---

[7] "Nationalism is a theoretical conception and a practical activity which tends to overvalue the nation and to make it a dominant, nay, an absolute ethical-political principle." (Don Luigi Sturzo, *Nationalism and Internationalism* [New York, 1946], p. 25.)

public, French nationalism was shaped by the loss of Alsace-Lorraine, but soon showed its natural characteristics, becoming antidemocratic, antisocialist, and anti-Semitic. Nationalism in Germany was on the whole anti-Catholic, but in France it was born pro-Catholic. The Dreyfus case attracted the attention of the most rabid nationalists and anti-Semites. There was no real theorist of nationalism like Treitschke or Gobineau, none who could compare with the celebrity later attained by Charles Maurras.

Italian Nationalism: Italian nationalism appeared relatively late in the nineteenth century. There was *irredentismo,* the tendency to look forward to the reunion of the mother country with Trentino and Trieste, then under Austrian domination. True Italian nationalism was of a later date and came of aping Maurras; its poet was D'Annunzio.

British Nationalism: Joseph Chamberlain, Cecil Rhodes, and Rudyard Kipling were representatives of British nationalistic imperialism, but leaving aside the eccentricities of this group, we find that theoretical and practical nationalism of the nineteenth-century variety never developed in England. There were two reasons for this: first, because the British are pragmatists and do not care for theories; and second, because the British already had an empire that was expanding almost automatically and without struggle in Africa and the Pacific. The Jubilee ceremonies of 1887 and 1897 were tinged less with nationalism than imperialism.

American Nationalism: The word nationalism did not take on the same meaning in the United States that it had in Europe. The idea of American nationalism was linked with federalist policies, the increase in the number of federated states, and their cultural and linguistic assimilation. From the national point of view, says Sturzo, the problem of the Negroes is a complex one and imparts to American nationalism a racial tinge. American domestic nationalism never overstepped the boundaries of pragmatism and sentiment in order to become a sociological or political theory.

Psychological Distinctions

Since some psychologists consider the group mind an integration of individual minds functioning as a unit,[8] they are inclined to stress the community in behavior when classifying the types of nationalism. The essential point of departure is the real or imaginary working of the mind and the group acceptance of ideas, ideals, and symbols.

An example of the distinction made in the types of nationalism from the psychological point of view is that by Gustav Ichheiser,[9] who finds two major forms.

Conscious Nationalism: When the members of a certain national group profess in an open and more or less vociferous way their national values and ideals, when they consciously and with awareness strive toward certain national goals, when they tend to glorify the real or imaginary peculiarities of their own national community, at the same time rejecting positively any feelings of hostility to the values, ideals, symbols, and aims of other nations, they then fall into the category of conscious nationalism.

Subconscious (or Unconscious) Nationalism: When members of a national group, even though they do not formulate or pronounce in any articulate way their special national ideas and beliefs, are nevertheless so influenced by naturally prejudiced concepts that, without being aware of it, they see and judge everything from their own national point of view, they may be classified in the general category of subconscious or unconscious nationalism.

This distinction is one that recognizes the peculiarities of human behavior. It is claimed that conscious nationalism is an old and well established human reaction, running from the early tribes to the modern nation. As a matter of self-preservation, the group, whether large or small, is conditioned to regard the for-

[8] Hans Kohn, *The Idea of Nationalism, op. cit.,* p. 580. Cf. also Michael Demiashkevich, *The National Mind: English, French, German* (New York, 1938); W. B. Pillsbury, *The Psychology of Nationalism and Internationalism* (New York, 1919); and Alfred J. É. Fouillée, *Esquisse psychologique des peuples européens* (Paris, 1902).

[9] Gustav Ichheiser, "Some Psychological Obstacles to an Understanding between Nations," *Journal of Abnormal and Social Psychology,* XXXVI (1941), pp. 427–32.

eign, the "other," as something wrong. Thus, a given national group may consider another people as un-English, un-German, or un-American. The quality of awareness is not always present.

On the other hand, subconscious or unconscious nationalism, being based upon irrationalist reactions, is far more dangerous and peculiar. The individual in this group sees everything through national spectacles, "but not knowing he carries them in his nose—he lives in the naive belief that he sees things objectively 'as they are' and as they should be seen by 'every reasonable person.'" The strange and the unfamiliar then become "unhuman," "uncivilized," not merely "un-American." The pattern of behavior of unconscious nationalism is called a dangerous one because it is not controlled and easily gets out of hand. The great problem of psychologists, it is said, is to apply to mass groups the techniques that have been rewarding in the treatment of individuals whose subconscious ideas have attained a dominating influence in their everyday behavior. The correction of irrationalist, aggressive hostilities on a mass scale thus becomes one of the most vital tasks of the modern age, a task not only of importance to psychologists but to the whole range of scholars and activists.

Classification by George Orwell

It is an indication of the enormous range of nationalism and its penetration into all branches of our social life that it has drawn the deep interest of writers, poets, and artists as well as social scientists. The late British novelist, George Orwell, who one day may be considered one of the most important writers on the literary scene of the twentieth century, presents an interesting classification of nationalism as it occurs among the English intelligentsia.[10] He warns that the picture is oversimplified because 1) no one has the right to assume that *everyone,* or even every intellectual, is infected by nationalism; 2) nationalism can be intermittent and limited; 3) a nationalistic creed may be adopted in good faith from non-nationalist motives; and 4) several kinds of nationalism, even kinds that cancel out, can exist in the same

[10] George Orwell, *Such, Such Were the Joys* (New York, 1953), pp. 86–93.

person. He selects the English intelligentsia because "in them, much more often than in ordinary English people, nationalism is unmixed with patriotism and can therefore be studied pure." He uses three headings, Positive, Transferred, and Negative, though some varieties will fit into more than one category.

1) *Positive Nationalism*

a) *Neo-Toryism:* The real motive of Neo-Toryism, giving it its nationalistic character and differentiating it from ordinary Conservatism, is the desire not to recognize that British power and influence have declined. "English ideas," usually left undefined, must dominate the world. All Neo-Tories are anti-Russian, but sometimes the main emphasis is anti-American.

b) *Celtic Nationalism:* Welsh, Irish, and Scottish nationalism have points of difference but are alike in their anti-English orientation. The motive force is a belief in the past and future greatness of the Celtic peoples; hence, Celtic nationalism has a strong element of racialism.

c) *Zionism:* This has the usual characteristics of a nationalist movement, but the American variant is more violent and malignant than the British. Orwell classifies it under direct and not transferred nationalism because it flourishes almost exclusively among the Jews themselves.

2) *Transferred Nationalism*

a) *Communism*

b) *Political Catholicism*

c) *Color Feeling:* The old contemptuous attitude to "natives" has been much weakened in England. Among the intelligentsia, color feeling occurs only in the transposed form, i.e., a belief in the innate superiority of the colored races.

d) *Class Feeling:* This exists among upper-class and middle-class intellectuals, only in the transposed form—i.e., as a belief in the superiority of the proletariat.

e) *Pacifism:* Although the majority of pacifists either belong to obscure religious sects or are simply humanitarians, there is a minority of intellectual pacifists whose real though unadmitted motive seems to be hatred of Western democracy and admiration for totalitarianism. Orwell concludes that pacifism, as it appears among a section of the English intelligentsia, is secretly inspired by an admiration for power and successful cruelty. "The mistake was made of pinning this emotion to Hitler, but it could easily be re-transferred."

3) *Negative Nationalism*

a) *Anglophobia:* Within the intelligentsia, a decisive and mildly hostile attitude towards Britain is considered to be compulsory, but it is an unfaked emotion in many cases. Since Anglophobia is always liable to reversal, there is the fairly common spectacle of the pacifist of one war who is a warmonger in the next.

b) *Anti-Semitism:* Anti-Semitism appears to be widespread, even among intellectuals, and it is strengthened by the general conspiracy of silence. Many claim as a matter of course to be free of it. People of left-wing tendencies are not immune to it, but it comes more naturally to people of Conservative tendency. Neo-Tories and political Catholics are always liable to succumb to anti-Semitism, at least intermittently.

c) *Trotskyism:* Orwell here means the Marxist doctrinaire whose main motive was hostility to the Stalinist régime. "Although in some places, for instance in the United States, Trotskyism is able to attract a fairly large number of adherents and develop into an organized movement with a petty *Fuehrer* of its own, its inspiration is essentially negative. The Trotskyist is *against* Stalin just as the Communist is *for* him."

This classification by Orwell is an ingenious one because it emphasizes the idea that nationalism, in its extended sense, includes such movements as Communism, political Catholicism, Zionism, and anti-Semitism. It shows that nationalism does not necessarily mean loyalty to a government or a country, nor is it necessary that the units with which it deals should actually exist (Jewry, Islam, Christendom, the Proletariat, and the White Race). From this broader and all-inclusive view, nationalism, in Orwell's words, becomes "power-hunger tempered by self-deception."

Nationalism: Curse or Blessing?

Our final classification of types of nationalism is a more general one which Hayes has called "curse or blessing?" L. S. Greenberg differentiates between these two broad categories by terming the present dominant forms of nationalism "Material Nationalism" (curse) and "Spiritual Nationalism" (blessing).[11]

Material Nationalism: This type of nationalism, so well-known today, ceases to be a legal, historical process, and degenerates, instead, into an abominable movement threatening the world with retrogression and decay. It promotes intolerance, chauvinism, and provincialism, and is chiefly responsible for wars. It is deeply rooted in the psychology of the masses. It has a primitive and gregarious aspect which promotes a spirit of exclusiveness and egotism. Although material in its manifestations, it speaks to the emotions of the masses. A corrupting influence, it is inimical to the continuance of good relations among peoples.

Spiritual Nationalism: Greenberg, perhaps somewhat optimistically, regards spiritual nationalism as the next evolutionary step in the history of the phenomenon. People will learn to respect others not because of their material wealth or the size of their military forces, but because of their culture and valuable contributions to human civilization. The ultimate goal of spiritual nationalism should be a cooperating humanity regardless of race, class, sex, creed, and nationality. It would be indestructible because it is based on culture and represents a spiritual phenomenon. "It is like a pillar of white light which will illumine the path of mankind in its search for a better world." [12]

The distinction made here is a basic one—that there is a good and an evil form of nationalism. The good form, it is said, is essential to the healthy and normal political and economic life of a nation. The evil form comes into existence when policies of nationalism—political, economic, social, and moral—are carried to such extremes as to exclude and prevent necessary policies of international cooperation. Then it becomes dangerous and deadly. This contrast was expressed by Pope Pius XI in a speech delivered on December 3, 1930:

> Right order of Christian charity does not disapprove of lawful love of country and a sentiment of justifiable nationalism: on the contrary, it

[11] L. S. Greenberg, *Nationalism in a Changing World* (New York, 1937), pp. 14–16, 19–20.
[12] *Ibid.*, p. 20.

controls, sanctifies, and enlivens them. If, however, egoism abusing this love of country and exaggerating this sentiment of nationalism, insinuates itself into the relations between people and people, there is no excess that will not seem justified; and that which between individuals would be judged blameworthy by all is now considered lawful and praiseworthy if it is done in the name of this exaggerated nationalism.[13]

[13] *Osservatore Romano*, No. 208 (1938), quoted in Don Luigi Sturzo, *Nationalism and Internationalism* (New York, 1946), pp. 5–6.

VI

Economic Nationalism

The fact that the nation-state must be accepted as the main unit of economic policy, even on problems that are world-wide, need not prevent constructive action. The self-interest of every nation is fundamentally on the side of economic cooperation and exchange, if national efforts can be directed towards improving the lot of the people rather than towards a competitive struggle for power. The more enlightened the self-interest the more clearly does this appear. Even in a world of self-centered nations, all have more to gain in terms of economic welfare (not power) by a concerted drive forward to better use of resources than by snatching real or temporary advantages from each other in a game of beggar-my-neighbor.

—Eugene Staley *

Economic Motives in Nationalism

The discipline of economics deals with social phenomena centering on provision for the material needs of the individual and organized groups. Since nationalism is one of the most powerful of such social phenomena, its expression is closely bound up with the economic process. A proper understanding of nationalism takes into account both economic and psychological factors, since the economic process is anchored in the psychological structure of society. The elimination of one or the other inevitably results in a blurred picture.

While recognizing nationalism as an expression of collective consciousness, historians,[1] social psychologists,[2] and scholars in

* World Economy in Transition (New York, Council on Foreign Relations, 1939), p. 227.
[1] "It was but natural that [the intensification of national spirit and rivalry all over Europe and America in the 1860's and 1870's] should find expression in the economic and industrial field as well as in strictly cultural and political domains." (Carlton J. H. Hayes, Contemporary Europe Since 1870 [2 vols., New York, 1953], II, p. 34.)
[2] "It is probable that the exaggerated nationalism which is often the direct basis

other social sciences direct careful attention to the economic motives in nationalism. Economists seldom use the term nationalism, substituting for it either the dual term economic nationalism or the professional term neo-mercantilism (nationalism working in the field of economics). It is a curious fact that in the vast range of the literature of economics there is little discussion of the various nuances in the meaning of nationalism. The malaise of definition and method is left to other disciplines.

The Meaning of Economic Nationalism

Economic nationalism is merely another term for nationalism as it has developed along economic lines. It is a philosophy of security, designed to make the nation safe in times of peace and self-sufficient in times of war.[3] It holds that any nation obtains for its people the highest possible standard of living when it devotes its industrial efforts to lines of production in which it has a comparative advantage, and depends for other products upon other parts of the world.[4] It believes that each major nation can be assigned a special industrial activity which best fits its national endowment, e.g., the English in the coal industry and fiberstuffs; the Germans in chemicals, optics, lithography, and the potash industry; the French in wine-growing; and the Americans in mass production.[5] It is further held that the nation must be free,

---

of conflict has originally an economic basis." (Otto Klineberg, *Social Psychology* [New York, 1940], p. 394.)

"[Nationalism] usually implies economic power, and hence the predominance of economic motives in national life, large authority of political leadership, the constant need of defense, the duty of military service, and the subservience of education to national welfare." (Bernard C. Ewer, *Social Psychology* [New York, 1929], p. 405.)

[3] John F. Cronin, *Economics and Society* (New York, 1939), p. 333.

[4] This idea is closely associated with the ideal of an international division of labor. Some economists regard this as a persistent mode of behavior stemming from primitive times. (Cf. Fred Rogers Fairchild, Edgar Stevenson Furniss, and Norman Sydney Buck, *Economics* [New York, 1948], p. 595.)

[5] Rudolf Rocker regards this concept of economic nationalism as "hopelessly outflown." "Men have rather prematurely drawn the conclusion that all economy is to be transformed and reconstructed on the basis of the special endowments and capabilities resident in each people because of their national peculiarities. . . . This illusion long ago went into the discard. . . . Men as individuals can be subjected to industrial specialization: whole peoples and nations, never." (Rudolf Rocker, *Nationalism and Culture*, tr. by Ray E. Chase [New York, 1937], p. 47.)

as far as humanly possible, from relying upon the industry of other nations.

It becomes apparent at once that economic nationalism is certain to result in international friction, unless it is controlled on a world-wide basis. Nations have retained, frozen as it were, the idea that their economy must be constructed on the basis of special endowments and capabilities, but at the same time, they have refused to accept fully as a matter of common sense the corollary of freedom of international trade. Economic nationalism does not always react to the advantage of each specific country. Moreover, it tends to keep the world divided, beset by fear, and on the edge of war. The economic expedients of nationalism include a whole network of tariffs (designed for maximizing the exports and minimizing the imports of all nations simultaneously); import quotas and licenses; bounties for home industries; subsidized railway fares to the frontiers; restrictions of international exchange; and discouragement of the export and import of capital. It is granted that economic isolation is no longer possible in the modern world, yet the system of economic nationalism is retained as if the very existence of each nation depends upon it. "The all-supreme nation-state, like the coal-driven locomotive, is on the way out, but in the meantime, we have to depend on the coal-driven locomotive to pull most of our freight cars and on the loyalties to the nation-state as the chief basis of government." [6] Sentiment, traditions, and the reluctance to extend world government make the nation-state the supreme agent of economic control.

The Growth of Economic Nationalism

The development of economic nationalism closely parallels the emergence of political and cultural nationalism. The profound changes that took place at the end of the Middle Ages and at the opening of the modern period have been attributed variously to the decay of feudal society associated with the introduction of gunpowder, to the revival of learning in the Renaissance, and to the destruction of the solidarity of the medieval Catholic state

[6] Eugene Staley, *World Economy in Transition* (New York, 1939), p. 226.

during the Reformation. Economists find the most significant reasons for the rise of nationalism in the voyages of discovery, the economic interests served by them, the resultant influx of precious metals, and the Commercial Revolution.[7] With these new economic forces the state began to be regarded as an economic unit. The old medieval policy of local protectionism was succeeded by the national protectionism typical of economic nationalism.[8]

The emergence of economic nationalism was associated with the whole complex development of industrial civilization. It flourished most in the national states which had become most industrialized. It was given great impetus with the First Industrial Revolution (*ca.* 1750–1850)—the introduction of the factory system, the improvement of means of communication and transportation, the growth of the middle class and proletariat, and the rivalries of nations for economic advantage.

When the First Industrial Revolution was centered in England and was just beginning to affect other countries,[9] economic nationalism was liberal in character and inspired chiefly by Adam Smith's concept of laissez faire. In the 1860's and 1870's, at a time when big business began to appear on the Continent and in America, a series of wars took place as Germans, Italians, and various Balkan peoples sought to achieve national unification. In the United States this intensification of the national spirit took the form of the repression of sectionalism in the Civil War. The New Industrial Revolution further encouraged the practice of economic nationalism. Stimulated by propaganda, the masses of all nations became convinced that their security and purchasing power were closely linked with their national wealth, the extent

---

[7] Cf. Huntly Macdonald Sinclair, *A Preface to Economic History* (New York, 1934), p. 111.

[8] "We can say that national protectionism was the natural outgrowth of the synchronization of the nationalism associated with the voyages of discovery and the emergence of the national economy." (Sinclair, *op. cit.,* p. 113.)

[9] The economic impulses arising from the Commercial Revolution in Europe were of great importance in promoting unity among the American colonists; a century of ignoring British commercial restrictions gave the Thirteen Colonies a strong motive for unifying action. According to Arthur M. Schlesinger, this has fully proved to have been far more powerful than any theoretical or legal abstractions involved in colonial restrictions on British imperial power. (Cf. Arthur M. Schlesinger, *The Colonial Merchants and the American Revolution* [New York, 1918]; and K. C. Babcock, *The Rise of American Nationality* [New York, 1906].)

of their industries, and the maintenance of a favorable balance of trade. Such phrases as national resources, national productive capacity, national self-sufficiency, national system of credit, and national welfare became normal in the world's vocabulary.[10] It is unnecessary to recount the subsequent historical development to the catastrophes of 1914–1918 and 1939–1945. Sir Norman Angell's warning went unheeded when he called it a "great illusion" that the economic needs of each country are served by nationalism and militarism.[11] Even today, economic nationalism, with its perpetual struggle for economic advantage, is responsible for the quixotic state of the world market and the concomitant threat to peace.

Economic Nationalism as a Persistent Form of Mercantilism

To understand more fully the growth and development of economic nationalism, let us turn our attention to its relation with mercantilism. During the Middle Ages, economic control was decentralized and jealously guarded in each relatively small district. The rise of national states and the expansion of trade made it necessary to do away with the old restrictions of both manorial and municipal administrations. In an age of expanding economic frontiers, the need arose for some new form of national control of commerce to take the place of the weakened guilds. The search for a satisfactory set of economic principles that would increase the wealth and power of the state produced a set of ideas now termed mercantilism.[12] While a definite, clear-cut system was never developed, certain general economic policies arose which gave unity to the character of the times and which were a factor in the transformation of European feudal society into an aggregation of national states.

[10] In his magnum opus, *Das nationale System der politischen Oekonomie* (Stuttgart, 1841; tr. by S. S. Lloyd, London, 1885), the German economist, Friedrich List, coined some sixty compound words using the adjective national—from national division of labor to national productive powers.

[11] Sir Norman Angell, *The Great Illusion* (New York and London, 1910).

[12] On mercantilism, see Charles W. Cole, *French Mercantilist Doctrines before Colbert* (New York, 1931); J. W. Horrocks, *A Short History of Mercantilism* (London, 1925); J. Morini-Comby, *Mercantilisme et protectionisme* (Paris, 1930); and Eli F. Heckscher, *Merkantilismen* (2 vols., Stockholm, 1931).

The principles of early modern mercantilism were: *the bullionist theory,* which identified the precious metals as the basic form of national wealth; *the merchandizing theory,* which called for the encouragement of trade as the most desirable form of economic activity; *the protectionist theory,* which advocated the elimination of competition from other nations by placing high tariffs upon imported goods and which called for support of home industries; and *a favorable balance of trade,* by which the state acquired bullion by making certain that it exported more goods than it imported.

The methods of mercantilism encouraged domestic industries by subsidies, bounties, tariffs, regulation of manufacturing, and national improvements. The acquisition of colonies was considered necessary to provide convenient sources of raw materials at little expense to the mother country. To protect both mother country and colonies, a powerful navy was considered indispensable to guard the merchant fleet at sea and to uphold the nation's position and prestige in wartime.[13]

Mercantilism was of greater interest for what it attempted than for what it achieved. It was more or less successful in promoting the interests of national states at a time when their foreign trade was comparatively ill-organized, although it did not have the same effects in all countries. It was, moreover, a decisive factor in the development of political centralization; it promoted the power of the national monarch, and the economic prosperity of the middle class. On the other hand, mercantilist efforts to achieve internal economic reform (for instance, to abolish internal tolls and tariffs) and to institute national improvements were not altogether successful. Mercantilism in practice brought graft, corruption, favoritism, and generally low ethical standards.

By the latter part of the eighteenth century, the elaborate structure of economic control built up by the mercantilists was beginning to crack. Businessmen who resented state interference in their affairs began to demand freedom of enterprise. In his

---

[13] The best example of mercantilist theory in practice is to be found in the measures inaugurated by Jean Baptiste Colbert, minister of Louis XIV. Colbert cleaned up the financial administration, reduced the public debt, increased taxation, encouraged industry and commerce, set up great trading organizations, constructed model factories, standardized all phases of domestic production, instituted high protective tariffs, improved the roads and canals, established the French merchant marine, and expanded the royal navy.

Wealth of Nations, Adam Smith insisted that since trade was a matter of mutual advantage, complete freedom should be allowed in the field of production (laissez faire) and in the movement of goods both within the country and to and from it.

It was precisely at this time that modern nationalism was being moulded into the image we know today. At this time, in its later phase, mercantilism came to be considered a restrictive influence and its regulations regarded as burdensome, but its emphasis upon a shift from local to national economic policy remained paramount.[14] Neo-mercantilism, a rebirth of the older form, emerged in the nineteenth century, repeating the principles of high tariff walls, the plethora of quota arrangements, the ideal of the restricted market, and the monopolized preserve—all in a more perfected form.[15] All the varied, numerous, and extremely vigorous measures of national control typical of early mercantilism found a place in the new economic nationalism. The idea of industrial nationalism gained a stronger hold upon popular thinking than at any time since the days of the mercantilists.[16]

There was little possibility for the success of economic liberalism in this age of increasing economic nationalism. Between 1830 and 1870 there had been an attempt to insure industrial progress by laissez faire, but after 1870 there was a rebirth of the restrictive policies of seventeenth and eighteenth century mercantilism, which had existed before the advent of liberalism. This economic development was a concomitant phenomenon to the heightening political nationalism of the late nineteenth century. The victory of the persistent apostles of national self-sufficiency meant the triumph of an integral form of violent nationalism.

The Application of Nationalism to a System of Political Economy

We can see evidences of nationalism at work in the struggle against the Classical School of economic thought. This latter school, led by Adam Smith and Jean Baptiste Say, demolished

[14] A. E. Burns and D. S. Watson, "Some Government Problems," in *Economic Problems in a Changing World,* ed. by Willard L. Thorp (New York, 1939), p. 646.
[15] Maurice Dobb, *Political Economy and Capitalism: Some Essays in Economic Tradition* (London, 1937), p. 244.
[16] Fairchild, Furniss, and Buck, *op. cit.,* p. 596.

the theoretical foundations of the older system of mercantilism by insisting that the economic life of society rests upon the principle, among others, that economic freedom yields greater and more beneficial returns to society than governmental intervention in economic affairs.[17] The proponents of laissez faire held that there was a divinely ordained harmony of the egoistic and selfish impulses in man. They believed that every individual should seek to outrun his rival in external economic competition but that he should never hinder that rival by unfair means.

Under the influence of the rising nationalism, critics of the Adam Smith-Say position denounced it as suffering from three main defects: boundless cosmopolitanism, dead materialism, and a disorganizing particularism and individualism. It was plagued, they said, by an out-moded liberalism. The laissez-faire philosophy, said the critics, took no account of nations, but simply of the entire human race on the one hand, or of single individuals on the other. Between each individual and entire humanity stands the nation, which must recognize the law of right for and within itself, and in its united character is still opposed to other societies of a similar kind in their national liberty. Consequently, in an era of nationalism, each nation can, under existing conditions, maintain its self-existence and independence only by its own power and resources.

The champions of a national system of political economy were objecting, in effect, to the rationalistic concept that political economy resembles a natural science in the universal applicability of its laws. For the theoretical postulations of rationalism they preferred to substitute what they regarded as the realistic demands of nationalism. They called themselves the Historical School,[18]

[17] On the Classical School, see Walter Bagehot, *Economic Studies* (London, 1898); Edwin Cannan, *A History of the Theories of Production and Distribution in English Political Economy, from 1776 to 1848* (3rd ed., London, 1917); Wilhelm Hasbach, *Untersuchungen über Adam Smith und die Entwicklung der politischen Ökonomie* (Leipzig, 1891); and G. Briefs, *Untersuchungen zur klassischen Nationalökonomie* (Jena, 1915).

[18] A similar development among historians may be noted. The Historical School, or "historicism," arose among historians partly as a reaction against the abstract principles of the Enlightenment. Originating with Justus Möser, Hegel, and Marx, historicism was later revived and altered by Max Weber, Wilhelm Dilthey, and Ernst Troeltsch, and was given a brilliantly subtle interpretation by Friedrich Meinecke. The rationalists spoke of a *Weltgeist* (world-spirit, cosmopolitanism); the historicists thought in terms of the *Volksgeist* (national spirit). Funda-

on the ground that, as realists, they were simply facing an historical situation as it exists and not seeking to mould their actions, as did the rationalists, to vague and inscrutable natural laws. They saw a desirable economic mode of conduct in the practical politics of the mercantilists and consciously gave a new lease of life to mercantilism.

The two chief proponents of the Historical School in the United States in the early nineteenth century were Daniel Raymond [19] and Matthew Carey,[20] both of whom believed that classical economy with its individualistic philosophy was unsuited to American needs, and who called for governmental paternalism as opposed to laissez faire, protective tariffs, and internal improvements at governmental expense.

The national system of political economy, however, received a most powerful expression in Germany, where it was considered to be a response to the practical needs of German economic life at the time. A succession of German economists (List, Roscher, Knie, Hildebrand, Schmoller, Bücher, Knapp, and Häusser), convinced that it was the chief task of the economic policy of Germany to defend the country against the superiority of England, demanded a national economic policy independent of the English tradition and a new national economic science to represent and promote this policy.

The most influential apostle of German economic nationalism was Friedrich List (1789–1846),[21] whose work was the first expression in the Germanies of the national concept at the economic level. In the struggle between a steadily intensifying nationalism and a progressively weakening liberalism, List maintained in his system of national economy very much the same ideas as the

mentally, historicism was an attempt to work politically through history (*durch die Geschichte politisch zu wirken*).

[19] Daniel Raymond, a native of Connecticut, prepared for the bar there and in 1814 appeared as a member of the bar in Baltimore. In 1820 he published his *Thoughts on Political Economy,* the first systematic treatise on the subject to be written by an American.

[20] Matthew Carey, an Irish immigrant, became a leading writer on political economy and a publisher in Philadelphia. A lively polemicist, he issued a long series of pamphlets presenting his view on a national system of political economy.

[21] For a fuller description of List's theories, see "The Rôle of Friedrich List in the Establishment of the Zollverein," in Louis L. Snyder, *German Nationalism: The Tragedy of a People* (Harrisburg, Pa., 1952), pp. 75–100.

literary romanticists and the early nationalists. He directed attention to "dynamic national enrichment" as vastly preferable to static national wealth. He protested against the cosmopolitan principles of the Classical School and demanded instead a wholehearted devotion to the *national* idea, on the ground that national unity is always the logical culmination of past developments. In his eyes the establishment of the *Zollverein* was a necessary prerequisite for German unification and for German national greatness. Originally a prophet without honor in his own country, List was later, after German national unification, hailed as "a great German without Germany," as "Germany's *verhinderten* Colbert," and as an economic genius who embodied the finest thinking of Cromwell, Canning, Quesnay, Robert Peel, even Aristotle.[22]

The Marxist-Leninist Interpretation of Nationalism

The Marxist-Leninist interpretation of nationalism is predicated upon the principle of historical materialism: the causes of all social changes and political revolutions are to be sought, not in men's brains, but in changes in the modes of production and exchange; not in the philosophy but in the economics of each particular epoch. It is held that emphasis must be placed on the socio-economic and historical appraisal of social phenomena. From the viewpoint of this rigid formula, any explanation of nationalism by a psychological or ideological approach concerns itself only with surface appearances. The nation, nationality, nationalism, and national character are all parts of the political and ideological superstructure of human society. These concepts may temporarily dominate society, but in the final analysis, according to Marxism-Leninism, they simply reflect the bitter, deeply rooted history of class societies and class struggles.

The Marxist-Leninist attitude towards nationalism is closely associated with its conception of the state. Every state in history was and is, it is maintained, a state of classes, a polity of superior and inferior social groups, based upon distinctions of either rank

---

[22] List and the Historical School extended their influence beyond Germany to England, the United States, France, Italy, and the Scandinavian countries.

or property.[23] The state is the product and manifestation of the irreconcilability of class antagonisms.[24] In modern states the capitalist class controls the mode of production of the state and hence determines its social, political, and intellectual character. Modern nationalism, say the Marxists, is a form of social action utilized by capitalists to retain a stranglehold on society. It is "the logical and inevitable consequence of the growth of monopoly within each state." [25] It is not the externalization of old and familiar aggressive instincts and fears, but rather reflects a social order in which capitalism is dominant.[26] It arose originally as a consequence of the appearance of modern monopoly capitalism and parallels its development. In its later stages it merges with imperialism and is responsible for modern wars. But, say the Marxists, it lags behind historical development, both in time and in structural form. It can be eliminated, the Marxists conclude, only by the destruction of monopoly capitalism, and peace can be permanently secured in the future only when a socialist society, based on socialist production, takes the place of capitalist society.[27]

Criticism of the Marxist-Leninist Position

Critics point out that the Marxist-Leninist conception of nationalism is defended with an emotional vehemence somewhat out of line with its claims for historical objectivity. It suffers from

[23] In the words of Engels: "The state is by no means a power imposed from the outside; just as little is it 'the reality of the moral idea,' 'the image and reality of reason,' as Hegel asserts. Rather, it is the product of society at a certain stage of development." (Friedrich Engels, *The Origins of the Family, Private Property, and the State* [Stuttgart, 1894], pp. 177-78.)

[24] "The state arises when, where and to the extent that class antagonisms *cannot* be objectively reconciled. And, conversely, the existence of the state proves that the class antagonisms are irreconcilable." (V. I. Lenin, *The State and Revolution* [London, 1933], pp. 12-13.)

[25] John Strachey, *The Coming Struggle for Power* (New York, 1933), p. 75.

[26] Alexander Szalai, "Social Tensions and Social Changes: A Marxian Analysis," in *Tensions That Cause Wars,* ed. by Hadley Cantril (Urbana, Illinois, 1950). p. 25.

[27] "When . . . all production has been concentrated in the hands of a vast association of the whole nation, the public power will lose its political character. . . . The proletariat . . . will have swept away the conditions for the existence of class antagonisms, and of classes generally, and will thereby have abolished its own supremacy as a class." (Karl Marx and Friedrich Engels, *The Communist Manifesto* [Chicago, 1888], p. 42. Originally published in 1848, the *Manifesto* was translated by Samuel Moore.)

the faults of all stratified, monolithic, and monistic interpretations of history, in which all the complexities of history are reduced to a comparatively simple formula. Several criticisms of
the Marxist-Leninist view of nationalism may be noted here.

In attributing war to the nature of capitalist society, Marxist-
Leninists do not add that no social system has yet succeeded in
abolishing war. Aggressive nationalism, far from existing only in
capitalist countries, has flourished under Communism, in Christian and non-Christian countries, among illiterate and literate peoples, under authoritarian as well as under democratic political
structures.[28]

The Marxist-Leninist attitude towards aggressive nationalism
indicates a double standard which betrays a political desire rather
than an objective historical observation. In this contradictory position, Marxists condemn aggressive nationalism in capitalistic
countries and, at the same time, defend it as something "positive,
essential, and fundamentally good" when it is displayed by op-
pressed colonial peoples.[29]

Marxism-Leninism predicted a diminution of nationalism as the
proletariat became economically ready for the overthrow of the
capitalist mode of production. But nationalism, far from diminishing, has increased and has failed to be conquered by the
cosmopolitan tendencies which Marx perceived in finance.[30]

Even if it be granted that one set of causes dominates the rest
and that it tends to shape the course of social development, there
are many motivations at work in history. If a particular people
exhibits a spirit of violent nationalism, it does not necessarily
follow that this nationalism is actually a perverted form of class-
feeling, or that it depends, in the final analysis, upon economic
grounds. Possibly it is, and does: probably not.[31]

The critics say that it is historically inaccurate to regard nationalism as the creature of a coherent economic class. While the
commercial classes in early modern history gave it their support
and were strong allies of the monarchs in their struggle against

[28] Gordon W. Allport, "The Role of Expectancy," in *Tensions That Cause Wars,*
op. cit., p. 45.
[29] Szalai, *op. cit.,* p. 24.
[30] Bertrand Russell, *Proposed Roads to Freedom* (New York, n.d.), p. 26.
[31] G. D. H. Cole, *What Marx Really Meant* (New York, 1934), pp. 40–41.

the medieval polity, these classes were not powerful enough to accomplish the task single-handedly. Most of their power came after the battle for the nation-state had been decisively won.[32]

The Marxist-Leninist view of nationalism, limited to objective, socio-economic processes, blandly pretends to ignore the subjective factors in history—the ideology of the masses, their emotional attitudes, and the development and contradictions of their ideologies. Political reality can be comprehended, say the critics, only if both the politico-economic actions of men and their psychological motivations are taken into consideration. Latter-day Marxism brushes aside the structure and dynamics of ideology and contemptuously labels it as "psychology" which is not Marxist, and, therefore, fallacious. The process is an interesting one. As a materialist, the Marxist repudiates as idealistic all such factors as instincts, needs, or psychological processes. Yet, his everyday political practice forces him to use such terms as "revolutionary consciousness," "the will to strike," and "the needs of the masses." The more he attacks psychology, the more he himself turns to applied psychology for ammunition for his excoriation of the social order. An understanding of national character depends not only upon social economics, but also upon political psychology. Marxist materialism is so concerned with the human stomach that it tends to forget what happens in the human brain. It places great significance on the class struggle, yet it denies the existence of mass psychology.[33]

Conclusions and Summary

Nearly all social scientists direct careful attention to the economic motives in nationalism. Economic factors are vital for an understanding of nationalism, since the economic process is anchored in the psychological structure of society. The growth of economic nationalism parallels the development of political

[32] *Ibid.*, p. 88.

[33] Marx himself did not neglect to mention the importance of actual individuals, their actions, and their living conditions: "Man himself is the basis of material production as well as of any other. Therefore, all the conditions which affect man, the subject of production, also modify, more or less, all his functions and activities as the creator of material wealth, of commodities." (Karl Marx, *Theorien über den Mehrwert* [Stuttgart, 1905], I, p. 388.)

and cultural nationalism. Economic nationalism was intensified along with political rivalries and the hardening of national cultural differences. With the nation-state as the supreme agent of economic control, economic nationalism seeks to make the nation safe in times of peace and self-sufficient in times of war.

The designation of recent economic nationalism as neo-mercantilism is justifiable considering the close correlation between the principles and methods of early modern mercantilism and present-day economic nationalism. The Adam Smith-Say Classical School of economics advocated a liberal economic philosophy on a cosmopolitan basis, but the Historical School developed a national system of political economy dedicated to the proposition that the needs of the national state were above all other needs. The historicists rejected rationalism in favor of nationalism.

Marxist-Leninist historical materialism regards nationalism as a part of the ideological superstructure of human society and as a reflection of the deeply rooted history of class struggles. It denounces any subjective, psychological explanations of nationalism as un-Marxian and inconsequential. Critics of this position point out that attributing aggressive nationalism to monopoly capitalism is historically inaccurate, that the prediction of a diminution of nationalism has not materialized, that many motivations work in history, that nationalism is not the creature of one coherent economic class, and that Marxists themselves, while professing to ignore subjective, psychological factors in nationalism, unconsciously utilize psychological terms in their everyday political practice.

VII

Patriotism and Nationalism

Our country! In her intercourse with foreign nations may she always be in the right; but our country right or wrong.

—Stephen Decatur *

Patriotism is the last refuge of a scoundrel.

—Dr. Samuel Johnson

What is Patriotism?

It would seem that here at last is a word that may be defined simply: patriotism is love of country. But once again it is not easy to find a precise definition. What is meant by one's country? Who are one's fellow countrymen? What is the relationship of patriotism to other loyalties? What kind of social conduct is implicit in patriotism?

Etymologically, the word patriotism is derived from the root word, father,[1] thereby indicating a sentiment based upon close parental loyalty. The definition is complicated by shades of meaning. Patriotism may be either: an affection (love of country; contentment with the physical features of the land and the characteristic speech, manners, and institutions of one's fellow countrymen); a wish (a desire that one's country be wealthy, powerful, civilized, and just); or an act of service (the willingness to serve one's country, on the assumption that the best proof and test

---

* "Toast given at Norfolk," April, 1816.

[1] The root of patriotism may be traced from "patriot"; French, *patriote*, from Late Latin *patriota*, a fellow countryman, from Greek *patriōtēs*, from *patrios*, established by forefathers, from *pater*, father. Use of the word patriot to mean a fellow countryman is now considered to be obsolete.

of love is willing service.[2] Patriotism may be used in two senses: patriotism satisfied means a willingness to be active in the country's service; or patriotism dissatisfied expresses bitter opposition and revolt against the ruling principles and practices of the community. It may mean a final ethical loyalty or it may be used as a term of derision.[3] It may be considered either a blessing or a curse. Any definition of patriotism is liable to challenge.

No matter what distinction is made between the words patriotism and nationalism, there has been a tendency in the popular mind to consider them equivalent. Yet, to confound patriotism with nationalism is to err not only linguistically but also politically.[4] Nationalism is primarily concerned with the independence and unity of the nation, whereas patriotism is more specifically the passion that influences the individual to serve the object of his devotion—his country, either in defending it from invasion, or in protecting its rights, or in maintaining its laws and institutions in vigor and purity. Nationalism is inseparable from the idea of power; patriotism, on the other hand, is by nature defensive, both culturally and militarily. But so ambivalent is the character of patriotism that it can easily be used to justify aggression.

There is also an important chronological difference between the two terms. Patriotism in some form has been a universal attribute of man in society throughout history. It was present among primitive groups, and it is present among contemporary primitive peoples; it is a powerful sentiment among all current peoples. Nationalism, however, is a relatively new phenomenon in modern history. Patriotism, nevertheless, has come to be associated with nationalism in recent centuries, even though it retains a distinct meaning.

Karl W. Deutsch makes the following apt distinction between patriotism and nationalism:

> Strictly speaking, patriotism is an effort or readiness to promote the interests of all those persons born or living with the same *patria,* i.e.,

---

[2] Cf. J. L. Stocks, *Patriotism and the Super-State* (London and New York, 1920), pp. 14–44, *passim.*
[3] For example, in England in the eighteenth century the word Patriot was used ironically to describe a seditious disturber of the government, since the name was assumed by persons whose right to it was questioned or ridiculed by others.
[4] Don Luigi Sturzo, *Nationalism and Internationalism* (New York, 1946), p. 5.

country, whereas nationalism aims at promoting the interests of all those of the same *natio,* i.e., literally a group of common descent and up-bringing, or rather of common culture, that is to say, of complementary habits of communication. Patriotism appeals to all residents of an ethnic group, regardless of their ethnic background. Nationalism appeals to all members of an ethnic group, regardless of their country of residence. Patriotism, based on residence, often appears at an earlier stage of economic and social mobilization, such as was found in Europe during the later Mercantilist era, and up to the middle of the nineteenth century. As mobilization progresses and comes to involve larger masses of the population in more intense competition and greater political insecurity, patriotism is replaced by nationalism which is based on far more intimate and slow-changing personal characteristics and communication habits of each individual.[5]

Chauvinism and Jingoism

The confusion is further compounded by the widespread tendency to use the word patriotism synonymously with two of its variations, "chauvinism" and "jingoism." Chauvinism [6] and jingoism [7] are, respectively, French and British terms denoting the belief, policy, or practice of a vainglorious, exaggerated patriotism, which boasts of the country's preparedness to fight and supports a bellicose policy in foreign affairs.[8] Both terms indicate a blend of patriotism, nationalism, militarism, and imperialism. Designed to appeal to the emotions, most chauvinistic and jingoistic boasts and threats are used as propagandistic devices to organize heightened group tensions so that they can be used instantly for attack or defense.

[5] Karl W. Deutsch, *Nationalism and Social Communication: An Inquiry into the Foundations of Nationality* (New York, Technology Press of M.I.T. and John Wiley and Sons, 1953), p. 232, footnote 40. Cf. H. M. Chadwick, *The Nationalities of Europe* (Cambridge, England, 1945), p. 3.

[6] Chauvinism is derived from the French surname of Nicholas Chauvin of Rochefort, a much wounded soldier of the First Republic and the Empire, whose demonstrative patriotism and blind idolatry of Napoleon came to be ridiculed by his comrades.

[7] Jingoism arose in England, where it was used originally as a nickname for the practice of praising Lord Beaconfield's action in sending a fleet to Turkish waters in 1878 to oppose Russia's drive to the sea. It came from a popular music-hall song:
"We don't want to fight, but *by jingo,* if we do,
　We've got the ships ,we've got the men, we've got
　　the money, too!"

[8] On chauvinism and jingoism, see Harold D. Lasswell, *Propaganda Technique in the World War* (London, 1927); G. M. Stratton, *Social Psychology of International Conduct* (New York, 1929); and J. A. Hobson, *The Psychology of Jingoism* (London, 1901).

The writings and speeches of jingoists in all major countries gave evidence of grandiose programs of national expansion and aroused mutual suspicions and antagonisms.[9] A classic jingoistic utterance is the famous dictum of Friedrich von Bernhardi: "War is a biological necessity of the first importance, a regulative element in the life of mankind which cannot be dispensed with, since without it an unhealthy development will follow, which excludes every advancement of the race, and therefore all real civilization.[10] British, French, and American jingoists spoke along similar lines.

Chauvinistic sentiment is revealed in such slogans as *Deutschland Über Alles,* Britannia Rules the Waves, *Sinn Fein,* or America First.[11] Only a few examples need be cited from chauvinistic literature. A stage of intoxicating exuberance may be reached, as witness this passage from Richard Wagner:

> When Goethe's *Götz* appeared, its joyous cry went up: "That's German!" And, beholding his likeness, the German also knew how to show himself, to show his world, what Shakespeare is, whom his own people do not understand. These deeds the German Spirit brought forth of itself, from its inmost longing to grow conscious of itself. . . . Everything done in the sense of this teaching is *deutsch,* and therefore is the German great.[12]

Chauvinism may become irrational in its intensity, as indicated by this strange paean from the works of Adolf Stoecker, Christian-Socialist pastor in Imperial Germany:

> Ten years ago much blood was spilled to win freedom and unity for the Fatherland; one cannot think enough of the Fatherland, and it is inspiring when young men give their Fatherland more than themselves, and give their blood and lives for the Fatherland. But when one makes a repulsive idol of the earthly Fatherland, when there is no heavenly Fatherland above the earthly Fatherland, then the spirit of

[9] For example, Rhodes, Kipling, Maxse, and Balfour in England; Déroulède, Delcassé, Barrès, and Maurras in France; D'Annunzio and Crispi in Italy; Pobiedonostev, Plehve, and Izvolsky in Russia; and Treitschke, Bernhardi, and Banse in Germany.
[10] Friedrich von Bernhardi, *Germany and the Next War,* tr. by A. H. Powles (New York, 1914), p. 18.
[11] Germans have insisted that "Germany Above All" indicates merely that the individual German owes his first loyalty to his country and that there is no connotation of a world-mission.
[12] Richard Wagner, *Works,* tr. by W. A. Ellis (8 vols., London, 1892–99), IV, p. 164.

the Fatherland remains dark; in many souls today a wrong idea of the Fatherland exists.[13]

Ubiquitous as a phenomenon, chauvinism appeared in Soviet Russia around 1935 when Lenin's social democracy was turned into Russian nationalism by orders from above. Here it assumed a kind of aphrodisiac pattern:

> Soviet patriotism—the flaming feeling of infinite love, unconditional submission to one's own land, of deepest responsibility for its fate and its defense—rises mightily from the depths of our people. Never before has the heroic fight for one's own land risen to the skies as with us. . . . The Soviet land is nurtured and made great by Lenin and Stalin! How it is caressed by the rays of the spring which came with the October Revolution! . . . Soviet patriotism is the love for the wonderful life which our great people have created; it is the mighty guard in the West and the East; it is the surrender to the great cultural heritage of human genius which has come to flower in our land and only in our land. . . . Soviet Union—spring of humanity! [14]

Patriotism as an Ennobling Virtue

On the other hand, patriotism may be considered to be the natural love for country, a deep and serious attachment to a particular place and a particular way of life, which the individual believes to be the best in the world but has no wish to force on other people. This type of patriotism manifests itself in such love of country that he is willing to give all he possesses, his life if need be, to lift the life standards of his people.[15] It was expressed by Frederick the Great in a famous passage:

> I love my country ardently. It is to her that I owe my education, my fortune, my existence, my all. Had I a thousand lives, I should with pleasure sacrifice them all, if I could thereby render her any service and show her my gratitude.[16]

It appears in the lines by Charles Churchill:

> Be England what she will,
> With all her faults she is my country still.[17]

[13] Adolf Stoecker, *Christlich-Sozial: Reden und Aufsätze* (Bielefeld and Leipzig, 1889), p. 11.
[14] *Pravda*, March 19, 1935.
[15] Cf. Bishop G. Bromley Oxnam, Indianapolis *Star*, February 13, 1930.
[16] *Frederick the Great*, tr. from French original (London, 1870).
[17] Charles Churchill, *The Farewell*, quoted in *Bartlett's Familiar Quotations* (New York, 1919), p. 413.

It was the subject of a famous toast:

> Our Country.—whether bounded by the St. John's and the Sabine, or however otherwise bounded or described, and be the measurement more or less—still our Country, to be cherished in all our hearts, to be defended by all our hands.[18]

It received its best expression in these lines by Shakespeare:

> This fortress built by Nature for herself
> Against infection and the hand of war,
> This happy breed of men, this little world,
> This precious stone set in a silver sea,
> Which serves it in the office of a wall
> Or as a moat defensive to a house
> Against the envy of less happier lands—
> This blessed spot, this earth, this realm, this England! [19]

This is a noble kind of patriotism, based on deep and human emotions and the object of rational social guidance, which all men of good-will, Americans, Britons, French, and German alike, desire in a world endangered by excesses of patriotic fervor. "We must substitute," says Albert Schweitzer, "a noble kind of patriotism which aims at ends that are worthy of the whole of mankind, for the patriotism current today; we must substitute a humanity with a common civilization, for idolized nationalisms." [20]

Criticism of Patriotism

The widespread perversion of modest patriotism into aggressive chauvinism has aroused a critical response which rejects it altogether as "the passion of fools," "a stupid doctrine," or "a scoundrel's refuge." "The greater the Fatherland," said Voltaire, "the less one can love it." [21] Tolstoy described patriotism as a bad and harmful sentiment: "It is an immoral feeling, because instead of confessing oneself a son of God, as Christianity teaches us, or even a free man guided by his own reason, each man under the influ-

[18] Robert Charles Winthrop, "Toast at Faneuil Hall on the Fourth of July, 1845," quoted in *ibid.*, p. 687.
[19] William Shakespeare, *King Richard II,* Act II, Scene 1.
[20] C. R. Joy and M. Arnold, *The Africa of Albert Schweitzer* (Boston, 1948), chap. 4.
[21] Quoted in Adam de Hegedus, *Patriotism or Peace* (New York, 1947), p. 22.

ence of patriotism confesses himself the son of his Fatherland and the slave of his government, and commits actions contrary to his reason and conscience." [22] Lord Hugh Cecil believed that patriotism "has become the convenient cudgel of the scoundrel to batter critics dumb." [23] Karl Marx and Friedrich Engels denounced patriotism as an instrument of capitalist exploitation and imperialist war and stated categorically that "the proletariat has no Fatherland." Yet, in 1914, and again in 1939, many Socialist parties in Europe succumbed to the lure of patriotism, while Stalinist Russia, supposed to be the generating focus of world revolution, discovered a supposedly new type of Soviet patriotism and elevated it to a fanatical level.

Anthropological Views of Patriotism

Let us turn now from these generalized views of patriotism and examine the attitudes of individual disciplines toward it. According to the anthropologist, Alexander A. Goldenweiser, the dominant elements in the rise of human society were the biological unit of the family and next the geographical factor of locality.[24] More or less unconsciously, by the trial and error process, primitive man found that through cooperative endeavor he was better able to obtain food, to promote specific types of enterprise, and, in general, to realize his wants.[25] To the primordial local unit of society, the family, or to its variation, the kinship group,[26] the individual gave his loyalty and devotion. Primitive man made

[22] Quoted in Stocks, *op. cit.*, p. 26.
[23] Quoted in Bernard Joseph, *Nationality: Its Nature and Problems* (New Haven, 1929), p. 345.
[24] A. A. Goldenweiser, *Early Civilization* (New York, 1932), pp. 235 ff. Among other unifying agencies are matrimonial status and community of religious or social interest. On this general problem see W. H. R. Rivers, *Kinship and Social Organization* (London, 1914); A. M. Tozzer, *Social Origins and Social Continuities* (New York, 1925); and W. Goodsell, *History of the Family as a Social and Educational Institution* (New York, 1913).
[25] Cf. L. H. D. Buxton, *Primitive Labour* (London, 1924), chap. 2.
[26] Ruth Benedict points out that among the Dubuans, one of the most southerly of the peoples of northwestern Melanesia, the trusted circle is the matrilineal line, to which the individual turns for backing throughout his life. It is not the family, for it does not include the father or his brothers and sisters or a man's own children. "It is the firm undissolving group of the mother's line." (Ruth Benedict, *Patterns of Culture* [9th printing, New York, 1952], p. 122.)

little differentiation between himself and the group to which he belonged. He knew only that those who did not have such protection were in a bad way.[27]

Patriotism, as the sentimental love for one's own country, was widespread and perhaps universal even among the lowest savages.[28] Tribes with nomadic habits showed an attachment to some particular valley especially associated with their life.[29] Some anthropologists claim that patriotism was stronger among primitives than it is among civilized peoples, for the outcast from primitive society found himself not only a man without a country but a man without the means of self-preservation.

Anthropologists differ as to whether or not the zealous patriotic behavior of primitive men was a gregarious instinct or an acquired characteristic. According to Hankins, there is nothing improbable in the idea that this primitive form of patriotism was inherited by man from his animal ancestors.[30] He calls for support from the naturalists, who tell us that sex, familial life, and recognition of territorial rights, all part of, or connected with, the gregarious instincts, are basic in the life of the higher animals. Margaret Mead, on the other hand, places much greater emphasis upon cultural conditioning.[31]

Historical Origins of Patriotism

Although historians agree that patriotism is as old as human association,[32] they believe that it attained its most characteristic form only after the full development of the state, when individuals took on the obligations and responsibilities of civic duties. Love of

[27] Robert H. Lowie, *Primitive Society* (New York, 1920), pp. 111 ff.
[28] E. Westermarck, *The Origin and Development of the Moral Ideas* (2nd ed., London, 1926), II, p. 168.
[29] E. Hanbury Hankins, *Nationalism and the Communal Mind* (London, 1937), pp. 132–33.
[30] *Ibid.*, p. 132.
[31] "We are forced to conclude that human nature is almost unbelievably malleable, responding accurately and contrastingly to contrasting cultural conditions. The differences between individuals who are members of different cultures, like the differences between individuals within a culture, are almost entirely to be laid to differences in conditioning, especially during early childhood, and the form of this conditioning is culturally determined." (Margaret Mead, *Sex and Temperament in Three Primitive Societies* [3rd printing, New York, 1952], p. 191.)
[32] George P. Gooch, *Nationalism* (London and New York, 1920), p. 5.

country came to be regarded as the supreme virtue in the early historic period. Homer revealed a universal belief when he said that "for our country 'tis a bliss to die." [33] During the thousand-year period of the Middle Ages, with Occidental unity centered in the church-state dualism, patriotism was submerged in favor of other group loyalties. The individual transferred his loyalty from the state to the church, or to his feudal superiors, his manorial lord, or his municipality. He did not think of himself as a Frenchman, an Italian, or a German, but as a Christian, a vassal, or a townsman.

With the beginning of the modern era, as national states arose, ecclesiastical and social loyalties gave way to political loyalty. Gradually, the nation itself, not dynasty, monarch, or government, became the object of the individual's allegiance. During this process of political consolidation, there was some confusion about the meaning of the term patriotism. Most civil wars, such as those of monarchists against republicans, Catholics against Protestants, and colonials against the mother country were considered to be wars between patriots.

In its more recent phase, patriotism came to be associated closely with nationalism. Carlton J. H. Hayes has defined nationalism as "an emotional fusion of nationality and patriotism." [34] George P. Gooch distinguishes between them by calling patriotism an emotion and nationalism a doctrine.[35]

Socio-Psychological Springs of Patriotism

The assumption that the love of country characteristic of patriotism is an innate disposition (McDougall) or a biological and instinctual orientation (Freud) has been criticized by other psy-

---

[33] Alexander Pope's translation of *The Iliad of Homer*, line 583, quoted in *Bartlett's Familiar Quotations, op. cit.*, p. 340.
[34] Cf. Wayland F. Vaughan, *Social Psychology* (New York, 1948), p. 895.
[35] "The core of nationalism is group-consciousness, the love of the community, great or small, to which we belong; but for the larger portion of the prehistoric and historic life of mankind such love of our unit has been an instinctive emotion, not a doctrine. While patriotism is as old as human association and has gradually widened its sphere from the clan and the tribe to the city and the state, nationalism as an operative principle and an articulate creed only made its appearance among the more complicated intellectual processes of the modern world." (Gooch, *op. cit.*, p. 5.)

chologists. Anthropologists are inclined to attribute the herd instinct and pooled self-interest of primitive tribes to a common
descent; [36] psychologists differ on the question of how much
common blood means in the creation and consolidation of the
political community. Most dismiss it as a negligible factor in an
age of complex ethnic intermixture. Another explanation is that
when the community is confronted by threats and provocations,
there is a concurrent regression among the individual members
toward powerful primitive impulses.[37]

Whether they call it instinct, impulse, need, motive, or drive,
psychologists and sociologists see in patriotism an underlying
common-human characteristic, in which the emotional processes
are rampant. Bernard C. Ewer defines patriotism as "the sentiment of devotion to one's country and people, a devotion which
expresses itself in various forms of service, especially in fighting
to repel aggression and to attain national aggrandizement." [38]
G. E. Partridge breaks down patriotism into five more or less
distinct factors, or five objects of attachment, the emotional love
of which all together constitute patriotism: 1) home as physical
country; 2) the group as a collection of individuals; 3) *mores,*
the sum of the customs of a people; 4) country as personality or
historical object, and its various symbols; and 5) leaders, or organized government or state, its conventions and representations.
Patriotism then becomes "the sum of the affections a people has
for that which is its own." [39] The English humanitarian, Clutton-
Brock, referred to this sentiment as "pooled self-esteem." [40]

Patriotism is the most significant of all the emotions that move
men to action. It is a passion that all normal men feel. So great is
its power that the average individual believes treason to be the
worst of all crimes, worse even than matricide, patricide, or in-
fanticide. Treason endangers the life of the community, hence it

[36] "The mythology of primitive tribes is quite commonly filled with stories of
descent from heroic or divine ancestors stressing the antiquity of the tribe and
often equating its origin with the origin of the world." (Francis W. Coker,
"Patriotism," *Encyclopedia of the Social Sciences* [New York, 1937], XI, p. 26.)
[37] Harold D. Lasswell, "Chauvinism," *Encyclopedia of the Social Sciences, op. cit.,*
III, p. 360.
[38] Bernard C. Ewer, *Social Psychology* (New York, 1929), p. 402.
[39] G. E. Partridge, *The Psychology of Nations* (New York, 1919), p. 79.
[40] Quoted in Crane Brinton, *The Shaping of the Modern Mind* (New York, 1953),
p. 153.

is murder compounded. Those "sons" who refuse as conscientious objectors in war time to rise to the defense of their motherland are described as contemptible. Any resistance to such an appeal implies rebellion against one of the most powerfully entrenched forms of traditional authority.[41] When patriotism is aroused, there are few, if any, other forces comparable to it in its emotional appeal. In Bernard Joseph's estimation, "patriotism is that part of nationality which may be compared to faith in religion." [42]

The groups of which Le Bon spoke disparagingly are of basic importance in the understanding of patriotism. Civilized man follows his savage ancestors in identifying group and group members.[43] The varied potentialities of which the group is capable are part of the universal experiences of mankind and may be regarded psychologically as the deposit of psychic development in which the individual has shared. Patriotism is one of the symbols elicited from this reservoir. It may be used for a group of any size, from the neighborhood, to the town, to the nation.[44]

Psychiatric Aspects of Patriotism

We have seen that neurotic and psychotic factors are important in motivating a sense of nationalism. They bear equal significance for patriotism. In times of peace, patriotism may be relatively dormant, but in its most intensive form during war periods, it assumes a quality of mass irrationalism. The danger is that it can easily be perverted to malevolent forms and base uses. Reflection in war time is at a minimum; any defense of toleration is fiercely denounced. Hate, love, self-punishment, and many other nuanced motives are brought into action, especially the use of such intangible symbols as "national honor." [45] Suspicions of a paranoid type are aroused; people are accused of violating ancient taboos.

[41] Cf. J. C. Flugel, *Man, Morals and Society* (New York, 1945), p. 291. For a further excellent account of the nature of patriotism, see Frank H. Hankins, *Patriotism and Peace* (Worcester, Mass., 1919).

[42] Bernard Joseph, *Nationality: Its Nature and Problems* (New Haven, 1929), p. 342.

[43] Robert Lowie, in *Are We Civilized?* (New York, 1929), believes that primitive man solves his simple task of living in a small society relatively well, but civilized man living in great units has a far more difficult task and succeeds but poorly.

[44] Vaughan, *op. cit.,* p. 895.

[45] Lasswell, *op. cit.,* III, p. 360.

As in the days of witchcraft, suspects are denounced, ostracized, and even put to death.

It is characteristic of patriotism in war time that the group personality becomes temporarily deranged as it is beset by neurotic fears and anxieties and is engulfed in a torrent of deceit and delusion. The emotional fervor becomes so great that the enemy is always accused, whether justly or unjustly, of having committed the most horrible atrocities. Military units which sacrifice themselves in the interest of patriotism, such as the Spartans at Thermopylae and the Kamikaze pilots at Okinawa, are hailed in their own countries as the most noble of heroes. Every social institution is brought into line and every objection to national policy is stifled as anathema.[46] Domestic feuds are forgotten, and differences between party, class, and creed are eliminated for the moment. The appearance of this type of patriotism is a sure sign that rational social guidance has failed.[47] No longer a benign love of country, patriotism becomes an epidemic.

Psychoanalytic Motivations in Patriotism

From the Freudian point of view, patriotism may be regarded as an emotion of the mass psyche, in which psychic processes occur just as they do in the psychic life of the individual.[48] Each person, in his psychic activity, possesses an "apparatus," [49] which helps him interpret his reaction to others. This unconscious understanding enables him to absorb such powerful social emotions as patriotism.

[46] Freud spoke of World War I as destructive of much that was valuable in the commonwealth of humanity: "Science herself has lost her passionless impartiality; in their deep embitterment her servants seek for weapons from her with which to contribute towards the defeat of the enemy. The anthropologist is driven to declare the opponent inferior and degenerate; the psychiatrist to publish his diagnosis of the enemy's disease of mind or spirit." (Sigmund Freud, "Thoughts for the Times on War and Death" [1915], in *Collected Papers* [London, 1924], IV, p. 288.)
[47] Perhaps the most striking example of this failure of rational social guidance can be found in the mass psychology of Fascism.
[48] Cf. Patrick Mullahy, *Oedipus Myth and Complex* (New York, 1948), pp. 69–70.
[49] Freud did not clarify the nature of this mechanism, but Mullahy gathers that it is related to empathy (a term later used by Harry Stack Sullivan to describe "an emotional contagion or communion" between infant and adult). (See Mullahy, *op. cit.*, pp. 284–85.)

Psychoanalytic motivations of patriotism are much the same as those of nationalism. Several theoretical variations, all closely related motivations, may be added.

Patriotism may be described as the logical emotional outcome of a psychic identification process. Psychoanalysts agree that the earliest emotional ties of the child become the most easily formed group emotional ties. Just as the infant's early mechanisms are attached to the parent figures, so does the community-impulse of patriotism become identified with the symbol of the state.[50] When draft boards placed the question to conscientious objectors: "What would you do if a Jap (or any other enemy) attacked your mother?", the questioners were on psychologically firm ground.

Patriotism is a substitute object which satisfies the individual's need for security. For the infant the nipple means security. The emotionally retarded child finds great survival value in thumb sucking. As he passes through the succeeding stages of juvenile era, preadolescence, early adolescence, and late adolescence to maturity,[51] he never surrenders his desire to retain his original source of security, but is always in search of substitutes. In this way his attachments to parents, family, kinship groups, and nation are formed. All are substitute needs for security.[52] Loyalty to the nation, as expressed in patriotism, becomes a wholly desirable attitude, psychologically rewarding and socially recognized.

Patriotism provides a means for the projection of hostile feelings and aggression. Whether they be classified as instincts, persistent modes of behavior, or regressions toward primitive impulses, the aggressive elements are important in very early life. The acculturation process requires repression of these hostilities and aggressiveness. Then the mechanism of projection comes into play, by which the individual can remove the stimuli from himself

[50] "When we are exhorted to fight (and perhaps to die) for 'king and country,' we are in effect asked to defend a person and a social organization which in large part derive their emotional appeal from displacements of the earlier loyalty and obedience to the parents." (Pflugel, *op. cit.*, p. 290.)

[51] These "epochs" or "eras" of personality development were named by Harry Stack Sullivan.

[52] "But, this is the tragedy of mankind, as substitutes increase in quantity and area they decrease in quality, they become more and more remote from a 'good object,' from a yielding nipple." (Géza Róheim, *The Origins and Functions of Culture* [New York, 1943], p. 84.)

by projecting them on those against whom he feels hostile. As Money-Kyrle has suggested, the capacity for the outward displacement and projection of his own hostile feelings is the only condition in which man could have successfully combined two of his chief characteristics which at first sight might appear to be incompatible—his aggressiveness and his gregariousness.[53] Since it is socially acceptable to consider hatred for the enemy consistent with love of country, patriotism becomes a highly satisfactory object for the projection of hostility and aggression.

Patriotism may be, in part, a manifestation of a psychic defense against fear and anxiety. All persons, in one way or another, set up defenses against fear and anxiety. Since fears are transparent and objective, they can be handled better, but anxiety, which is hidden and subjective, has even more deleterious effects. One can react courageously to fear, but anxiety provokes a feeling of utter helplessness, especially because of its seeming irrationality. Horney says that "hostile impulses of various kinds form the main source from which neurotic anxiety springs." [54] According to Róheim, "defence systems against anxiety are the stuff that culture is made of and therefore specific cultures are structurally similar to specific neuroses." [55] From this point of view, patriotism provides a satisfactory outlet by which a neurotic society seeks to allay its conflict-ridden objective situations.

Conclusions and Summary

Patriotism has been defined simply as love of country, but here again the problem of definition is complicated by shades of meaning. Though similar psychical sentiments, patriotism and nationalism are not equivalent. Nationalism is primarily concerned with the independence and unity of the nation; patriotism is more specifically the passion that influences the individual to serve the object of his devotion—his country. In its exaggerated

[53] Roger Money-Kyrle, "The Development of War," *British Journal of Medical Psychology,* XVI (1937), p. 219. Money-Kyrle points out further that, on this view, man became "exoctonous," to avoid conflict with the social group, much as be became exogamous to ensure peace within the family. Similar behavior has been noted for the aggressive human nation and the wolf pack.
[54] Karen Horney, *The Neurotic Personality of Our Time* (New York, 1937), p. 63.
[55] Róheim, *op. cit.,* pp. 81–82.

form, patriotism becomes chauvinism and jingoism, which boast of a country's preparedness to fight and which support a bellicose policy in foreign affairs. Attitudes toward patriotism vary: some regard it as an ennobling virtue, while others criticize it as "a stupid doctrine" and as "the passion of fools."

Individual disciplines contribute varying ideas to the meaning of patriotism. Anthropologists say that patriotism was widespread even among the lowest savages, but they are not certain whether to designate patriotism as gregarious instinct or acquired characteristic. Historians say that patriotism is as old as human association, but they believe that it attained its most characteristic form after the full development of the state. They add that in its recent phase it has come to be associated with nationalism. Most sociologists and psychologists reject the idea of patriotism as an innate disposition. They see in it, however, an underlying common-human characteristic, in which the emotional processes are dominant. They are inclined to describe patriotism as one of the symbols elicited from the reservoir of psychic development of the group in which the individual has shared. Psychiatrists stress the neurotic and psychotic factors in patriotism and call attention to the fact that in periods of war patriotism changes from benign love of country to a contagious epidemic, characterized by mass irrationalism. Psychoanalysts say that the motivations of patriotism are much the same as those of nationalism. Patriotism may be, in part, a logical outcome of a psychic identification process, a substitute object that satisfies the need for security, a means for the projection of hostility and aggression, and/or a manifestation of a psychic defense against fear and anxiety.

VIII

The Problem of National Character

Germany since the earliest times had a fixed national spirit in all classes, still has it at the present time, and according to its organization will have it everlastingly. —JOHANN GOTTFRIED VON HERDER

A complete constancy of national character can hardly be maintained. Single characteristics of a people, however, often show extraordinary powers of survival and self-assertion. —MAX HILDEBERT BOEHM

Rejection of the Idea of National Character

There is a strong difference of opinion on the existence of national character. One point of view rejects it entirely as only a metaphysical dream shot through with fallacious generalizations and unreflecting prejudice. It is said that collectivity is an abstract idea and the collective organism is a mystical delusion.[1] Any notion of national character suffers from the same defect that is to be found in the foundation of every collective concept.[2] Differences within nations are so great as to eliminate the possibility of

---

[1] "The explanation of the fact that large groups appear to possess decided characteristics of their own, in so far as it is not due to the illusion of a prejudicial or superficial observer, lies simply and solely in the stage of civilization attained by them, and the decisive influence of example upon them. A super-psychology has no more existence than a super-soul. . . . Life and actuality are found only in the study of the individual." (Max Nordau, *The Interpretation of History*, tr. by M. A. Hamilton [New York, 1910], p. 130.)

[2] "A man may well, because of certain inborn characteristics and capabilities, belong among the chemists, the farmers, the painters or the philosophers, but a people as a whole never permits itself to be subject to an abstract assumption, because every one of its members exhibits peculiar inclinations and requirements, which became apparent in the rich manifoldness of their undertakings." (Rudolf Rocker, *Nationalism and Culture*, tr. by Ray E. Chase [New York, 1937], pp. 46–47.)

defining a truly national character.[3] It is not only difficult to isolate national characteristics, but once they are ascertained they turn out to be trivialities unworthy of attention. With a little ingenuity, it is possible to deduce two entirely different sets of characteristics for any nation.[4] The contention that each nation has a character of its own, it is further claimed, is mere superstition, and so-called national differences can be accounted for fully by the undeniable characteristics of individual psychology.

"Permanent" National Character

A second point of view holds that national character is a demonstrable historical reality produced by variable social influences, and it remains constant among a people from first to last. "In the literature of any people," said Henry Morley, "we perceive under all contrasts of form produced by variable social influences the one national character from first to last."[5] The idea of national character as a permanent, stable entity was borrowed by Herder and others from Montesquieu in the late eighteenth century, and developed in the nineteenth century into so fixed a persuasion that it helped mould the destiny of nations.[6] With it came a host of popular stereotypes.[7]

[3] Cf. Hamilton Fyfe, *The Illusion of National Character* (London, 1940).
[4] "If we assumed group constitutional differences as basic factor, national character would have to be a stable entity through the centuries based on the recurrence of the same infancy situation. We know, however, that the 'personality' of nations is extremely variable." (Géza Róheim, "Psychoanalysis and Anthropology," in *Psychoanalysis Today,* ed. by Sandor Lorand [New York, 1944], p. 390.)
[5] Quoted in Hans Kohn, *The Idea of Nationalism* (New York, 1944), p. 10.
[6] Cf. Louis Gottschalk, *Understanding History* (New York, 1950), p. 215. Herder's confidence in the *Volksgeist* (which may be translated roughly as national character) as a means of effecting changes in history influenced such historians as Sybel, Treitschke, Macaulay, Michelet, and Bancroft.
[7] Such as the frugal Scotsman, the realistic and volatile Frenchman, the emotional and cynical Italian, the phlegmatic and self-assured Englishman, and the aggressive and naïve American.

The instability and opportunism in stereotypes is revealed in this table of adjectives chosen by Americans in 1942 and 1948 to characterize the Russians:

	1942	1948
Hardworking	61%	49%
Intelligent	16%	12%
Practical	18%	13%
Conceited	3%	28%
Cruel	9%	50%
Brave	48%	28%
Progressive	24%	15%

Historically, the notion of a permanent national character cannot be sustained. Transformations can and do take place in the "personality" of nations. In the early eighteenth century, the French were known as a stolid, peace-loving people; yet, within a century, they had a violent revolution and afterwards sought to impress their ideas of liberty, equality, and fraternity upon the rest of Europe by means of Napoleon's armies. In similar fashion, the formerly impractical, comfortable Germans of the Holy Roman Empire and the Confederation, petty and bourgeois in their habits, emerged in the nineteenth century into a leading position in industry and business, and found themselves involved in two world wars. The English, once regarded as a people inclined to revolution, are today generally looked upon as one of the most stolid and stable people on earth.

The Relative Uniformity of National Character

A third point of view, equidistant between the two extremes, recognizes the existence of national character, but without minimizing the difficulties of determining its meaning and nature. National character, it is held, has a limited validity if it intends to convey the idea that certain values have been inculcated within cultures by responses to different calls from without—by environmental conditions, historical traditions, and formal education.

This position holds that there is a relative uniformity of national character as shown in the extraordinary persistence and power of survival of national traits. Each individual is exposed to those forces which make up the idea of nationalism, and each tends to identify himself with the predominant group of the age in which he lives.[8] He treats the events that happen to his group

(The results of this poll are taken from William Buchanan, "Stereotypes and Tensions as Revealed by the UNESCO International Poll," *International Social Science Bulletin,* III [1951], p. 526.)

"Many of the unfavorable stereotyped conceptions that various ethnic groups have of each other may be related to . . . historically precipitated animosities, while others are more obscure in their origins. Whether the prejudices and stereotypes were ever justified by these historic conflicts, even at the time, is beside the point. . . . The fact that they *persist* for many generations, even for centuries, is the main problem." (G. M. Gilbert, *The Psychology of Dictatorship* [New York, 1950], p. 287.)

[8] "The phenomenon of the identification of the individual with the group is far

precisely as if they happened to him. This process of identification, partly sensible and objective, and partly imaginative and false, accounts for the obvious intensity of group life. The individual may or may not absorb all the qualities of the national character, especially since in modern complex societies the factors conditioning character may be involved or contradictory.[9]

Those who advocate the concept of limited validity protest that their critics tend to confuse national character with racial character. Since they regard racialism as a meaningless fraud, few scholars speak of national character as if it were something inheritable. Aware of this confusion of meaning, many observers tend to shy away altogether from the term national character, on the assumption that, no matter how carefully they distinguish between nationalism and racialism, they will be accused of propagandistic and unscientific thinking.

An increasingly popular term among psychologists is "basic personality structure" of given groups instead of national character. Both terms indicate personal characteristics that are shared by individuals who live within the framework of a common culture. Those who use the new term say that, on occasion, the studies of national character are devoted to relatively superficial aspects of behavior, such as manners and morals, but that "basic personality" studies turn their attention to the integrative processes (the inculcation of a given set of principles for the governing of behavior, the way in which these are inculcated, and the over-all physical conditions under which the development takes place). The important point is that no matter which term is used—basic personality structure or national character—there is recognition that certain common patterns of functioning can be observed in individuals who comprise the nation and that these patterns will

from simple. It does not mean that there is any universal tendency to feel at one with the existing régime. Persons hate the State as well as love it. . . . In general, it may be affirmed that the vast majority of human beings feel themselves strongly identified with the fortunes of some group outside themselves." (E. F. M. Durbin and John Bowlby, *Personal Aggressiveness and War* [New York, 1939], p. 37.)

[9] It is not held here that the national character is the sum total of the individuals concerned, since there may be extraneous factors over which the individual has little or no control. The majority of people in a given country may abhor war, yet they may find themselves carried along by the war spirit. There are always large numbers in any society who fail to conform to type and who act atypically on occasion.

not be found in those who live in different cultural conditions. There may be individual deviations within the nation, but the fact remains that those who have lived in the same cultural framework show definite similarities in personality patterning. No matter what their origins, the characteristic patterns of behavior of different nations do differ.

Anthropology and National Character

Anthropologists may be assured of grateful remembrance by other scholars for having centered their attention upon folkways and folk-customs, "the very heartbeats of nationality." [10] Of particular value has been their work in banishing for all time the bogies of racial character and its related inconsistencies and contradictions. [11] There is no adequate proof that the different behavior of racial groups is organically determined, nor can it be demonstrated that any race, because of its hereditary character, must be placed outside the pale of existing civilizations.

The existence of group character or different personality norms among the members of different, small, culturally homogeneous societies has been established, and techniques for their study have been well developed. [12] Until recently, the work done by anthropologists along these lines has been exclusively on primitive societies. But on the larger question, as to whether character on a national scale is similar to that of group character found among primitive peoples, there is some difference of opinion. According to Franz Boas, the opportunities for expressions of crowd psychology are numerous in all societies in which enterprises are common,

[10] Carlton J. H. Hayes, *Essays on Nationalism* (New York, 1941), p. 65.
[11] Cf. Franz Boas, *The Mind of Primitive Man* (New York, 1911), and *Anthropology and Modern Life* (New York, 1928); R. H. Lowie, *Culture and Ethnology* (New York, 1917); Jean Finot, *Le préjugé des races* (Paris, 1906); Théophile Simar, *The Race Myth* (New York, 1925); J. S. Huxley and A. C. Haddon, *We Europeans* (New York, 1936); and I. Zollschan, *Das Rassenproblem* (3rd ed., Vienna, 1912).
[12] A few examples of this productive work may be cited: Franz Boas, *The Social Organization and Secret Societies of the Kwakiutl Indians* (Washington, 1897); Bronislaw Malinowski, *Argonauts of the Western Pacific* (London, 1922); George Bird Grinnel, *The Cheyenne Indians* (New Haven, 1923); G. Bateson and M. Mead, *Balinese Character* (New York, 1942); and Géza Róheim, *Australian Totemism* (London, 1925).

whether they be primitive or civilized.[13] The crowd spirit is evoked, and the emotionally conditioned associative acts are emphasized. There is no essential difference in capacity for control, but the conditions for exciting strong emotions may be different. Géza Róheim agrees that both in primitive societies and also in modern nations we have a group ideal, that is, a certain standard of the way a member of the group should think and behave. But, in Róheim's view, there is an important distinction: the more primitive a society, the less difference there will be between the group ideal and the ego-ideal.[14]

Ralph Linton points out that the crux of the problem of national character lies in the degree to which modern civilized nations have distinct national cultures and extent to which the culture elements shared by the social units which compose such a nation reflect a common denominator of the personalities of the nation's members.[15] Linton believes that a considerable number of culture patterns are normally shared by the members of any modern nation irrespective of their class or regional differences. He holds further that from these, the existence of certain common value-attitude systems can be deduced, and that a knowledge of these systems should make it possible to predict with fair accuracy the behavior of the average national in certain situations.[16]

The concept of national character hinges on a controversy which we have discussed at several places in preceding chapters— whether or not society is an organism. Many observers insist that society is not and can never be anything over and above the in-

---

[13] Franz Boas, "Anthropology," *Encyclopedia of the Social Sciences* (New York, 1937), II, pp. 108–09.

[14] Géza Róheim, "Psychoanalysis and Anthropology," in *Psychoanalysis Today, op. cit.,* p. 393. "It is improbable that groups (tribes, nations) can maintain a stable personality for more than a few generations. With nations whose history we know we can definitely show how external factors change the idealized 'imago' of a nation. Hungary had a revolutionary, liberal Son Hero type of idealism as long as the ruler was an alien, a German (Austrian), a Hapsburg. But as soon as the Hungarian ruling classes wrested the power from their foreign rulers, they became reactionaries. It is very questionable, however, whether these *'imagines'* of modern nations idealized by propaganda and literature really mean much, whether they correspond to the personality structure of the people within that group." (*Ibid.,* pp. 393–94.)

[15] Ralph Linton, "The Concept of National Character," in *Personality and Political Crisis,* ed. by Alfred H. Stanton and Stewart E. Perry (Glencoe, Illinois, 1951), pp. 133–34.

[16] *Ibid.,* p. 144.

dividual minds that compose it, and that it is a fallacy to conceive of a mythical entity—the group—thinking and acting. Yet, in the words of Margaret Mead, this is largely a verbal quarrel. "Character," she says, "is an abstraction, a way of talking about the results in human personality, of having been reared by and among human beings whose behavior was culturally regular." [17] According to Ruth Benedict, "group phenomena must be studied if we are to understand the history of human behavior, and individual psychology cannot itself account for the facts with which we are confronted." [18]

The development of objective techniques for the study of national character has hardly begun. The study of group personality norms, or what Linton calls "status personalities," by projective techniques and other scientific methods promises to throw much light on the dynamics of personality formation. The sheer labor involved in sampling methods, statistics, and other scientific techniques (Rorschach Test, Thematic Apperception Test, life histories, etc.) applied on the large group scale is a staggering one. New measurement devices will undoubtedly be invented to replace the present crude and time-consuming tools. Research on a now unthinkable scale may one day throw more light on the problem of national character.

Eric Fromm's Theory of Social Character

The tremendous strides in our knowledge of anthropology, sociology, psychology, and psychoanalysis in the last several decades have enabled us to achieve a better understanding of the irrational phenomena which operate in society. The publication of Eric Fromm's *Escape From Freedom* in 1941 [19] marked a milestone in modern thought on the nature of society.[20] Fundamen-

---

[17] Margaret Mead, *And Keep Your Powder Dry* (New York, 1942), p. 21.
[18] Ruth Benedict, *Patterns of Culture* (9th printing, New York, 1924), p. 214. "In all studies of social custom, the crux of the matter is that the behavior under consideration must pass through the needle's eye of social acceptance, and only history in its widest sense can give an account of these social acceptances and rejections. . . . Those explanations of custom which derive our economic scheme from human competitiveness . . . and all the rest . . . have for the anthropologist a hollow ring." (*Ibid.*)
[19] Eric Fromm, *Escape From Freedom* (New York, Rinehart, 1941).
[20] Although primarily a psychologist, Fromm embodied the best of multidisciplinary

tally, this book presented a revision of Freud's theory of the relationship of man and society. In Fromm's view, Freud made a great discovery in directing attention to the irrational and unconscious forces which determine parts of human behavior. Moreover, it was Freud who showed us that these irrationalities and the whole character structure of an individual are reactions to the influences exercised by the outside world.[21] But man, to Freud, is fundamentally anti-social. In Fromm's words:

> . . . society must domesticate him, must allow some direct satisfaction of biological—and hence, ineradicable—drives; but for the most part society must refine and adroitly check man's basic impulses. . . . Freud chose the word sublimation for this strange transformation from suppression into civilized behavior. . . . The relation of the individual to society in Freud's theory is essentially a static one: the individual remains virtually the same and becomes changed only in so far as society exercises greater pressure on his natural drives (and thus enforces more sublimation) or allows more satisfaction (and thus sacrifices culture).[22]

Fromm objects to Freud's thesis that the culture of man is eternally rooted in his biological constitution. Fromm seeks to show that man's adaptation to nature is based on the process of learning, on culture, not on instinct, and that the latter is a diminishing if not a disappearing category in human beings. Fromm's idea of the acculturation process may be summarized as follows:

The child achieves a sense of security and belonging in the family, "the psychic agency of society." In the process of growth, as the child emerges from his state of un-self-conscious unity with his milieu, he has to stand alone and face the world in all its perilous and overpowering aspects. Threatened by isolation and powerlessness, the human being now is impelled to abandon his individuality by completely submerging himself in the world outside. There are several "psychic mechanisms of escape" which enable the individual to avoid his sense of aloneness in the social

---

thinking on the nature of society. With the publication of his book, Fromm became, in the judgment of many social scientists, one of the foremost thinkers in psychoanalysis, ranking at a level with Adler, Jung, Rank, Horney, and Sullivan; (Cf. Patrick Mullahy, *Oedipus Myth and Complex* [New York, 1948], p. 238 and *passim*).

[21] Fromm, *op. cit.*, p. 9.

[22] *Ibid.*, pp. 10–11.

world: moral masochism, sadism, destructiveness, and automaton conformity.

We need not concern ourselves here with the technical elaboration of these various forms of escape. But it is clear that among the irrational, pathogenic factors in society, communicated to the individual through his family, school, and social milieu, are patriotism and nationalism. Patriotism, or love of country, is, in part, a disguise for masochistic feeling and destructiveness. Nationalism as a form of behavior enables the individual to wipe out the differences between himself and others, at least to the extent of overcoming his conscious fear of aloneness. "He therefore becomes exactly as all others are and as they expect him to be." [23]

Fromm constructs a theory of social character, which may be considered as a more elaborate category which includes national character. An understanding of this social character is a key concept for an understanding of the social process. According to Fromm, "character in the dynamic sense of analytic psychology is the specific form in which human energy is shaped by the dynamic adaptation of human needs to the particular mode of existence of a given society. Character in its turn determines the thinking, feeling, and acting of individuals." [24] The social character is necessarily less specific than the individual character. In the latter we deal with the whole of the traits which in their particular configuration form the personality structure of this or that individual. On the other hand, "the social character comprises only a selection of traits, the essential nucleus of the character structure of most members of a group that has developed as the result of basic experiences and mode of living common to that group." [25] By means of internalizing external necessities, the social character harnesses human energy for the task of a given economic and social system. [26] Granting that physiologically determined needs like hunger, thirst, and sex may be called "instincts," the form of expression and satisfaction of these needs in the social structure are culturally determined. "Although character development is shaped by the basic conditions of life and although there

[23] *Ibid.*, p. 186.
[24] *Ibid.*, p. 278.
[25] *Ibid.*, p. 277.
[26] *Ibid.*, p. 284.

is no biologically fixed human nature, human nature has a dynamism of its own that constitutes an active factor in the evolution of the social process." [27]

Fromm further develops this thesis in a historical frame of reference by showing how European and American history since the end of the Middle Ages saw a process of growing freedom accompanied by a growing isolation.[28] We may assume that nationalism and its concomitant, national character, are modern forms of group emotions to which the individual automatically conforms in his eternal search for security and a sense of belonging.[29] Primitive man found his primary ties in the soil on which he lived and the people within his kinship group. Similarly, modern man seeks his roots in "an organized, structuralized totality," which will protect him from falling into complete isolation.[30] Whether rightly or wrongly, whether consciously or unconsciously, the individual feels that his automatic conformity to what is called the national character is the *sine qua non* for attaining good and warding off evil. The need for such sublimation to achieve security is found today in nationalism.

Other Sociological Views of National Character

The keen interest of sociologists in national character may be traced to their belief that it is to be approached through an investigation not of individual differences in behavior, but of the qualities manifested in the collective life of nations. That a pattern of agreement is being reached is indicated by a brief summary of conclusions made by several leading sociologists. Alex Inkeles, associated with the Russian Research Center at Harvard University, makes these germane points: [31]

While there is yet no satisfactory formulation which precisely

[27] *Ibid.,* p. 289.

[28] This is the type of conflict situation to which psychoanalysts attribute the emergence of neuroses.

[29] "An individual, in his measure, moves unconsciously towards the settled form which is his character. . . . This is even more true of the history of nations and their characters than it is of the individual man." (Ernest Barker, *National Character and the Factors in Its Formation* [New York and London, 1927], pp. 5–6.)

[30] Cf. *ibid.,* pp. 6–10.

[31] Alex Inkeles, "National Character and Social Structure," *Antioch Review,* IX (1949), pp. 161–62.

defines the existence of a national mind, there can be no serious question but that there are important characteristic value systems, symbols, and patterns of reaction which may be meaningfully used to distinguish the populations of particular national states.

These distinctive patterns are products of unique social, economic, and political conditions, and not products of race or innate national traits.

As such they are mutable, subject to change and in some respects to control and planned development. There is frequently a range of alternatives as to which pattern will be predominant in future social developments.

Changes in these distinctive patterns cannot ordinarily be effected by a direct assault on the patterns themselves, but must come from changes in the political and socio-economic situation which gave rise to them.

The views of Morris Ginsberg, the British social psychologist, may be summarized as follows: [32]

The difficulties to be faced in the study of national character are 1) personal bias in observation and interpretation; 2) the great complexity of national groups in inner unity and homogeneity; and 3) the lack of a generally accepted theory of the structure of individual character. But it is a mistake to dismiss national character as an "illusion."

Nations like other groups behave in distinctive ways and if their behavior shows some unity and continuity we may perhaps speak of a group character without committing ourselves to any theory of the group mind or group personality.

The indirect method of studying national characteristics by an analysis of the psychological basis of the collective achievements of peoples has undoubtedly proved more fruitful than the direct method based on the observation of individual behavior.

The mental characteristics of the racial elements which have entered into the composition of the European elements are entirely unknown, and to explain national traits by reference to them is to explain the obscure by the more obscure. This is not to say that genetic qualities do not count. Unless we are prepared to

[32] Morris Ginsberg, *Reason and Unreason in Society* (Cambridge, 1948), pp. 131–55.

deny the inheritance of mental characteristics we must regard it as highly probable that just as there are individual differences there are also group differences and that these play their part in shaping the collective life of groups.

Differences in national character are not in the main to be traced to variations in innate tendencies, but rather to variations in the ways in which these are expressed, balanced, and directed.

The object of the study of national character is to discover whether these manifestations of the collective life reveal the existence of relatively permanent and stable traits and dispositions and how far these form congruent systems.

National character is something always in the making, moulding and being moulded by the circumstances in which nations find themselves.

A similar pattern of conclusions may be noted in the work of another British sociologist, Frederick Hertz: [33]

The chief arguments against the idea of a national character are: 1) the wide diversity of individual and cultural traits in each nation; 2) the absence of any very marked and decisive differences of individual characters and cultural traits between nations, provided that comparable social types only are compared; and 3) the frequent and fundamental changes which have taken place in views held of the character of specific nations.

The so-called unity, persistence, and peculiarity of national traits (as held by all racial interpretations) are fallacious notions.

We may speak of a national character by analogy only, as we also speak of the character of a landscape which comprises many different things. It would be desirable to replace the term "national character" by the more correct designation, "national mentality."

National character can only be defined as the totality of traditions, interests, and ideals which are so widespread and influential in a nation that they mould its image, both in the mind of the nation concerned and in that of others.

The persistency of national traits is by no means an invariable rule. The history of most nations shows also sudden changes in the national mentality.

[33] Frederick Hertz, *Nationality in History and Politics* (3rd ed., London), pp. 37–51.

Natural environment and social structure comprise many factors which partly favor the development of a certain unity of character, partly discourage it.

The national ideology tends to determine the private character, especially in countries where the individual is totally subordinated to the nation.

The New Multidisciplinary Science of National Character

Until the period after World War I, most scholars, assuming that people all over the world are basically the same, rejected the idea of national character as *contra bonos mores*. In recent years, however, there has been an abrupt reversal of opinion, and a new generation of scholars is busily at work creating what amounts to a new science of national character.[34] The idea of different behavior patterns of national groups is now accepted as valid and worthy of intensive study.[35] The old McDougall-Freudian theory of attributing national differences to instincts on a biological basis has fallen into disrepute, and in its place is the concept that such differences are due to the acculturation process. The trend is towards a modified Freudian approach, utilizing Freud's studies on the unconscious, on child behavior, and on personality, but considering these characteristics in their social setting.

The new approach is multidisciplinary in character. The rôle of the historian is predicated on the assumption that institutions often reflect mainly the influence of dominant groups, hence analysis of a nation's current institutions must be supplemented

---

[34] For an excellent review of recent studies on national character, see Morroe Berger, "Understanding National Character—and War," *Commentary*, II (1951), pp. 375–86.

[35] "The burden of the available work in the scholarly disciplines concerned with social relations indicates that there are distinctive patterns of reaction to given situations which may be used to distinguish the populations of particular national states. These patterned responses, along with the symbols and value systems . . . are not independent of political and economic institutions; indeed they are intimately interwoven with them. But they may exercise an independent influence in the selective apprehension of experience, and have a profound effect on the opportunities for success of *new* institutional forms in the political and economic realm." (Alex Inkeles, *op. cit.*, p. 159.)

by historical and causal studies.[36] Anthropologists, who are well versed in handling whole cultures, are now applying to the larger civilized communities the same techniques they have used in the past for the study of primitive societies.[37] The relatively new discipline of social psychology has cut across departmental lines and, as recorded below, has begun a systematic and unified study of group behavior. Psychiatrists and psychoanalysts, as noted in previous chapters, have been directing increasing attention to group emotions and the problems of nationalism and patriotism. Even the disciplines of education, social work, and industrial engineering are being drawn into the rapidly enlarging field of study. We are witnessing what amounts to a revolutionary development in modern scholarship.

Two major trends are emerging in this multidisciplinary approach to national character—one psychological and one political. The former holds that a psychological approach to the roots of social phenomena can be most meaningfully understood in terms of national, and not institutional, character. The political school attacks this frame of reference as unscientific, beset with an inadequate methodology, and politically defeatist, and maintains that societies and social movements can be best understood in terms of political and socio-economic analysis (systems of economic organization, power structure, and class and caste differences). Social change, according to political scientists, is mainly institutional change rather than changes in national character. By providing socially correct conditions one can insure socially correct behavior, the national character notwithstanding.[38]

[36] "The difficulties of comparative study can be removed gradually as our knowledge of the different nations grows and is supplemented by more detailed study of the character of groups within the nations." (Ginsberg, *op. cit.*, p. 135.)

[37] For example, the previously cited anthropological studies by Mead, Benedict, Gower, *et al.*

[38] Inkeles, *op. cit.*, pp. 156–57. Inkeles finds two fundamental objections to the views of the political school: 1) it assumes the existence of a set of "objective" circumstances which have the same reality for all participants in the total situation; and 2) it completely neglects the rôle played by psychological factors such as the symbols and stereotypes a people orients towards, the rôle of their sentiments and values, their frustrations, or their aggressions. "These elements have no necessary connection with any group mind, and however much they may be the direct outcome of any given political and socio-economic system, they must still be accounted for." (*Op. cit.*, p. 158.)

The UNESCO Tensions Project

The social science division of the United Nations Educational, Scientific, and Cultural Organization (UNESCO) was established in 1945 as a specialized agency of the United Nations. At the Second Session of the UNESCO General Assembly in 1947, a series of resolutions authorizing a study of "Tensions Affecting International Understanding" was passed.[39] The plan was to engage the help and the cooperation of social scientists and of academic and learned institutions in many parts of the world. For the first time in history the peoples of many lands have turned officially to the social scientist in the quest to achieve the most important goal of mankind—enduring peace.

Much of the UNESCO research is psychologically oriented, and it has the advantage of being multidisciplinary and multinational in character. The work of two distinguished social psychologists, Hadley Cantril, of Princeton University, and Otto Klineberg, of Columbia University, successive directors of the UNESCO Tensions Project, deserves special mention.

As a practical first step, eight specialists from different countries[40] were brought together in a two weeks' conference at

[39] *Resolution 5.1.1.1.:* Inquiries into the distinctive character of the various national cultures, ideas and legal systems, with the aim of stimulating the sympathy and respect of nations for each other's ideals and aspirations and appreciation of national problems.
Resolution 5.2.2.2.: Inquiries into the conceptions which the people of one nation entertain of their own and other nations.
Resolution 5.1.1.3.: Inquiries into modern techniques which have been developed in education, political science, philosophy and psychology for changing mental attitudes and for revealing the processes and forces involved when human minds are in conflict.
Resolution 5.1.1.4.: Inquiry into the influences which predispose towards international understanding on the one hand and aggressive nationalism on the other.
Resolution 5.1.1.5.: The preparation of a Source Book describing the work already under way in the study of tensions that arise from technological improvements and the resulting shift of populations.
[40] Alexander Szalai, professor of sociology, University of Budapest; Gordon W. Allport, professor of social relations, Harvard University; Harry Stack Sullivan, M.D., former chairman, Council of Fellows, Washington School of Psychiatry; Gilberto Freye, professor of sociology, University of Bahia, Brazil; John Rickman, M.D., editor, British Journal of Medical Psychology; Max Horkheimer, director of the Institute of Social Research, New York City; Georges Gurvitch, professor of sociology, University of Paris; and Arne Naess, professor of philosophy, University of Oslo.

Paris during the summer of 1948. In 1950 Dr. Cantril edited and published *Tensions That Cause Wars,*[41] which included a common statement and individual papers of the eight social scientists. In the twelve paragraphs accepted as a basis of agreement, it was held that there is no evidence that wars are necessary and inevitable consequences of human nature as such, but that they are fostered by many of the myths, traditions, and symbols of national pride handed down from one generation to another, and that the social sciences have a vital part to play in the task of acquiring self-knowledge and social insight.[42] Included in the many conclusions reached in the individual papers were these: "the task of social and psychological research is to analyze the character traits that have emerged from the new socio-cultural pattern";[43] "the method of upbringing children should be studied in relation to national character" and other factors;[44] and answers to such problems as national character "must be, if they are to prove tenable, highly conditioned, complicated, and piecemeal."[45]

The divergent points of view expressed in *Tensions That Cause Wars* indicate that even among supposedly objective social scientists each scholar writes within the atmosphere of his own familiar culture. Each contributor was given the opportunity of recording his observations on his colleagues' statements. Alexander Szalai, the Hungarian sociologist, who represented the Marxist-Leninist view of historical materialism, took the opportunity to engage in critical, sometimes bad-tempered controversy with nearly all the others, his remarks being duly entered throughout the book.[46] The book itself was received critically, a reflection, perhaps, of present attitudes. The British weekly, *The Economist,* asked: "What practical use is this to anyone? . . . If the organization is determined to go on making itself ridiculous by attempt-

---

[41] Hadley Cantril, ed., *Tensions That Cause Wars* (Urbana, Illinois, 1950).
[42] *Ibid.,* pp. 17–21.
[43] Max Horkheimer, "The Lessons of Fascism," in *ibid.,* p. 229.
[44] John Rickman, "Psychodynamic Notes," in *ibid.,* p. 202.
[45] Arne Naess, "The Function of Ideological Convictions," in *ibid.,* p. 259.
[46] A typical heckling footnote by Szalai: "Naess becomes increasingly unable to write down the word 'communism' without associating 'fascism.' That is exactly the neurosis all imperialistic warmongers are trying to spread in the world. No such neurosis ever existed in the conference room of UNESCO where this symposium was conducted." (*Ibid.,* p. 272.)

ing to run before it can walk, there may be something to be said
for holding the present conference in the comparative obscurity
of Lebanon." [47]

The second major preliminary study of the UNESCO project
was published, also in 1950, by Otto Klineberg.[48] *Tensions Affecting International Understanding* is a skillful survey of scattered and fragmentary products of research on human behavior
and serves to give form and direction to the study of national
character. Klineberg leans towards a belief in the importance of
a combination of historical and socio-psychological factors in
eliciting the meaning of national personality. However, at the
same time, he points to the fact that our current concern is with
the facts of national differences. "Whatever their origins, the
characteristic patterns of behavior do differ, and we need to know
precisely how they differ." [49] In his second chapter, "Personality
in Relation to Nationality," [50] Klineberg performs the valuable
service of forming an organized structure based on past work on
national character. A précis of this important research is in order
here.

Descriptive Accounts: Tocqueville, Madariaga, Siegfried, and
others have written brilliantly on the characteristics of various
national groups. Commager, Nevins, and other historians have
compared observations about a particular nation made by a large
number of interpreters. The Institute of World Affairs of the
New School for Social Research, under the direction of Adolph
Lowe, has begun a study of "The Image of America as Reflected
in the Writings of Various Observers."

Descriptions and Interpretations by Anthropologists: Such
anthropologists as Mead, Gorer, Benedict, La Barre, Haring,
Hsien Chin Hu, and others, have applied to complex modern
societies some of the techniques developed in the study of rela-

---

[47] *The Economist*, November 20, 1948. To this Cantril replied properly that "*The
Economist* made one mistake, namely, that a child must do a lot of staggering,
tumbling and learning before it can walk, let alone run." (Cantril, *op. cit.*, p. 14.)
[48] Otto Klineberg, *Tensions Affecting International Understanding* (New York,
1950). This work was done in cooperation with the Social Science Research Council, which published it as Bulletin 62 in its series of monographs dedicated to
research in the social sciences.
[49] *Ibid.*, pp. 91–92.
[50] *Ibid.*, pp. 8–92.

tively simple primitive societies. Similar work has been done by such ethnologists as Kluckhohn, Bateson, and others. In Klineberg's view, valuable insight into the behavior of groups has given a more systematic picture of national character, though at times an impression of universality is given which is probably not in accord with the facts.

Vital and Social Statistics: The census reports of most countries, dealing with phenomena relating to forms of mental disease, crime, births, marriage, and divorce, as well as many aspects of normal and abnormal behavior, are highly suggestive of at least one way in which differences in national culture may be revealed. There are, however, such difficulties as unreliable statistics, the large number of variables, and differences in interpretation. With more adequate statistics for a large variety of national cultures, we may be able to get at national differences in general and also at the degree of homogeneity within each nation.

Psychiatric Interpretations: Attempts have been made to explain the behavior of national communities in terms paralleling the behavior observed in individual psychotic patients. Klineberg finds this extension not justifiable without further evidence.

Psychoanalytic and Modified Psychoanalytic Approaches: Róheim, Gorer, La Barre, Sikkema, and other anthropologists have sought to understand national psychological characteristics through study of the earliest experiences of the child. Kardiner, the psychiatrist, believes that a basic personality does exist and can be reconstructed from the institutional description of a particular community. Some psychoanalysts lean more heavily on an instinctual interpretation of personality dynamics, others on a social viewpoint. Fruitful results await depth interviewing of different populations.

Psychomatic Relationships: Differences between nations emerge also in connection with somatic or bodily reactions which appear to have, in part, a psychological origin (lower average systolic blood pressure of Chinese, Hindus, Filipinos, possibly due to chronic differences in emotional attitudes). More complete data is needed.

Content Analysis of Cultural Products: Kracauer, Wolfenstein, Leites, Dorothy Jones, Powdermaker, Lasswell, Lewin,

Lazarsfeld, and others have sought to explain national character in terms of certain cultural aspects of national groups—in their plays, books, moving pictures, radio programs, advertisements, etc. Historical as well as contemporary material is consulted.

Community Studies: The Lynds, Warner, West, Embree, Redfield, Yang, Hsü, Child, Arensberg, Kimball, and others have attempted to give a relatively complete picture of the life of a single community.

Public Opinion Surveys: Polling devices (British Institute of Public Opinion, American Institute of Public Opinion, Gallup Institute, etc.) can and should be used, but interpretation of results will be doubtful without independent information on the total background of the culture.

Attitude Studies: Katz, Chang, McGranahan, Schaffner, and others have used attitude measurement to record the ideologies of peoples. Psychological measuring scales are applied cross-nationally to indicate the range of individual differences.

Intensive Interviews: Cantril, Campbell, and others have used planned interviews as a means of yielding more information than the single questions of the polling type. Careful interviewing may yield "patterns of attitudes."

Tests and Measurements: A vast amount of work is being done by psychologists in testing intelligence and personality. Interpreted with the greatest possible caution, these techniques (Rorschach, Thematic Apperception Test, etc.) may possibly yield a number of cross-cultural comparisons.

The Semantic Approach: Schaffner, Thorner, Kecskemeti, Leites, and others have raised the question as to whether the current vocabulary of a particular national group may give some information about that group. In other words, language may be used as at least one source of information regarding national character.

No one of these techniques has been judged completely satisfactory, since their validity has not yet been fully established. More knowledge is possible in cases where a number of techniques can be used in conjunction.

The importance of Klineberg's study is that, for the first time, on an inductive basis, the vast amount of seemingly unrelated work being done on national character is sifted, analyzed, and brought together in a meaningful pattern. With this book, a significant step has been taken in the construction of a science of national character.

The UNESCO Tensions Project has initiated a number of pilot studies designed to develop methods that can be applied later on a wider, international scale. A series of monographs on the "Way of Life" of some sixteen nations is being prepared to throw light on different national cultures. Another series of studies is devoted to national stereotypes, such as stereotypes in English children and adolescents, by H. O. James of the University of London. The range of investigation extends to studies of attitude change, as, for example, the production of a sample textbook on French history showing the interdependence of French and other cultures, by Lucien Febvre and Fernand Braudel of the University of Paris. Other studies are being made on the issue of aggressive nationalism, population problems, and modern technology. In all these projects, the UNESCO Department of Education is cooperating with other research organizations, including the Carnegie Endowment for International Peace, the New Education Fellowship, and the International Council for Philosophy and Humanistic Studies.

Typical of the fruitful work being done by these research teams was the publication in 1953 of an international scientific study of the causes of prejudice and intergroup hostilities. Written by Gardner Murphy, American psychologist and director of research at the Menninger Foundation, this book describes a study carried out in India by teams of psychiatrists, psychologists, and sociologists investigating mass tensions and violence.[51] The importance of such studies cannot be overestimated in the critical task of maintaining world peace.

Cybernetics and the Quantitative Approach: Karl W. Deutsch

An important step forward in understanding the nature of nationalism and national character has been made by Karl W.

---

[51] Gardner Murphy, *In the Minds of Men* (New York, 1953). While carried out under UNESCO auspices, this study was made in response to a request from the Government of India.

Deutsch, professor of history and political science at the Massachusetts Institute of Technology, in his recently published study, *Nationalism and Social Communication*.[52] Deutsch believes that our present knowledge of nationalism, based on the direct approach by specialized students, has given us a wealth of empirical data, as well as excellent techniques for the qualitative recognition of its characteristics and symptoms. At the same time, he finds that this approach, which gives intuitive descriptions of nationalistic situations and behavior patterns of peoples, is insufficient for our needs, since it has not yielded quantitative measurements or predictions. He, therefore, devotes his attention to suggested methods of research and offers a new set of tools for the quantitative measurement of nationalistic movements. An interdisciplinary study, world-wide in its scope, Deutsch's work applies the new ideas of communication theory and cybernetics to the theory of nationalism.[53]

Despite the disparate and often contradictory views of the meaning of nationalism, Deutsch finds in them an underlying unity, a recurrence of certain themes, and a structural correspondence. Examining the social sciences concerned with nationalism, he finds a structural correspondence between certain key concepts in each field. "The picture revealed by all these together is a world not of flat uniformity but of uneven cluster distributions. It is a world in which clusters of settlement, nodes of transport, centers of culture, areas and centers of language, divisions of caste and class, barriers between markets, sharp regional differences in wealth and interdependence, and the uneven impact of critical historical events and social institutions all act together to produce a highly differentiated and clustered world of regions, peoples, and nations. Techniques of mapping in each concrete case the areas of these overlapping influences, and the density or scarcity of social communications that result from them promise to shed light on some of the conditions and prospects of national or supranational integration." [54]

[52] Karl W. Deutsch, *Nationalism and Social Communication: An Inquiry into the Foundations of Nationality* (New York, Technology Press of M.I.T. and John Wiley and Sons, 1953).
[53] Cybernetics, or the control and communication in the animal and the machine, is a discipline conceived by Norbert Wiener, mathematician at the Massachusetts Institute of Technology.
[54] Deutsch, *op. cit.*, p. 161.

Inquiring into the nature of political power, Deutsch finds all such power dependent upon the highly uneven distribution of social communication facilities and of economic, cultural, and geographical interdependence. A people is a crucial unit within each cluster of intensive social communication. The essential aspect of the unity of a people is the complementarity or relative efficiency of communication among individuals, something which might be called "mutual rapport," but on a larger scale. It is this complementarity which can and should be tested. Deutsch reviews a number of ways in which complementarity can be measured in individuals, especially their assimilation and differentiation within the group. National assimilation and differentiation, he says, are related to social learning. He recommends that, in such testing, the specific findings and methods of social psychology, sociology, and anthropology should be related more closely with those of history, economics, and social science.

The next step in the Deutsch approach is the quantitative study of large-scale processes of national assimilation and differentiation, based on the data and methods of economic history, population theory, and statistics which permit the identification of crucial population groups, the charting of long-run trends of national assimilation and differentiation, and their tentative projection into the future. A decisive factor in this study is the fundamental process of social mobilization which accompanies the growth of markets, industries, and towns, and, eventually, of literacy and mass communication. The gross quantitative processes of national assimilation and differentiation, as measured by statistics, are dependent, in turn, upon a number of qualitative and quantitative factors. Some of these balances which lend themselves to measurement include supply and demand, frequency of contact of different kinds, and economic rewards and penalties. Other balances are either technical, linguistic, cultural, or political in nature. With the assistance of Robert M. Solow, Deutsch then presents a "Crude Mathematical Model of Assimilation and Mobilization Processes," [55] which is designed to calculate probable national assimilation or differentiation periods.

Deutsch finds, in addition, that national consciousness and

[55] *Ibid.*, Appendix V, pp. 209–13.

will are accessible in principle to the same structural and quantitative approach. He believes that crude models for the processes
of consciousness and will could be derived from the theory of
communication and control, with the help of which the consciousness of nations could be mapped or measured in some
respects. The destructive as well as the constructive aspects of
national development, consciousness, and will, he believes, are
accessible to charting and measurement by social scientists. "Development and application of such methods by social scientists
could do much to indicate potential danger spots, and application
of their findings by policy makers could serve to forestall or
minimize destruction and to guide fundamental processes of
social mobilization and national development into constructive
channels." [56]

In focusing his attention upon social communication—the
ability to convey messages and to have them quickly and accurately understood—Deutsch has sought to open nationalism to
techniques for measurement and prediction. The great advances
made in recent years in statistical methods, particularly in sociology and psychology, can be used, Deutsch is convinced, to clear
away much of the confusion that has existed in the past on such
questions as why economic growth in certain areas has led to
national unification, while in others it has led to greater diversity.
Whether or not one agrees with the Deutsch approach, it is clear
that this is the type of study that should be encouraged by all
scholars who have been dissatisfied with the results of current
empirical studies, intuitive descriptions of nationalistic situations
and behavior patterns, and abstract inferences from theory.

To some extent, Deutsch has disarmed potential critics by his
modest refusal to jump to conclusions and by his centering of
interest on research not yet done and that could be done by the
methods he suggests. He urges the use of better tools, such as
longer series of more complete and accurate data, more realistic
assumptions, and more refined mathematical techniques. He
feels that none of these tools should be impossible to obtain. In
good scientific fashion he recommends that constructions of pro-
jections should correspond to matters of fact, that there be no

[56] *Ibid.*, p. 163.

significant inaccuracies or distortions in historical data, statistics, and calculating methods, and that no significant elements or factors be omitted from the calculations.

Granting that progress can be made in the measurement of national assimilation or differentiation of mixed populations in a given territory, some historians will express doubt as to the possibility of predictability in this field.[57] The problem hinges around the meaning of history itself. In considering past treatments of nationalism, Deutsch finds a structural agreement that nationalism and nationality are in some sense historical in origin and development. Nationalism, though it concerns the psychology of human behavior, is essentially an historical phenomenon, and, as such, it takes on the quality of the historical process. Historians have found that spiritual and accidental factors in both history and nationalism do not lend themselves easily to predictability. Nor have historians been altogether successful in the quest for objective criteria of causes, value, and influence. When historians discuss the problem of underlying causes for any historical development, including nationalism, they disagree among themselves, because causal explanations of events rest upon the multiple philosophies of history.

The problem of understanding history is complicated by the fact that history is being compounded day by day by the addition of new history. Furthermore, few historians have been able to extricate themselves completely from their milieu and write history, as Ranke recommended, *wie es eigentlich gewesen ist*. The unknowable, actual universe of history differs from the clock-like cosmos regulated by natural law. While natural scientists may disagree on fundamental interpretations of the universe, what they lack in knowledge will have no effect upon the physical universe. The social scientist is faced with an infinitely more

[57] I am indebted to John M. Firestone, of the Department of Economics at The City College of New York and a specialist in statistics, for the gist of the following remarks: Any forecasting or prediction must be based on a set of assumptions, which, if correct, will permit an accurate or reasonably accurate forecast. If premises are false, no matter how accurate are the facts on which the forecast is based, the forecast will be incorrect. The basis of forecasting is past experience. Statistics are used to summarize past experience (such as in weather forecasting, polls for elections, or business forecasts). Statistics provide an aid for forecasting but not the means. A better result can be achieved with the aid of statistics, but everything, in the final analysis, depends upon the basic assumptions.

difficult task, since there are no generally accepted "laws" of history comparable to Kepler's Third Law. New discoveries are constantly being made in astronomy and medicine, but neither the stars nor disease germs change because of changes in the observer.

This does not necessarily mean that predictability of a nation's behavior is impossible and that scholars should give up the task of applying structural and quantitative analysis to historical data. What it does mean is that there are enormous difficulties involved, not the least of which is the training of a generation of statistically minded young historians. Deutsch has broken ground with his excellent data and calculations used for a diagram of Swedes and Finns and of the rural populations in Finland, 1749–2000, and with his statistical sources and data for an example of economic mobilization in a nationally mixed area (Bohemia-Moravia-Silesia, 1900–1971). Interested scholars will await with interest further work by Deutsch in applying quantitative concepts to nationalism. It may be possible that much of the vagueness now surrounding the phenomenon of nationalism may be cleared away by the use of social, educational, political, and economic statistics.

Conclusions and Summary

There is a wide diversity of opinion on national character. One extreme view holds that the idea of national character is a metaphysical dream shot through with fallacious generalizations. Another extremist position contends that national character is a permanent, stable entity. A third view recognizes the existence of national character as a concept of limited validity, and holds that there is a relative uniformity of personality among nations.

The concept of national character is of special interest to anthropologists and sociologists. Rejecting racial character, anthropologists have, nevertheless, applied to national societies the same techniques that they have used in their study of primitive societies. Most anthropologists feel that cultural patterns exist on a national scale. Other scholars, notably Inkeles, Ginsberg, and Hertz, recognize the obstacles in the study of national character but agree that distinctive national patterns of personality exist and that these patterns are mutable. The psychologist, Eric Fromm, in a significant work, *Escape From Freedom,* uses a combination of approaches to show the existence of what he terms "social character."

A multidisciplinary "science of national character" is currently in process of formation. The UNESCO Tensions Project, under the direction of the social psychologists, Hadley Cantril and Otto Klineberg, is a vital and important contribution to an understanding of national character. The work of Karl W. Deutsch gives promise of developing valuable techniques for the quantitative measurement of nationalism and its symptoms.

IX

The Idea of a National Soul

He who hears anything else from the wailing masses than the call, "Help me," he does not know the national soul.

—THOMAS CARLYLE

National Character and National Soul

Much of the criticism directed at the concept of national character is the result of confusing it with the vague and shifting idea of a national soul. Even careful scholars, when considering nationalism based on a conscious determination, fall into the trap of searching for a mystical national soul to complement the body of the nation. "Where there is a soul," said George P. Gooch, "there should be a body in which it may dwell. Here is the master-key to the political history of the nineteenth century." [1]

We have seen that national character refers to the totality of certain fundamental psychical characteristics peculiar to a certain people, influencing their behavior, and manifested with greater or less continuity in a succession of generations.[2] Scholars of many disciplines and many nations agree on the existence of collective conduct, collective attitudes, social symbols, and collective mentality (emotions, desires, and aspirations). Granted that a satisfactory methodology for measuring national character has not yet emerged, there is little ground for rejecting it as a figment of the imagination. This is not to say that national character may

[1] George P. Gooch, *Nationalism* (London and New York, 1920), p. 8.
[2] Morris Ginsberg, *The Psychology of Nationalism* (New York, 1921), p. 103. Ginsberg is careful to add that any notion of a *Volksgeist*, or national soul, in any other sense than this is not required in social psychology nor is it of any value as a principle of explanation.

not have both a rational and an irrational base. Part of it comes about by accident and part by the education. Irrational elements may, indeed, play a rôle in the determination of national character, but those irrational elements themselves may be attacked by rational control.

The ideal of a national soul—an impressionistic, mystical entity hovering over the individuals that constitute a nation—is an entirely different matter. Here we must wander blindfolded into the realm of fanciful abstraction. The national soul resists any effort at rational control or definition. There is no possibility of establishing any scientific validity for the claims of its proponents. It is said that rooted deep in the national soul are to be found "the mysticism of the life process" and "the ascent and decline of nations." [3] It is precisely this kind of mystical phraseology that may exert the greatest psychological effectiveness on the national mind.

Genesis of the Idea

The original stimulus to the idea of a national soul came in Germany, where, during the course of the nineteenth century, certain vague and mystical theories about *Volksgeist* (national spirit), *Volksseele* (national soul), and *Volksstimme* (national voice) emerged out of Romanticism. Such early Romantics as the Schlegel brothers, the Grimm brothers, Tieck, Novalis, Herder, Fichte, Schelling, Schleiermacher, and others saw the organic-genetic conception of culture as an expression of the national soul,[4] which had its beginnings in the heroic Middle Ages.[5] They issued a plea for the claims of the imagination, of emotion and feeling, of individualism, and, above all, for a synthetic expression of the national genius in all its manifold aspects of literature, art, religion, and politics. Though at first little concerned with

[3] Most scientists agree that science has been unable to comprehend the enormous emotional problem of mysticism.
[4] Cf. Robert R. Ergang, *Herder and the Foundations of German Nationalism* (New York, 1931), p. 234.
[5] Cf. G. Salomon, *Das Mittelalter als Ideal in der Romantik* (Munich, 1922), pp. 46 ff. It should be added that German Romanticism as an element in nationalism was fully matched by Slavophile Romanticism in the case of the Russians or Poles and by Biblical Romanticism in the case of messianistic nationalism.

politics and the state, Romanticism in Germany and in other countries after 1800 played an important rôle in the development of nationalism.

The effect of Romanticism on the German mind has been widely discussed. German Romanticism wished to be more than poetry: it was an interpretation of life, nature, and history.[6] According to Nietzsche, "as everything loves its symbol, so the German loves the clouds and all that is obscure, evolving, crepuscular, damp and shrouded; it seems to him that everything uncertain, undeveloped and growing is 'deep.'"[7] Constant repetition of this theme has led to the stereotype that the Germans are hamstrung by a predilection for philosophic mysticism, abstract subjectivism, vague mysticism, and admiration for the demonic, the heroic, and the like.[8] All such generalizations, while convenient and possibly containing a germ of truth, have not been substantiated scientifically. Certainly they would not explain Germany's leading part in the New Industrial Revolution and her extraordinary economic recovery after the holocaust of World War II. The German consciousness of national uniqueness was part of a European-wide phenomenon, differing possibly in details but similar in the over-all pattern.

The classic expression of the meaning of the national soul was given by Adolf Stoecker, court-chaplain to William I and later leader of the anti-Semitic Christian-Social Workers' Party. As a neo-Romanticist, Stoecker considered his duties as "care-taker of the national soul" the most important task before him in life.[9] To the contention that no national soul could exist, since the soul is the immortal part of the individual, Stoecker replied that this objection is merely "pietistic-individualism."[10] It is the important task of the missionary, said Stoecker, to save the national as well as the individual soul. He reasoned in this way: there is a certain

[6] See Hans Kohn, "Romanticism and the Rise of German Nationalism," *Review of Politics*, XII (1950), p. 443.
[7] Freidrich Nietzsche, *Beyond Good and Evil*, tr. by Helen Zimmern (London, 1907), p. 198.
[8] For example: "No doubt this can be said also of other peoples, but it does seem to be true that Germans are more apt to be moved by large but vague ends. . . ." (Morris Ginsberg, *Reason and Unreason in Society* [Cambridge, 1948], p. 143.)
[9] Dietrich von Oertzen, *Adolf Stoecker, Lebensbild und Zeitgeschichte* (Schwerin i. Mecklenburg, 1912), p. 261.
[10] *Ibid.*

relation between all portions of the national body; German blood flows in every German body, and the soul is to be found in the blood (*und im Blut ist die Seele*); when one has a German brother before him, not merely a brother from common mankind, a certain reaction takes place if the brother is not German; people can be compared to birds, of which there are different species; Germans and Frenchmen differ in their souls; there is no individual soul which exists for itself alone, as it lives, feels, thinks, and hears together with other souls.[11] "Man is not body, he is soul and the immortal soul is his best part. So a nation has not only a body to work and to shed blood in case of war, but also a soul, and this soul must be protected against all disintegrating influences." [12] The national soul, he said, exists in eternity among a huge nation of people with its capital at Jerusalem.[13] Through the golden streets uncounted millions wander.

As an example of the sensitiveness of the national soul, Stoecker pointed to the Reformation, "that popular event, that great movement of the national soul, in which the Germanic world was caught in the storm of Luther's ideals and in which the individual was swept along with the majority." [14] He was certain that the national soul existed even in Biblical times, for did not Paul, journeying to Philippi, Thessalonica, and Corinth, take up the missionary battles in the larger cities, where the national soul was much more in evidence than in the smallest villages? [15]

This point of view appears again and again in the writings of German as well as non-German irrationalist philosophers. The writings of Richard Wagner are filled with paeans of praise to the glorious German Spirit, such as: "If we wish to account for the amazing rebirth of the German Spirit in the field of poetic and philosophic literature, too, we can do so only by learning from Bach what the German Spirit is in truth, where it dwelt, and how it restlessly shaped itself anew, when it seemed to have

[11] *Ibid.*
[12] Adolf Stoecker, *Christlich-Sozial, Reden und Aufsätze* (Bielefeld and Leipzig, 1885), p. 230.
[13] Oertzen, *op. cit.,* p. 262.
[14] Adolf Stoecker, *Wach' Auf, evangelisches Volk!* (Berlin, 1896), p. 541. The Nazi battle-cry *"Deutschland Erwache!"* ("Germany Awake!") may be traced to Stoecker.
[15] Adolf Stoecker, quoted in *Die Stadtmission,* LI (1928), p. 34.

altogether vanished from the earth." [16] It was passages like this one that led even an understanding observer, the Wagnerian expert, Ernest Newman, to throw up his hands at Wagner's mysticism, which the critic called "wild rhetoric," "amateurish to the point of stupidity," "a peculiarly offensive form of national vanity," and "the cheapest and crudest spirit of national self-adulation." [17]

Richard Wagner was not alone in this realm of mysticism. Julius Langbehn asserted that "knowledge alone produces only pigmies, but faith produces heroes." [18] According to Arthur de Gobineau, "a society is great and brilliant only so far as it preserves the blood of the noble group that created it." [19] Houston Stewart Chamberlain insisted that "pure blood is sacred." [20] Oswald Spengler wrote in a similar vein: "Besides the energy of the blood—which coins the same living features [family traits] over and over again for centuries—and the power of the soil—as evidenced in its stamp on man—there is that mysterious cosmic force of the syntony of close human connections." [21] This type of thinking reached its culmination in Alfred Rosenberg, the high priest of Nazi mythology, who claimed that "each race has its own soul and its own religion," [22] and that "the soul simply means race viewed from the interior, and, inversely, race is the external aspect of the soul." [23]

This was Romanticism in its most confused form, "a demoralization of the mind by intellectuals afraid of the intellect." [24] It should be emphasized again that the same type of irrationalist nonsense also appeared in non-German writing. By no means should all German philosophers be included among these mystics,

[16] Richard Wagner, *Works,* tr. by William Ashton Ellis (8 vols., London, 1892–99), IV, p. 157.
[17] Ernest Newman, *A Study of Wagner* (London, 1899), pp. 274–78.
[18] Julius Langbehn, *Der Rembrandtdeutsche* (Leipzig, 1893), p. 93.
[19] Arthur de Gobineau, *Essay on the Inequality of Human Races,* tr. by Adrian Collins (2 vols., New York, 1915), I, p. 210.
[20] Houston Stewart Chamberlain, *The Foundations of the Nineteenth Century,* tr. by John Lees (2 vols., London, 1911), I, p. 298.
[21] Oswald Spengler, *The Decline of the West,* tr. by Charles Francis Atkinson (2 vols., New York, 1932), II, pp. 125–26.
[22] Cf. Alfred Rosenberg, *Mythus des XX. Jahrhunderts* (37th ed., Munich, 1934), *passim.*
[23] Cf. Albert R. Chandler, *Rosenberg's Nazi Myth* (Ithaca, New York, 1945), p. 7.
[24] Frederic Lilge, *The Abuse of Learning* (New York, 1948), p. 131.

but only those pseudo-philosophers who, quite irrationally, accepted the idea of a national soul and helped spiritually to prepare the way for Hitler's "myth of the blood."

Were this belief in the existence of a national soul confined to the work of eccentric pseudo-philosophers, it could be dismissed without further consideration. But it was a contagious idea, which attracted the attention even of distinguished and solid scholars. Johann Kaspar Bluntschi, the German-Swiss jurist and political theorist, in his famous work, *Theory of the State*,[25] treated the state as a "moral-spiritual personality," comparable to a human organism. He described the body of the state, its constitutional organization, as subject to the law of growth, decay, and death; its soul, the national spirit, as embodied in the common language, customs, and outlook of the people. The earlier theories of *Volksgeist* and *Volksseele* were systematized by such psychologists as Wilhelm Wundt,[26] Eduard Wechssler,[27] and Elias Hurwicz.[28] This trend was not limited to Germany. We can see its influence in France, where Gustave Le Bon[29] and Alfred Fouillée[30] began to show an interest in crowd behavior, and in the United States, where William McDougall,[31] W. B. Pillsbury,[32] and others attempted a scientific approach to the study of group characteristics. Both pseudo-philosophers and reputable scientists sought to unravel the mysteries of national soul.

National Soul and National Consciousness

The mystical and unscientific concept of the national soul is distinct from the psychologically recognized idea of national consciousness. National consciousness is a specific kind of group

[25] Johann Kaspar Bluntschi, *Theory of the State* (6th ed., Oxford, 1892).
[26] Wilhelm Wundt, *Die Nationen und ihre Philosophie* (Leipzig, 1915).
[27] Eduard Wechssler, *Esprit und Geist: Versuch einer Wesenskunde der Deutschen und Franzosen* (Bielefeld, 1927).
[28] Elias Hurwicz, *Die Seele der Völker* (Gotha, 1920).
[29] Gustave Le Bon, *La psychologie des foules* (Paris, 1895), tr. as *The Crowd* (New York, 1896).
[30] Alfred J. E. Fouillée, *Esquisse psychologique des peuples européens* (Paris, 1902).
[31] William McDougall, *An Introduction to Social Psychology* (Boston, 1908), and *The Group Mind* (New York, 1920).
[32] W. B. Pillsbury, *The Psychology of Nationality and Internationalism* (New York, 1919).

consciousness, or group solidarity, in which the members of the group establish a bond for the purpose of implementing certain aims. It consists of imagery and of awareness of traditions that the individual supports in common with all the rest of his group. In the words of F. H. Allport, "nationalism has a supreme power over the behavior of the individual. The exaltation of self-consciousness through identification with the nation plays no small part in this control. Hatred and struggle against a common enemy bring the impression of universal patriotism and coopera-tion into the focus of attention, and thus foster national soli-darity." [33]

National consciousness is a complex structure, consisting of many variations, from a subconscious state of mind to a clear-cut ideology.[34] It is distinguished by pride in a number of different organizations. All these lesser groups with their allegiances keep alive the loyalty to the larger whole, since belonging to a nation is not a matter that can easily be contemplated and regularly emphasized.[35] Without national consciousness there would not be the consciousness of kind, which is the first sign of nationality and the acid test of its existence.[36]

The sociologist, Franz Oppenheimer, believes that we must not deduce national consciousness from the nation, but, quite to the contrary, we must deduce the nation from national conscious-ness.[37] There is some difference of opinion on this point. Rudolf Rocker holds that "the old opinion which ascribes the creation of the national state to the awakened national consciousness of the people is but a fairy tale, very serviceable to the supporters of the idea of a national state, but false none the less. The nation is not the cause but the result of the state. It is the state which creates the nation, not the nation the state. Indeed, from this point of

[33] F. H. Allport, Social Psychology (Boston, 1924), p. 388.
[34] Frederick Hertz, Nationality in History and Politics (3rd ed., London, 1951), p. 3.
[35] Pillsbury, op. cit., p. 244.
[36] Bernard Joseph, Nationality: Its Nature and Problems (New Haven, Conn., 1929), p. 127.
[37] "Wir müssen nicht aus der Nation das Nationalbewusstsein, sondern umgekehrt aus dem Nationalbewusstsein die Nation ableiten." (Franz Oppenheimer, System der Soziologie [Jena, 1923], I, p. 644.)

view there exists between people and nation the same distinction as between society and the state." [38]

Don Luigi Sturzo believes that as long as a people remains unconscious of its personality, there is no nation in the sociological meaning of the term.[39] There may be periods, he adds, when national consciousness weakens and then reasserts itself. An example may be found in Finland, where her great nineteenth-century poet, Elias Lonnrot, awakened the nation from a long sleep.

Just as physicians recognize symptoms of health and disease without altogether understanding their origins, so do social psychologists see the existence of national consciousness and seek to develop a satisfactory methodology to throw light upon its causes. The idea of a national soul, on the other hand, may be an unintelligible, enigmatic, vague, cryptic doctrine that, on occasion, may be motivated by considerations of political power. National consciousness lends itself to scholarly interrogation; the national soul should be taken as a matter of political faith.

Conclusions and Summary

Scholars of many disciplines and nations agree on the existence of national character, but they tend to reject the idea of a national soul as the product of vague speculation. The original stimulus to the doctrine of a national soul came from early nineteenth-century Romanticism. The earlier theories of *Volksgeist* and *Volksseele* were developed and systematized by a series of irrationalist scholars; even reputable scholars showed an interest in investigating these theories. The so-called national soul should not be confused with the scientifically demonstrable concept of national consciousness.

[38] Rudolf Rocker, *Nationalism and Culture,* tr. by Ray E. Chase (New York, 1937), p. 200.
[39] Don Luigi Sturzo, *Nationalism and Internationalism* (New York, 1946), p. 24.

Conclusion

It would seem proper to summarize the results of our analysis and answer the original query: What is nationalism? with a definitive statement designed to satisfy the scholars of all disciplines. Unfortunately, nationalism cannot be defined adequately in simple terms, since it takes many forms and expressions. Its essential elements should be sought in psychology, history, and the related disciplines, not in a dictionary. We have attempted to clarify its meaning not by definition but by description. The problems and approaches to nationalism have been summarized at the end of each chapter and need not be repeated here. The aim has been merely to achieve a starting point for further investigation.

For those who, nevertheless, insist that a definition is in order —on the ground that all words have meaning—perhaps the following is least objectionable: nationalism, a product of political, economic, social, and intellectual factors at a certain stage in history, is a condition of mind, feeling, or sentiment of a group of people living in a well-defined geographical area, speaking a common language, possessing a literature in which the aspirations of the nation have been expressed, attached to common traditions and common customs, venerating its own heroes, and, in some cases, having a common religion. To this projected definition it should be added immediately that there are exceptions, more or less pertinent, to nearly all the terms used in it. Nationalism has two major senses: concrete (geographical, linguistic, political, social, economic, and cultural); and ideal (psychological). It is my conviction, based on this survey, that nationalism should be considered first and foremost a state of mind, an act of consciousness, a psychological fact. It is that socially approved symbol used by modern society in its search for security.

Nationalism, as an expression of the human mind, takes on characteristics of an unending dichotomy in the thinking of man (Zoroaster's dualism of Good versus Evil; Goethe's Faust-Mephistopheles struggle). In its "good" form, nationalism is free from an attitude of superiority to the neighbor. Man has a natural attachment for his home, which he wants to protect against all dangers. He sees a solution for his task in community or national action. The individual gravitates towards the nation because to him it represents self-preservation, and safety. Furthermore, he takes pride in the history and culture of his own group.

In its "evil" form, nationalism has developed into a divisive force that exerts supreme power over the behavior of the individual and becomes the focal point for individual and group fears, anxieties, frustrations, and aggressions. This type of nationalism is the result of one of the most powerful emotions—blind, unreasoning fear. It is the fruit of mental and moral confusion and of maladjustments between thinking and action.

In either case, whether in its "good" or "evil" form, nationalism is the result of an arbitrary classification made on the body of humanity. This tendency is not new in history. In one of his *Dialogues,* Plato tells the story of a visitor to Athens from one of the Greek settlements in Magna Graecia who complained angrily about the Greek disposition to divide all the world's inhabitants into two species—Greeks and barbarians. The disgusted foreigner added a note of sarcasm: "Some wise and understanding creature, such as a crane is reputed to be, might in imitation of you make a similar division, and set up cranes against all other animals, to their own special glorification, at the same time jumbling together all the others, including man, under the appellation of brutes."

There is no necessity for nationalism to exist forever in its present form. It could possibly become outmoded in the new historical age which we are now entering. Man can split the atom, and he can wipe out the inhabitants of an entire continent if not the whole world. One result of modern technical development is the rapid shrinking of the world, by which nations of different colors, tongues, religions, philosophies, traditions, and prejudices are thrown together and compelled either to cooperate or fight. In few of these nations are the people educated to know the people who are different from themselves. Yet, in the words of George Brock Chisholm, there is now only one basic importance in the world on which the very existence of mankind depends—the emotional relationship between the peoples of the world.

It is a worn commonplace but it is vital for our existence—the safety of mankind in the Age of the Atom lies in the realization that the freedom and welfare of the individual are ultimately bound up with the freedom and welfare of all peoples on the earth. The desire for the well-being of one's own nation can be— and must be—made compatible with the welfare of all humanity.

Bibliographical Note

From the enormous literature on nationalism, reference will be made here to those works which have proved to be most useful in studying the meaning of nationalism. An old but still useful bibliography will be found in Edward B. Krehbiel, *Nationalism, War, and Society* (New York, 1916). Koppel S. Pinson's, *A Bibliographical Introduction to Nationalism* (New York, 1935), a critically annotated bibliography, is indispensable for any study of nationalism. It is to be hoped that Dr. Pinson will bring his excellent compendium up to date. There is a brief but carefully selected bibliography following the articles on "Nationalism" by Max Hildebert Boehm and Carlton J. H. Hayes in *Encyclopedia of the Social Sciences* (New York, 1937), VI, pp. 248–49. The best recent bibliography is in Karl W. Deutsch, *Nationalism and Social Communication* (New York, 1953), pp. 251–66.

Outstanding among the major surveys is *Nationalism: A Report by a Study Group of Members of the Royal Institute of International Affairs* (London, 1939), produced under the chairmanship of Professor E. H. Carr. The work of the UNESCO project and the Social Science Research Council is cited in the documentation of chapter 8 on "The Problem of National Character" in the present book.

The two most productive American scholars of nationalism are Hans Kohn and Carlton J. H. Hayes. Nearly all of Hans Kohn's works are concerned with nationalism: *History of Nationalism in the East* (New York, 1929); *Nationalism in the Soviet Union* (London, 1933); *Force or Reason* (Cambridge, Mass., 1937); "The Roots of Modern Nationalism," in *Bulletin of the International Committee of the Historical Sciences* (Paris, 1938), pp. 388–91; "Nationalism," in *Before America Decides,* ed. by Frank P. Davidson (Cambridge, Mass., 1938), pp. 13–26; *World Order in Historical Perspective* (Cambridge, Mass., 1941); *Revolutions and Dictatorships* (Cambridge, Mass., 1941); *The Idea of Nationalism* (New York, 1944); *Prophets and Peoples* (New York, 1946); *The Twentieth Century* (New York, 1949); and *Pan-Slavism: Its History and Ideology* (Notre Dame, Ind., 1953).

Among the many works by Carlton J. H. Hayes are *Essays on Nationalism* (New York, 1926); "Two Varieties of Nationalism, Original and Derived," *Proceedings of the Association of History Teachers of the Middle States and*

Maryland, XXVI (1928), pp. 71–83; *France, a Nation of Patriots* (New York, 1930); *The Historical Evolution of Modern Nationalism* (New York, 1931); and the article on "Nationalism" in *Encyclopedia of the Social Sciences* (New York, 1937), VI, pp. 240–48.

Important works by other American historians include: Oscar Janowsky, *Nationalities and National Minorities* (New York, 1945), which places special emphasis upon East-Central Europe; Robert R. Ergang, *Herder and the Foundations of German Nationalism* (New York, 1931); W. M. Gewehr, *The Rise of Nationalism in the Balkans* (New York, 1931); and Halvdan Koht, "The Dawn of Nationalism in Europe," *American Historical Review,* LII (1947), pp. 265–80. Among the political scientists are: William Ebenstein, *Man and the State* (New York, 1948); Carl J. Friedrich, *Constitutional Government and Politics* (Boston, 1950); Franz Neumann, *Behemoth* (New York, 1942); and F. L. Schuman, *International Politics* (New York, 1941). The most fruitful sociological works are: Florian Znaniecki, *Modern Nationalities* (Urbana, Ill., 1952); Max Sylvius Handman, "The Sentiment of Nationalism," *Political Science Quarterly,* XXXVI (1921), pp. 104–21; and Max Wirth, "Types of Nationalism," *American Journal of Sociology,* XLI (1936), pp. 723–37. Contributions by American psychologists, psychiatrists, and psychoanalysts are mentioned in the documentation.

Some of Britain's most astute scholars have been concerned with nationalism and its implications. Lord Acton's famous essay in "Nationality" was published in his *History of Freedom* (London, 1909). References to problems of nationalism are made in James Bryce, *Studies in History and Jurisprudence* (Oxford, 1901). The outbreak of World War I stimulated an intensive study of nationalism by British scholars: Arnold J. Toynbee, *Nationality and the War* (London, 1915); Ramsay Muir, *Nationalism and Internationalism* (London, 1916); J. Holland Rose, *Nationality in Modern History* (London, 1916), a collection of lectures; Israel Zangwill, *The Principle of Nationalities* (London, 1917); R. W. Seton-Watson, *The Rise of Nationality in the Balkans* (London, 1917); Sir Alfred Zimmern, *Nationality and Government* (London, 1918); John Oakesmith, *Race and Nationality* (London, 1919); and Sir Arthur Keith, *Nationality and Race* (London, 1919).

Other significant British works include: Ernest Barker, *National Character and the Factors in its Formation* (London and New York, 1927); George P. Gooch, *Nationalism* (London and New York, 1920); H. A. L. Fisher, *The Common Weal* (London, 1924); C. A. Macartney, *National States and National Minorities* (London, 1934); and H. J. Laski, *Grammar of Politics* (London and New Haven, 1925), and *The State in Theory and Practice* (London, 1938).

The work of German scholars in the field of nationalism has been outstanding. Studies in the psychology of nationality were begun in Germany as early as 1860 by Moritz Lazarus and Heymann Steinthal in *Zeitschrift für Völkerpsychologie und Sprachwissenschaft.* Additional studies along this line were made by Wilhelm Wundt, especially in his *Die Nationen und ihre*

Philosophie (Leipzig, 1915). The distinguished historian, Friedrich Meinecke, devoted much attention to nationalism, above all in his *Weltbürgertum und Nationalstaat* (5th ed., Munich, 1922). The most prolific German scholar in the field is Waldemar Mitscherlich, whose many books on nationalism include: *Nationalstaat und Nationalwirtschaft und ihre Zukunft* (Leipzig, 1916); *Der Nationalismus West-Europas* (Leipzig, 1920); *Nation und Nationalität* (Karlsruhe, 1927); and *Nationalismus: Die Geschichte einer Idee* (Leipzig, 1929). The intense interest in nationalism by German scholars is indicated by the recent *Report on the Third International Meeting of Historians, 17–20 October, 1949,* which was published in *Europa und der Nationalismus* (Baden Baden, 1950).

Among the good general accounts are: Eugen Lemberg, *Geschichte des Nationalismus in Europa* (Stuttgart, 1950); Otto Vossler, *Der Nationalgedanke von Rousseau bis Ranke* (Munich and Berlin, 1937); S. R. Steinmetz, *Die Nationalitäten in Europa* (Berlin, 1927); and Friedrich Julius Neumann, *Volk und Nation* (Leipzig, 1888).

Some important specialized studies by German scholars are: Alfred Fischel, *Der Panslawismus bis zum Weltkrieg* (Stuttgart, 1919); Robert Michels, *Der Patriotismus* (Munich, 1929); and Hermann Heller, *Sozialismus und Nation* (Berlin, 1925). Psychologically oriented studies include: Eduard Wechssler, *Esprit und Geist* (Bielefeld, 1927) and Elias Hurcwicz, *Die Seelen der Völker* (Gotha, 1920). A sociological approach to nationalism is used in: Franz Oppenheimer, *System der Sozologie* (Jena, 1923); Alfred Amonn, *Nationalgefühl und Staatsgefühl* (Munich, 1915); Heinz Ziegler, *Die moderne Nation* (Tübingen, 1931); and Joseph Fels, *Begriff und Wesen der Nation* (Münster, 1927). The relation of linguistics to nationalism is described in Georg Schmidt-Rohr, *Die Sprache als Bildnerin der Völker* (Jena, 1932).

In France, Ernest Renan published his famous essay, *Qu'est-ce qu'une nation?* (Paris, 1882), which, unfortunately, has not yet been translated into English. The Belgian ethnologist and sociologist, Arnold van Gennep, began his scholarly study of nationality from the anthropological point of view in his *Traité comparatif des nationalités* (Paris, 1922). One of the best French accounts is René Johannet, *Le principe des nationalités* (Paris, 1916), which treats the historical origins of nationalism. Henri Hauser, *Le principe des nationalités* (Paris, 1916) is a useful résumé, while Charles H. Pouthas, *Le mouvement des nationalités en Europe dans la première moitié du XIX siècle* (Paris, 1945) is more up to date. A. J. É. Fouillée, *Esquisse psychologique des peuples Européens* (Paris, 1902), and G. Le Bon, *Lois psychologiques de l'évolution des peuples* (17th ed., Paris, 1922), originally published in the late nineteenth century, were among the first important books on the group mind.

Several volumes of real worth have appeared in other countries. Argentina: Rudolf Rocker, *Nationalismo y cultura* (Buenos Aires, 1942). Austria: Otto Bauer, *Die Nationalitätenfrage und die Sozialdemokratie* (2nd ed., Vienna, 1924); Ignaz Seipel, *Nation und Staat* (Vienna, 1916); and Karl Renner,

Das Selbstbestimmungsrecht des Nationen (Vienna, 1918). Canada: W. S. Wallace, *The Growth of Canadian National Feeling* (Toronto, 1927). Italy: P. S. Mancini, *Il principio di nazionalità* (Rome, 1920); and Count Terenzio Mamiani Della Rovere, *D'un nuovo diritto Europeo* (Turin, 1859), which emphasizes the *Risorgimento*. Spain: F. Pi y Margall, *Las nacionalidades* (Madrid, 1876). Switzerland: Karl Hilty, *Vorlesungen über die Politik der Eidgenossenschaft* (Bern, 1875). The Marxist view of nationalism is stressed in N. Lenin, *Über die nationale Frage* (2 vols., Berlin, 1930–1931); and Iosif V. Stalin, *Marxism and the National Question* (New York, 1942).

Index